MIND

THE

GAP

MIND
THE
GAP

The New Class Divide in Britain

Ferdinand Mount

First published in 2004 by
Short Books
15 Highbury Terrace
London N5 1UP

This edition published in 2012
10 9 8 7 6 5 4 3 2 1

A CIP catalogue record for this book
is available from the British Library.

ISBN 978-1-96021-95-5

Printed and bound by CPI Group (UK) Ltd, Croydon, CR0 4YY

It's the same the whole world over,
It's the poor wot gets the blame,
It's the rich wot gets the gravy.
Ain't it all a bleeding shame?

Song of the First World War

The oligarchic character of the modern English
commonwealth does not rest, like many oligarchies, on
the cruelty of the rich to the poor. It does not even rest
on the kindness of the rich to the poor. It rests on the
perennial and unfailing kindness of the poor to the rich.

G.K. Chesterton, Heretics, chapter 15

Introduction

'Class doesn't count in Britain any more.' I must have read the words, or words very like them, dozens of times before. Sometimes it is only a phrase or a subordinate clause that slips off the tongue, such as 'in today's classless society', or 'now that class barriers are disappearing'. Fifty years ago, after winning the 1959 election, Harold Macmillan trumpeted that 'the class war is over'. In 1990, John Major declared it his ambition to turn Britain into a classless society, suggesting thereby that with one more heave this great goal might be achieved. If we were not actually there yet, we soon would be. Inexorable social forces had been set in motion years ago. We couldn't have stopped the process even if we had wanted to.

On lecture tours overseas I myself have spouted something of the sort to audiences of innocent Germans and amiable Americans. 'Class divisions are fading in Britain,' I told them, and they didn't utter a peep of protest, any more than most of us do when we read such assertions in the newspapers. In fact, it was only when one of these lectures was going to be reprinted and I was correcting the proofs that I came across the sentence again, and something made me stop.

It wasn't a conscious, rational hesitation, more an instructive twitch, the kind of apprehension you have when you open your front door and sense that something inside the house is wrong, though you cannot exactly pin it down. If pressed, I could still muster all the usual arguments supporting the claim of Britain's growing classlessness: these days everyone wears blue jeans, we are all on first-name terms, anyone can get to university or become Prime Minister. It was just as easy to think of the counter-arguments: how the gap between the fat cats and the low-paid is actually widening, how the rich still live longer than the poor.

But it wasn't that the balance between the pros and the cons had changed. It was more that to make the claim at all suddenly seemed glib. It tripped too quickly off the tongue, as though we wanted the claim to be true so badly that we were prepared to cut any corners, as though behind it there lay some sort of abiding embarrassment, possibly even a secret that we didn't want to confront.

My hesitation was not in any case prompted by the obvious, continuing and perhaps deepening economic inequalities in Britain. It was to do with something else, with what for want of a better word we call 'culture' and with the sense that the worst-off in this country live impoverished lives, more so than the worst-off on the Continent or in the United States. They seem to me impoverished not simply in relation to the better-off in Britain today but in relation to their own parents and grandparents. And the upper classes are uncomfortably aware of it, which is why they show so little respect and affection for the lower classes.

If that is true, then this becomes the most interesting and pressing social question around. And if it is true also that the gap between the upper and the lower classes has not been narrowing, as we fondly supposed, but steadily and remorselessly widening, then we have been not so much labouring as lounging under a gigantic delusion.

I am well aware that this is not what most of us believe. It is not what we want to believe. It is counter-intuitive and contrary to everything that we have been told. Besides, to reopen the whole question of class in Britain is to blunder into a minefield. Most of us find the subject painful and embarrassing. The words we have to choose from can sound patronising, crass or unkind — lower-class, lower-middle-class, working-class, let alone bourgeois or petit-bourgeois. Even middle-class is these days often used as a venomous synonym for smug, unadventurous or selfish.

And even if it is worth investigating, as an urgent matter of justice and equity, what has happened to the class system in general and the working classes in particular, the present author may not look like the ideal candidate to undertake the task. I was educated at expensive independent schools, I live in a very nice house in a conservation area, I have a languid upper-class voice and a semi-dormant baronetcy. I have always had interesting and usually well paid work and taken holidays abroad in sophisticated spots (Who knows ? Some of these things may be true of some of my readers too).

Worse than all of this is the fact that in the past I have worked for a Conservative government, and not just any government but the administration led by Margaret Thatcher, which its passionate opponents still believe did more to deepen class divisions than any other government since the war.

How can someone like me pretend to know what life was and is like for the worst-off of my fellow countrymen? My answer is that it is People Like Us who are largely responsible for the present state of the lower classes in Britain. It is our misunderstandings, meddlings and manipulations which have transformed a British working class that was the envy and amazement of foreign observers in the nineteenth century into a so-called underclass which is often the subject of baffled despair today both at home and abroad. My argument in this book is that we did the damage, or most of it. It is the least we can do to try to understand what we have done and help to undo it where we can.

In any case, this essay does not make any rash claims to inside knowledge of how the worst-off in Britain live, let alone of how they think. The book is based primarily on what the ruling class has said, and written, about the lower classes, on how it has treated their institutions and their aspirations, and on the facts of common observation. At the end, it is true, I do throw out a few suggestions of my own, which the reader is free to amend or discard. But the real meat of the whole business is to be found in the indictment drawn up in the book's middle chapters.

The tendencies in British culture and society that I criticise in this essay are not the unaided work of any single ideology or political party. Almost all postwar British Prime Ministers — Macmillan and Heath and Thatcher no less than Attlee and Blair and Brown – have sought to break down class barriers in one way or another. Sometimes they were at least half-right, sometimes they did lasting damage. My purpose here is not to keep a score sheet (though I am sure that the party-minded will not hesitate to do so). In fact the one thing I am certain of is that it is only by freeing ourselves of party-political mindsets that we can hope to identify exactly what has gone wrong and begin to formulate some suggestions as to how the damage might be repaired.

All I want to say at this point is that it would be false comfort to imagine that we are anywhere near out of the wood yet. What is striking is how many of Labour's more thoughtful ministers — Alan Milburn, Stephen Byers, Peter Mandelson, Estelle Morris to name but a few — have confessed, usually on leaving office, that, after years of Labour government, class divisions in this country not only persist but actually appear in some important ways to be deepening.

The second potential objection — which I do take account of now and again — is that I do not give sufficient value to the huge improvements in material conditions over the past century and a half: the improved expectation of life, the medical advances now available to everyone, the educational opportunities, the cars, the videos, the holidays in the sun. Surely these are a blessing, and a blessing in particular to the poorest. And along with them go the new freedoms: the gradual disappearance of unkindness to the wretched and the deviant, the uninhibited freedom of expression, the acceptance of minority races, the erosion of the social barriers preventing women from leading a fuller life. Surely the freedoms, opportunities and material comfort and security open to the worst-off in this country are immeasurably superior to those enjoyed by people in previous generations who found themselves at the bottom of the heap. We are the beneficiaries of a century and a half of social reform, are we not? How can it be that class division should survive into the 21st century as anything worse than a slightly absurd remnant of the bad old days?

Well, I have often drawn attention to these changes myself and in earlier essays have tried to open the eyes of those who believe that Britain is stuck in its straitlaced past. Anybody who bothers to refer back to these earlier writings (for example, 'Farewell to Pudding Island', *Times Literary Supplement*, April 28, 2000, or 'Dogmas of Decline', *Prospect*, August/September 2001) may find a certain dissonance, even a contradiction, between their relatively blithe tone and the grimmer notes struck here. I can only respond by asserting that modern Britain is a country complex enough and strange enough to accommodate a variety of descriptions that stand at awkward angles to one another: unbuttoned but also uneasy, dynamic but divided too, contented and yet apprehensive.

I am a latecomer to the subject myself. Even a few months ago, I did not imagine that, this far on in the day, I would be writing a book about class. The subject seemed to me exhausted, *passé*, fit only for style gurus and features editors with a page to fill. But now I feel that we have to go over — or perhaps *go through* — this well-trodden ground in order to get to something more interesting, more worrying, and sadder.

I shall begin by looking rather briefly at class distinction and class division in Britain today. But then we shall have to go back, a fairish way, if we are to catch some plausible glimpse of what has gone wrong and why.

I
Outworn Shibboleths

At a society wedding a couple of years ago, a friend of mine wandering into the marquee for the reception was greeted by a cousin of his who took him aside and muttered conspiratorially into his ear, 'Mind the gap'. Moving deeper into the tent, my friend again had this strange advice whispered into his ear by another acquaintance, this time intoned in the sonorous voice of the announcement on the Tube. Only on second hearing did he get it. 'Mind the gap' — in drawing attention to the social distance between the bride's family (unmistakably upper-class) and the groom's family (embarrassingly middle-class), the wedding guests were perpetuating, with a delight amounting to orgasm, the ancient English sport of class distinction.

Making such distinctions has been one of the treasured pastimes of the upper classes for centuries. Such phrases as 'milk in first', 'not quite our class, dear' and 'HMG' for 'homemade gent' could be heard until very recently. Some families and social sets even had a special private term to identify their social inferiors; the Bloomsbury group's word for 'common' was 'bedint'. Social putdowns could take many forms, from Estella's hurtful rebuke to Pip in *Great Expectations* for calling knaves 'jacks' to Alan Clark's remark that Michael Heseltine 'had had to buy his own furniture' (Clark's own fortune, based on a huge Scottish thread business, dated back only two generations, so that his grandfather too must have had to buy his own furniture).

These days, though, it is itself a sign of vulgarity to make such remarks. To 'mind the gap' so crudely and overtly is widely recognised as not only old-fashioned but disgusting. Snobbery, at least this sort of snobbery, no longer corresponds to the social reality, except perhaps among a tiny cluster of dinosaurs who continue to lead completely unreal lives on their reservations, so conscientiously maintained by the National Trust. The social revolution has swept away all that sort of nonsense.

This is largely true, as far as it goes. The intricate network of markers that once distinguished the upper from the middle classes has lost much of its potency. What I mean here are the distinctions set out so brilliantly by the professor of linguistics Alan S.C. Ross in his essay, 'U and Non U' published in *Encounter* and later taken up by Nancy Mitford and Evelyn Waugh, their contributions being gathered together by Mitford in a little volume *Noblesse Oblige* (1956). Ross, largely supported by Mitford, argued that members of the upper class in England were now distinguished by little more than their speech patterns. They were not necessarily better educated or cleaner or even richer than persons not of their class. Nor in general were they likely to play a more prominent part in public affairs, practise different professions or even engage in different pursuits or pastimes (Ross was curiously indifferent to blood sports, which then and now occupy the energies of the upper classes to an extent not found elsewhere. Despite all the efforts of the Countryside Alliance to depict fox-hunting as a classless sport, it remains largely patronised by and offers a rallying point for the rural upper class).

But speech was the thing. U-speakers ate 'lunch' in the middle of the day and 'dinner' in the evening. They said 'sorry', not 'pardon'. They went 'riding', not 'horseback-riding'. They sat in their 'drawing-rooms', not 'lounges'. They used 'lavatory paper', not 'toilet paper'. They listened to the 'wireless', not the 'radio'. They picked up the 'telephone', not the 'phone'. In later life they had recourse to 'false teeth' and 'spectacles', not to 'dentures' and 'glasses'. They ate 'puddings' rather than 'sweets', and, most famously of all, they kept the crumbs off by means of a 'table napkin', never, heaven forfend, by a 'serviette'.

Nancy Mitford confirmed most of these distinctions. She was, after all, the prime inventor of the game. It is Uncle Matthew's explosion in *The Pursuit of Love* (1945) that sets it all off:

Education! I was always led to suppose that no educated person ever spoke of notepaper, and yet I hear poor Fanny asking Sadie for notepaper. What is this education? Fanny talks about mirrors and mantelpieces, handbags and perfume, she takes sugar in her coffee, has a tassel on her umbrella, and I have no doubt that, if she is ever fortunate enough to catch a husband, she will call his father and mother Father and Mother.

Mitford did, a little nervously, question Ross's assertion that 'one word or phrase will suffice to brand an apparent U-speaker as originally non-U (for U-speakers themselves never make mistakes).' Usage changed very quickly, she conceded, and 'I even know undisputed U-speakers who pronounce girl "gurl", which 20 years ago would have been unthinkable.' So you could not be condemned to outer darkness by a single solecism.

In his essay, Evelyn Waugh condemned her classifications as absurdly capricious and unreliable. 'There is practically no human activity or form of expression which at one time or another in one place or another, I have not heard confidently condemned as plebeian, for generations of English have used the epithets "common" and "middle-class" as general pejoratives to describe anything which gets on their nerves.' Fish knives, for example, were condemned as non-U and indeed feature in the opening line of John Betjeman's poem 'How to Get on in Society':

Phone for the fish knives, Norman.

Yet in many English stately homes fish knives had been in continuous use for nearly a hundred years. Waugh argued that fashionable usage was always in constant transition. Every family and every set had its own private vocabulary and syntax. Words and phrases that were originally adopted facetiously, in inverted commas, passed into daily use. 'Posh', queried by Professor Ross, is a good example. Originally it was decidedly non-U — its non-Uness is echoed in the name of Murray Posh, the wealthy vulgarian in *The Diary of a Nobody* (1892). In Anthony Powell's novel, *The Acceptance World*, set in the late 20s, Peter Templer reproves his model wife Mona: '*Posh?* Sweetie, what an awful word. Please never use it in my presence again.'(1955, p62). But it then, as Ross points out, entered schoolboy slang, and is today used colloquially by all classes to denote the rich and smart.

Waugh is right in pointing out that language is irrepressibly fluid. Just as all sorts of words change meaning over time, migrating from the particular to the general and the benign to the pejorative or vice versa, so class-restricted usage may alter or fade away. Old-fashioned U pronunciations — 'gel' for 'gurl', 'lahnch' for 'launch', 'nurshry' for 'nursery', 'Millan' for 'Milan' simply disappear. U-usages may spread downwards to conquer the middle classes — loo, lunch. Or non-U usages may become general — mirror, radio, glasses (although 'wireless' has a facetious afterlife in all classes).

But in a larger and more important sense, Waugh's remarks about the impossibility of pinning down U-speak are beside the point, or at least disingenuous. It is not simply the fluidity of language that has washed away this whole disgraceful topic. What has gone is the *will* to erect, maintain and police such distinctions. Except in rare private moments, such as my friend's experience in the wedding tent, the upper class no longer dares to enforce its own code. This exclusive coinage has ceased to be legal tender. That may seem a pretentious phrase to describe what might seem to be no more than the small change of snobbery. Yet within living memory the code was used, quite fiercely, to maintain barriers, to inflict pain and to identify kindred spirits. Forms of address (well covered by Ross in his article, which deliciously first appeared in the Finnish philological periodical *Neuphilologische Mitteilungen*) were the heavy artillery in this campaign. It was crucially important to distinguish a knight's wife, 'Lady Smith', from an earl's daughter, 'Lady Jane Fellows'. On the envelope it was vital to distinguish a gentleman, 'A.C.L. Blair Esq', from a non-gent, 'Mr John Prescott'. A gentleman did not begin a letter 'Dear Gordon Brown', nor end it 'Yours truly'. All these distinctions are now obsolete. Where they are still maintained for reasons of habit and caprice, they have lost the power to wound.

And with this new tolerance in speech has come a similar tolerance in matters of dress. No longer would a room full of upper-class men freeze if someone entered wearing brown shoes with a blue suit. Some of the more arcane rules have simply vanished from view — my favourite was 'never wear a soft hat in town before Goodwood'. Some of these rules were recognised as fatuously baroque even when they were first enunciated, for example, Lord Curzon's claim that 'no gentleman eats soup for luncheon'. But the important point is not so much that these rules have all disappeared as that the social penalties for breaking them have gone. A young man will still feel uncomfortable if he turns up at a dinner party wearing an ordinary suit to find the rest of the company in dinner jackets — or more usually these days the other way round. But he will not be ostracised. The pretty girls will not refuse to speak to him on that account. And the episode will not be remembered against him.

There is more than fashion and linguistic fluidity at work here. These caste marks have not simply faded or mutated to be replaced by other such marks. Nor has the way the upper classes speak taken on a fresh set of inflections, in the way that Lady Caroline Lamb's drawl was supposed to have set fashionable speech patterns for the rest of the nineteenth century.

What has happened is much more dramatic and permanent. The old class markers have become taboo. To be caught using them (except, as I say, in deeply private circumstances) is to show yourself to be worse than a snob, although it certainly shows that. To remark on someone, for example, saying 'Pardon' where U-speak would use 'sorry' is now *unkulturny*, crass, out of it. U-speakers naturally carry on saying 'sorry', but they no longer preen themselves on their superior speech habits, nor despise others for the lack of them. It is now bad manners to remark on other people's language or accent. And when you hear someone — usually an elderly person living in the country — indulging in such old caste talk, you wince and try to change the subject.

To outsiders — anglophones from the United States or the Commonwealth, for example — upper-class English speech still sounds so bizarre, so affected that they imagine that the old class games are still being played. And English people with regional accents may still take elocution lessons to iron out their voices to what they regard as acceptable levels. The same is not, I think, true of the Scots, the Welsh, or the Irish — a significant difference which we shall come back to.

But an important social change has taken place, none the less, even if it does not always sound that way. The manners of classlessness have become de rigueur. Social difference in the old-fashioned sense is no longer a legitimate topic for discussion.

This is an admirable change. It removes a set of stultifying constraints. Lady Catherine de Bourgh no longer rules OK. Looking back, we may find it odd that the class code should have lasted so long after the material power of the aristocracy had unmistakably cracked. Perhaps that was the very reason why it lasted, as a consolation for the real differences in wealth and power which had crumbled away.

Does all this mean that we are at last moving towards a society that is more or less classless?

Surely this surge of feeling against overt class distinction must suggest that there is something new about the way we live now. If the upper classes no longer feel the need to cut themselves off, but on the contrary hasten to show that they are part of the populace, doesn't that demonstrate that there is a will for unity surging through the country, one which may as yet be imperfectly expressed in our institutions but which has such a head of steam behind it that it must soon prevail?

That is certainly the way our politicians talk. For the past half century every political party has talked of a classless society as its goal. But there has been rather less analysis of what exactly this might mean in practice and how it would differ from the Britain that we inherited and have been living in. Perhaps we need to spend a little time reflecting on the idea of a classless society before we can confidently claim that we are living in one.

And we may need to pause and reflect on something else too. All we have said so far relates to the diminishing gap between the upper classes and the rest of society. Could it be that we are so inordinately anxious to draw attention to this phenomenon because there is another gap that is not narrowing at all, one that we are rather less eager to mind?

II
Three Versions of Classlessness

(i) Economic equality and its eclipse

What then do we mean exactly by 'a classless society'? What would such a society look like in practice? How would it differ from the way we live now and from the way our parents lived? And what sort of evidence are we to count as relevant and cogent for this investigation?

The first answer to these questions, the most obvious and the most rigorous answer, is that a classless society would be a society of equals. The more thoroughly equal we are in every possible respect, the less will it be possible for anyone to claim that our society is divided into classes or castes or layers. And the first type of equality we think of is equality in the official rules governing society as a whole, what we have come to call political equality. A society in which some adults are not entitled to vote at all or in which their vote counts for less than the votes of other adults cannot claim to be either equal or classless. Within living memory, Britain has certainly been unequal in these ways. Until 1918, no woman could vote, nor could a very large number of adult males. The franchise was extended to women under 30, the 'flapper vote', only in 1930. Until 1948, businessmen and graduates of the older universities could vote in more than one constituency at parliamentary and local elections. Until 1972, you had to be a householder to sit on a jury, which naturally excluded the poor and the majority of women.

Such inequalities now seem intolerable and antediluvian. We all take it for granted that the State must treat us equally as citizens. And much of modern politics is about pushing forward the boundaries of this civic equality, reforming and redefining its implications. Equal access to the law, for example, implies that the poor must be entitled to some sort of legal aid. At first, that aid was largely confined to criminal cases, where the liberty and even the life of the accused might be at stake. But in recent times we have come to feel that people should not be debarred by lack of money from standing up for themselves. For example, if the State insists on regulating marriage, the most intimate of all human relations, then every citizen must be enabled to use the full resources of the law in this field, which means that legal aid must be extended to divorce.

And if the State is not only regulating other services such as education and health care but intervening as a near-monopoly provider of such services, then it follows that every family must be entitled to equal access to those services, and the quality of the services they receive should be as nearly equal as possible.

Difficult to achieve in practice, but the logic is impeccable and irresistible. And every recent government has at least paid lip service to the ideal. State schools were no longer to be divided into the elite grammar schools and the dustbin secondary moderns (the tripartite division envisaged by the 1944 Act had never come to much, because nobody could be bothered to set up the intended third element, the technical schools). Everyone was to be educated at comprehensive schools which would cater for all tastes and talents. The independent schools which educated only some seven per cent of the total would be allowed to continue, on grounds of individual liberty, but their existence was felt by many to be an embarrassing anomaly. The universities were to be largely State-controlled and State-financed, not least because it was the State rather than private philanthropists which had established the new universities in such huge numbers. Again, access to the universities was to be greatly enlarged, until anyone who could benefit from a university education would be able to find a place. The rough estimate (and soon the official target) was that to achieve this we needed to provide university places for 50 per cent of the age group.

But all this civic equality, though highly desirable in itself, would be scant comfort to the poorest if at the same time intolerable economic inequalities persisted. What good would all these rights and freedoms amount to if you were still on the breadline? It might be right for philosophers such as Isaiah Berlin to distinguish between two sorts of liberty, negative and positive, freedom from and freedom to, political and economic liberty, as they were variously called. But in ordinary speech, it would sound bizarre to claim you were

27

living in a classless society if the government of the day felt no obligation to remedy huge inequalities of income which were producing opulence on the one hand and indigence on the other.

Only the most extreme or idealistic socialists dreamed of exact mathematical equality of income. But it has generally been agreed in Britain, certainly ever since 1945, that the more intolerable inequalities should be levelled out by income tax, so that the top earners should be receiving after tax no more than, let us say, seven or ten times what the bottom earners took home. This process has not been a rapid one. On the contrary, it has been slow, jerky, sometimes imperceptible. But it did continue, off and on, throughout the first thirty years after the war. Left and Right would agree with Polly Toynbee that 'after the last war, the gap between rich and poor got steadily narrower: we have never been more equal than in the late 1970s' (*Guardian*, January 13, 2003).

Left and Right would, however, disagree as to how far this was an unmitigated Good Thing and also about what happened next. The Right would argue that taxation had become so severely progressive as to inhibit industrial and commercial enterprise and to drive potential entrepreneurs to emigrate. The reduction of the higher tax rates under Margaret Thatcher, they maintain, revived the British economy and enabled not only the top earners to prosper but opened up opportunities to acquire wealth and property to people in the lower-middle classes who had never owned anything before. The Left would argue that the change of direction created a selfish, get-rich-quick society in which the wealth never trickled down to the poor.

But both sides would agree, if pressed, that after 1980 there was a change of direction. Economic equality had ceased to be the prime objective, or even a prime objective of government policy. This change in direction has now lasted through a generation and three Prime Ministers. Far from the reduction in inequality achieving a sharply higher priority under New Labour, in some ways it is even less of a governing ideal. The figures from Incomes Data Services suggest that inequality of income actually increased over the first five years of the twenty-first century. Earnings of the top ten per cent of the workforce went up by nearly 54 per cent while the lowest earners in full-time employment saw their pay rise by only 46 per cent.

If you concentrate on the fattest of the fat cats, the Chief Executives of the FTSE100 companies, their pay doubled in the Blair years, while the average UK salary rose by less than half that figure — and of course top earners don't pay nearly as much tax as they used to, so the gap is even wider than it seems. True, Gordon Brown's 'stealth taxes' have reduced the total weight of taxation on the poorest and increased the burden on the middle classes. But until the credit crunch there was no serious attempt either to raise the top rates of tax beyond 40 per cent (apart from the increase in National Insurance contributions) or to deter large companies from paying enormous salaries to their senior executives. And the increase in the top rate to 50 per cent was more in the nature of hush money than a deliberate effort to remedy inequality.

These huge salaries to leading businessmen are matched by even huger compensatory pay-offs to them when they are sacked. That frugal investor, Warren Buffett of Omaha, Nebraska, goes so far as to say 'Chief executives just care about their comp' (*Sunday Telegraph*, May 11, 2003). Scarcely a day goes by without news of the vast rewards accorded to some Chief Executive Officer who has steered his company on to the rocks.

During the two years in which the share price of Reuters fell from 800p to 107p, its chief executive Tom Glocer received cash bonuses worth £1.1 million, salary payments worth £1.6 million and relocation payments of £1 million. At the same time, Reuters employees faced a reduction of one in five jobs over the following three years, 2,250 having already been axed. By 2003, the size of some chief executives' pension pots was already gigantic: Sir Richard Sykes of GlaxoSmithKline's stood at £15.3 million, Lord Browne of BP's at £12.7 million. Not entirely coincidentally, the employee pension schemes of these firms were in huge deficit.

These trends continued right through the Credit Crunch. Between 2000 and 2008 the FT All-Share Index fell by 30 per cent. But cash payments to executives increased by 80 per cent. In the worst crash year of 2008, stock markets fell by a third, but the salaries of top executives rose by ten per cent. While ordinary savers saw the value of their future pensions plummet, the pension pots of top executives went on bubbling. In that year, sixteen company chiefs saw the value of their pension pots jump by more than £1 million, the biggest jumper being that financial wizard Sir Fred Goodwin, whose pension pot increased by £8,3 million.

It was, of course, essential to offer some better incentives for performance. In the 60s and 70s, it really was true that business was hobbled not so much by the relatively modest rates of pay for top executives as by the ludicrous top rates of income tax they were expected to pay — 83p in the pound on earned income and 98p in the pound on investment income. But those absurdities were swept away when Nigel Lawson reduced both rates to 40p in the pound at the end of the 1980s. It is hard to argue that executives needed to double or treble their rates of pay on top of that if they were to be expected to get up earlier in the morning.

Nor is this disregard for equality as a prime value confined to purely economic matters. Whatever else Labour's recent proposals for the reform of education are motivated by, it is not an insatiable lust for equality. The Left complain that specialist schools are only grammar schools by another name and that to allow the universities to set the level of the fees they charge will be to introduce two or more tiers into higher education. Defenders of the government's proposals argue that several tiers already exist in practice, and that the monomania for equality has been a snare and delusion which has depressed standards all round.

But again both sides would agree that equality in the most straightforward sense has not been the principal driving factor in recent British politics. It may be a pleasant hope which now and then hovers in our minds. It may be an auxiliary motive in exercises to improve standards in public services. But it is not a fierce insatiable urge which governs all our waking moments. And we do not seem to be shocked by this. On the contrary, we read on one page of our newspaper of a multimillion-pound golden hello being paid to lure some foreign *wunderkind* to rescue a large British company and, on the next page, of continued degradation and poverty on a council estate, and at most we raise a weary eyebrow at the contrast. We do not demand a violent and immediate programme of levelling down.

Yet it is during this same period since the late 70s that we have been deafened by talk of Britain's growing classlessness. Ever since the Second World War — and indeed ever since the First — it has been generally agreed that the *ancien régime* was played out and that a new, more democratic, more flexible, less sclerotic, less snobbish society was on the way. But it is only within the last two decades that we have heard quite such confident assertions that the new classless society has actually arrived.

Whatever else we mean by 'classless' in talking about Britain now, it isn't economic equality, since we seem to be steaming in the opposite direction from that particular anchorage, and steaming quite blithely too.

So, if it is not a persistent drive to reduce inequality that underpins our claim to be increasingly classless, what is it? There are, I think, two further candidates, to which we must now turn.

(ii) One Volk, one lifestyle?
Is it possible that, after all, the turn towards a classless

society does not have much to do with politics in the official sense? Perhaps it does not derive — anyway, not primarily — from laws and governments and taxes and public services. Perhaps it is simply a matter of social behaviour, of the way we talk and dress and live our lives. We have already seen how the upper class no longer seeks to mark itself off from the middle class by enforcing its own linguistic taboos. Perhaps this benign relaxation is only one symptom of a more general convergence of manners.

That would surely be a legitimate type of a classless society. People might not be equal in incomes. Some people might be more powerful than others in other ways that were not entirely economic. But despite these differences, people of all classes might live in much the same way. It has often been suggested that the United States has been more or less classless in that way and has been so ever since Tocqueville first noticed the fact. Switzerland and the Scandinavian countries have also been put forward as candidates. So have Australia and New Zealand. In these regions and countries, we are told, considerable inequalities of income and wealth persist but are tolerated, even regarded as necessary for economic prosperity (though these inequalities may now and then be curbed by government action if they appear to be growing excessive). But they are also tolerated because the lifestyles of the rich do not seem so very different from those of the poor. The houses and gardens of the top earners do not seem inordinately larger or more luxurious than those of ordinary people. Their pleasures, habits of speech, opinions and allegiances do not seem sharply removed from the common run. They are better cushioned against life's discomforts, but not unimaginably so.

Strolling round the shores of Lake Michigan, for example, you will see the mansions of the senior executives of the great motor manufacturers up to and including members of the Ford family. They are roomy and luxurious but they are not in the same class as the English country houses built by the great merchants of the eighteenth and nineteenth centuries and often now inhabited by their present-day successors such as Michael Heseltine and James Dyson, the vacuum-cleaner wizard.

Is modern Britain, too, one of these 'quiet republics' (although some of them are 'crowned republics', as Britain too has been described)? Or, if we have not yet achieved this level of social convergence, are we on the way there?

That is unmistakably what many people, perhaps the majority, mean when they talk about classlessness. Indeed, this is a phenomenon which many people take for granted, because it seems to them so obvious and conspicuous.

What they mean is that we don't look or sound so class-divided or behave in such class-divided ways as our parents or grandparents. We seem more homogeneous and we wish to seem so — by dressing alike, in blue jeans and Marks & Spencer clothes, by talking alike, in classless accents — mockney, Estuary English, dj mid-Atlantic — and in other hybrid voices which are designed to conceal class origins and demonstrate solidarity with our fellow citizens.

Now people have been saying this kind of thing ever since the end of the Second World War (even since the end of the

First). The 20th century was, after all, destined to be the Century of the Common Man. The power of aristocracy had been broken by death duties and the universal franchise. The coming of the Welfare State would equalise our economic conditions. The coming of the BBC and the cinema would equalise our voices, so that regional dialects (which among other things served to identify the lower classes) would be a thing of the past.

In recent years, extra flourishes have been added to this diagnosis: for example, that the coming of Terence Conran's pots and pans and tables and chairs would bring simple good design to the masses; similarly, the rash of TV programmes and newspaper columns on cookery would teach the lower classes how to cook and wean them off junk food. Basically, though, the lines of the argument have remained the same for a long time now.

Have 'class markers' really disappeared to the extent we hope or pretend? And in so far as they have survived, do we really pay less attention to them? Are we more reluctant to point them out and spend time analysing them? If we hear less about class distinctions these days, is it because they are genuinely diminishing, or because we feel more inhibited about referring to them — which might also be a sign that they are diminishing, even if not as fast as we would like?

Let us try a few comparisons. Think of a photograph of a crowd before the war — walking along Piccadilly, say, or at a military parade or a race meeting. The men will all be dressed in suits, and most of them will be wearing hats. Don't we find it quite difficult to tell them apart, let alone be sure of

35

identifying to which class they belong?

You might suppose that the hats would help to distinguish them: flat caps for the poor, trilbies or bowlers perhaps for the middle classes, top hats for top people. But even there the matter is more complicated than that. Age and occasion come into it. At a golf tournament or out shooting in the 30s, for example, almost everyone up to and including the Prince of Wales will be wearing a flat cap. In the City, clerks and messengers and partners will all be wearing bowlers, although the Governor of the Bank of England and the Government Broker may be wearing toppers. I have in front of me a photograph of my uncle and my grandfather, Berkshire squires both, at a race meeting in the late 1920s. My uncle, then a young man, is wearing a flat cap; my grandfather, a retired Tory MP, is wearing a soft grey felt hat with a dark band of the type worn by bankers in Westerns. Both would have felt they were wearing a hat appropriate not so much to their class as to their age bracket.

Now let us take a cross-section of passers-by in a London street today and begin to sort them. First, there are the men in standard lounge suits, from Austin Reed or Cecil Gee. They will be hatless and wearing pale shirts and darkish ties. Their shoes may be polished. These men, we assume, will be working in banks, insurance offices, law firms or the civil service.

Then we see men who are on average somewhat younger, in baggy Armani-type suits with loafers on their feet. Their shirts are likely to be of a darker colour and half of them won't be wearing a tie. These are sometimes described as belonging to the New Class. They work in the media, advertising, PR, graphic design or publishing. They too will be hatless.

Then we can see men in track-suits, or track-suit bottoms and T-shirts if fine, or until recently shell suits. They will be wearing trainers and possibly a baseball cap or a hoodie of the type traditionally worn by serial rapists. If the wearer is under 25, the baseball cap may be worn reversed, and he may also sport an earring. All ages may well be shaven-headed.

Don't we have here the makings of a class system in clothes at least as strongly marked as the dress code of the 1930s? I am not confident enough to trace a similar system in women's clothes of either period, except to say that the similarities in style (not in quality or cut of cloth) between women of different classes in any period usually seem to us more strongly marked than their differences. In the late 1920s, for example, every woman from the Duchess of York (later the Queen Mother) downwards will be wearing a cloche hat. My grandmother, no fashion plate, is wearing one as she strides over the grass between my uncle and my grandfather in the photograph I mentioned. Ten years later, women of all classes will be switching over to turbans; skirt lengths similarly go up and down according to the dictates of fashion rather than social class.

Even if you concentrate on the young — who are famously addicted to an international classless style of dress — you can still find class markers today, fainter perhaps but not entirely erased. For example, straight upper-class young men these days will certainly possess several pairs of jeans, but on top, instead of a T-shirt, they will wear a polo shirt or a casual Friday shirt from Boden. And instead of a leather jacket, incongruously they will sometimes sport with their jeans a boating jacket of the type worn by Guards officers in summers long gone by. There are complicated feelings at work here, perhaps a desire to be both cool or hip and at the same time keep their distance and retain a separate group identity. At the weekend in London, upper-class men of all ages may still dress as if they were going for a walk in the country — tweed jacket, corduroys often of a lurid canary colour, and even a flat cap.

But even if there has been some equalising of dress — though in my view the uniformity is not much greater, except among the young, than it was in the 1930s — such a claim is harder to sustain when you look at other sides of life: at the way people furnish and decorate their homes, for example.

As always, city neighbourhoods are separated by price. And increasingly so are villages, as the pretty old cottages are bought up by the well-to-do, many of them retired people, and the old locals move out to the council estates. But in both city and country there are transitional areas where people from different income brackets live side by side, before the poorer sell up and are replaced by incoming professional people. And if we peer through the windows, we can once again establish a three-class system of sorts, this time in home furnishing.

In the older well-to-do streets, you will find dark, often mahogany furniture of a Georgian or Victorian type, sofas covered in chintz, antique clocks, Axminster or Wilton carpets, with landscapes or sometimes family portraits on the wall. There may be a bookcase, glass-fronted, often with fine-bound books in it. Here and there in such streets, but more probably in transitional areas, you will find other houses decorated very differently. These have plain modern furniture in paler woods, sofas and armchairs upholstered in plain materials, carpets also of a plain design or made of coir, jute or seagrass. On the walls will be prints and reproductions from various periods of the 20th century, from Picasso and Matisse through Warhol and Liechtenstein to Caulfield, Hockney and Hodgkin. The rugs will be kilims and other tribal types. The books will be paperbacks, though a large part of the shelves will be given over to tapes, CDs and DVDs.

Here and there in the transitional streets but abundantly in the poorer districts and on the new estates you will find a third kind of decor. Here the carpet will be of a violent highly coloured design, whorled and clustered and splashy. The wallpaper will also be colourful, often of a floral design and frequently textured with a flock finish or a crusty effect. There will be a matching three-piece suite. On the walls you are mostly likely to see family photographs, although there may be landscapes not entirely unlike those on the walls of the first type of house. If there is a bookshelf, it may contain china and glass ornaments as well as books.

If we move outdoors, through the French windows which are available as standard in the first class and quite often seen in the second but seldom in the third, we shall find two general types of garden. The first, modelled on Vita Sackville-West's garden at Sissinghurst, and also on Gertrude Jekyll's writings and garden designs, will be largely muted in its colour effects, specialising in delicate pinks, mauves and pale blues, allowing no bright red or yellow. The shrubs will be massed informally to give a natural impression. There may be wild flowers planted in the long grass.

The other type, more generally found in Class Three dwellings, though occasionally in old-fashioned Class One establishments, will go for bright colours, formal plantings with island beds in the lawn and herbaceous borders along the walls. Its favourite flowers are begonias, busy Lizzies, red-hot pokers, gladioli, while the first type prefers true geraniums, tobacco plants and old-fashioned roses.

Some gardens partake a little of both types, and a few gardeners like to cross over, but not many. When the doyen of gardening writers, Christopher Lloyd, in his old age decided to abandon the tasteful muted efforts he had been achieving all his life at his famous garden, Great Dixter, in Kent, and go for the brightest scarlet and orange flowers he could think of, there was a sharp intake of breath among his fellow gardeners. He had, so to speak, gone over to the other side. But he was soon forgiven for what was identifiable as a classic high camp gesture in which bad taste is, at the whim of the insider, decreed to be good.

Class distinction in gardening is relatively simple and lighthearted. By contrast, class distinction in voices is the most painful subject. It was, as I have said, supposed to have died out long ago. The public voices which we were subjected to all day long — on radio and television and in the cinema — were expected to flatten out our peculiarities, so that we would ultimately all be talking a modified BBC English.

Those who made this hopeful prophecy failed to specify exactly what sort of BBC English they meant. Was it the superbly articulated upper-middle class of the old newsreading tradition — which had lasted through from Alvar Liddell to Bryan Perkins? Or was it the jaunty mid-Atlantic of disc jockeys on the Light Programme and Radio Luxembourg? That was the first complication, but there was another thing which I don't think the prophets of sameness really took into account.

Even in its early days, the BBC was the first place that you heard the regional accents of Britain given any kind of public authority. Indeed, hearing your own local accent on the radio brought it to consciousness, and made you aware of its difference from the accent employed by neighbours just across the county boundary. Hearing the voice of the Dorset farmer Ralph Wightman on the radio, for example, made me more aware of how the people in our own village on Salisbury Plain spoke, and how different it was — harder, more sardonic — from the creamy Hampshire burr of the cricket commentator John Arlott or the rising Labour politician Jim Callaghan.

Perhaps as a result, far from dying out as expected, regional accents seem to have flowered as never before and are now often deliberately cultivated and rejoiced in. Even someone like the present writer, who has only an average ear for dialect, can detect at least a dozen in Great Britain, without attempting Ireland; the rude vowels of Lancashire, the rough gravelly Yorkshire, the gurgle and coo of the Tyne, the whining Scouse, the generic Midlands nasal, the flat hard Norfolk voice of the Singing Postman, old-fashioned Cockney, the South London vulgar diphthong, the Hampshire burr, the soft Bristolian, the rich cream Devon, the all-purpose Welsh lilt, genteel Morningside, guttural Glaswegian, soft peaty West Highland. Any self-respecting linguist should be able to double this tally.

Most of what I have said in the last couple of pages is well known to us, and some of it is actually voiced now and then, usually in order to amuse ourselves. Class still provides part of the underlying message in the style supplements, and anyone who identifies a new social sub-class is sure of a hearing, particularly if the new term reflects a reality that goes beneath the surface. The term 'Sloane Ranger', for example, coined by Peter York and Ann Barr in the 1980s, was immediately resonant, not just because it identified with deadly accuracy the social habits of that remnant of the old upper classes which lived within a stone's throw of Sloane Square, shopped at Peter Jones and wore waxed Barbour jackets, but because their description also captured both the nostalgia and the fortitude of such people as well as their snobbery.

The whole topic of class markers still has some mileage left in it. A *Daily Telegraph* feature a few years ago (September 28, 2002) proclaimed that 'it's now cool to be a Sloane' and that many of the old habits, aversions and haunts of the earlier Sloane Rangers continued 20 years after the tribe was first identified. Of Princes William and Harry, we were told that 'on the odd occasions that the Princes do venture up to London, it is usually to meet Old Etonian chums in the same Chelsea bars and clubs that their mother had frequented 20 years previously.' Smoking jackets and Burberry were back. The Volkswagen Golf DBI ('Daddy bought it') fulfilled the same social role as the Golf GTI had in its day. The Countryside March of September 2002, one of the largest single gatherings of the British upper classes in history (matched in world terms perhaps only by the Opus Dei gathering in St Peter's Square to celebrate the canonisation of its founder), featured an array of rural costume that had scarcely changed in my adult lifetime. Nor had the fierce belief of the upper classes in an unchanging countryside which must be preserved at all costs.

In fact, the cause of 'preserving the countryside' has a strong class element in it. For the upper classes, the ideal English landscape remains one in which villages keep within their pre-1914 limits and do not spread into the surrounding 'unspoilt' farmland — although, by any aesthetic standards, modern agriculture can produce some decidedly unappealing vistas, denuded of hedgerows, woods and wilderness. Ideally too, the population of those villages should be made up exclusively of gentry and peasantry, or 'country people', as the euphemism has it. Townees belong in towns and, if released into the country at all, should not wear brightly coloured anoraks and must keep to the footpaths at all times. The attitude of the old Duke of Portland who built underground passages at his country seat, Welbeck Abbey, so that he should not have to set eyes upon his staff, was regarded as somewhat eccentric. But it is implicit in many upper-class assumptions about the countryside that the lower classes are better neither seen nor heard, that the best service that they can render totheir social superiors is to remain as nearly invisible as possible.

This particularly applies to Essex Man with his loud mouth and his vulgar tastes and habits. When the journalist Simon Heffer coined this term to describe members of old working-class families who had moved out of the East End into suburbs and new towns but had refused to become genteel, he described a defiant social reality which lurked behind the sociologist's anodyne term 'blue-collar worker'. 'Essex Man' described that considerable fraction of the working class that had been expected to join the general process of embourgeoisement, but — along with Essex Girl — had refused to kowtow. British politics has spawned plenty of such stereotypes — Hampstead Liberal, Orpington Man, Worcester Woman, Mondeo Man, and most recently Islington Man. Some of these stereotypes speedily become out of date. Hampstead long ago became too expensive an area for most liberals, for example, but even when the stereotypes provide only a blurred snapshot of a fleeting social moment, they do remind us that diversity — which we applaud — also tends to imply division — which we don't.

I'm not saying that these class markers all carry some profound significance. Some are vestigial reminders of former, more deeply class-marked stages in our social history. Others are passing fads which we take up by way of amusement and will drop as soon as they pass out of fashion

It is not, however, as if the making of such distinctions has invariably become more lighthearted with the passage of time. On the contrary, quite often there is a sour, even malevolent note. Take, for example, the flock of websites that have sprung up which are devoted to the successors to Essex Man and Essex Girl, the Chatham Boys and Girls or Chavs. The homepage of Chavscum (webmaster@chavscum.co.uk) proclaims itself as 'a field guide to Britain's burgeoning peasant underclass': 'What makes the Chavs attire so funny is that they think they are at the cutting edge of fashion and by adorning their body with hunks of worthless 9ctgold crap they look rich! In reality what they do look like are a bunch of fucking pikeys!' — and so on, through the Chavs' deplorable taste in clothes and cars, their intellectual inadequacies ('the dumbed-down lunchtime news will still prove as inaccessible as Proust to most Chavs') to their mindless addiction to the most vacuous television shows and their drunken bickerings into the small hours. The hatred almost explodes off the computer screen.

We shall return to this weird loathing. But for the purposes of this chapter what matters are the continued obsession with class difference and the itch to scratch at it and caricature it. There is in fact a huge amount of evidence (and evidence being added to every day) that one thing we cannot argue in support of the thesis that Britain has become, or is well on the way to becoming, a classless society is that there is now uniformity in the way we show ourselves to the world.

There remains then only one candidate to justify the classlessness claim, and that is the most formidable and interesting of the three. After rejecting equality of income and equality in lifestyle as the prime mover in the emergence of our supposedly classless society, we must turn to equality of opportunity.

(iii) Opportunity knocks but doesn't answer

There is no doubt that equality of opportunity has been the declared goal of most British politicians since the war. Indeed, you can date this general consensus further back. Disraeli, in his *Vindication of the English Constitution*, wrote that 'the basis of English society is equality, but here let us distinguish: there are two kinds of equality; there is the equality that levels and destroys and the equality that elevates and creates.'

The first kind implied an equality of result, in which the tall poppies would be beheaded and the talented reduced to the ranks. The second kind rested on equality before the law, on equality of liberties and hence the freedom to make the best of your talents. 'One of the great achievements of modern Conservatism', Rab Butler boasted, 'is to bring in as a reality *la carrière ouverte aux talents*.' Now this is not as thoroughgoing an equality of opportunity as that envisaged by the Labour Party throughout most of its existence. Most leading Labour thinkers would argue that a proper equality of opportunity demanded an equal starting point. Unfair differences in health and education must be eliminated in order to give the worst-off a chance of competing on reasonably equal terms. For Conservatives, by contrast, achieving this would demand an excessive degree of social engineering. 'Complete equality of opportunity', Ian Gilmour argues, 'could only be achieved by taking children away from their parents and bringing them up in baby farms, which is, or should be unthinkable... Everybody should have a chance to get on in the world and rise as high as his abilities permit, unhindered by antique privilege.' (*Inside Right*, 1977, p.151) And Gilmour went on daringly to declare: 'In this country that aim is near achievement.'

Socialists, and most liberals too, would dispute that confident judgment, and argue that the worst off were still unfairly handicapped in the race. None the less, they would surely agree that the aim was desirable, and that some considerable progress had been made over the course of the 20th century, even though reactionary Tory governments might now and then halt or derail the process.

And what politicians put forward in their election programmes, most people accept as the natural direction of modern politics. And they see signs of this equality all around them; the spread of home ownership and the huge expansion of student numbers in further and higher education offer the most striking evidence of it.

There is then a form of argument which is widely accepted both in political circles and in the broader population. It runs roughly like this: in the old days — let us say up to 1914 — there was not much social mobility, class barriers were rigid, and only the luckiest or most energetic men (very few women) escaped from the class into which they were born. These days, opportunities have hugely expanded for everyone, even the poorest (though they are still handicapped). Almost everyone has a chance to realise his or her potential. The life chances of our children are likely to be better still.

Britain is a more flexible and open place, and as a result the old class rigmarole is fading and lifestyles are converging. All this adds up to an increasingly classless society, and one of the symptoms of it is that equality of opportunity is generally accepted as a guiding principle. It is up to the government to realise and strengthen this principle in practice, for example, by improving standards in the public services and ensuring through taxation and benefits that the poor receive a fair share of the cake.

Thus in asserting this equality of opportunity, we bring in the other two ways of being classless: some equalising of incomes and some consequential converging of lifestyles. But it is this third principle, the equality of opportunity, which is the one that really counts. And it is on that principle that we base our claim to be on our way to a classless society, differing only in our estimates as to how near we are to that splendid goal. Equality of opportunity is what distinguishes us from Britain in the past and from many other benighted countries in the present.

Now there are several things to be said about this claim. The riders and qualifications I shall offer may not by themselves destroy the claim or nullify it. But, taken together, these qualifications do suggest that there is a dangerous simplicity, a thoughtless over-confidence at work here. We ought at the very least to take the argument a little more carefully and sceptically before rushing to conclusions.

The first point to note is that Britain always has been a notoriously *open* society. We may not see this ourselves. Often it takes outside observers like Stein Ringen, the American sociologist working at Oxford, or the economist P.T. Bauer, a Hungarian Jewish refugee, to point out that for many centuries, of all major European countries, Britain has been the easiest place for a young man of talent to make his fortune and to rise within his own lifetime to an accepted social position among the gentry or even the nobility. Marriage, too, provided a handy leg-up to many a likely lad, from Dick Whittington onwards. 'Mind the Gap' weddings have been a staple of English farce, and a social reality, for five centuries and more.

Neither political nor social power has ever been closed off to the upwardly mobile. It may seem remarkable to us today that a music-hall entertainer's son, brought up in furnished lodgings, with scarcely an O-level to his name and no higher education, should become Prime Minister, as John Major did. But was that any more remarkable than that the illegitimate son of a ploughman should do the same seventy years earlier and go on to hobnob with duchesses into the bargain, as Ramsay MacDonald did? Or that Benjamin Disraeli, a Jew who never attended public school or university and could become a Member of Parliament only because he had been hastily baptised as a child, should become Prime Minister of Britain at the height of her imperial power in the mid-nineteenth century?

Yet we are reluctant to acknowledge these obvious facts, a reluctance which perceptive observers find rather perplexing. Professor Ringen argues that 'Britain continues to portray itself as an exotic and archaic class society, although it is now an ordinary class society, much like Germany or Sweden.

What is peculiar in Britain is not the reality of the class system and its continuing existence, but class psychology: the preoccupation with class, the belief in class, and the symbols of class in manners, dress and language.' (*Times Literary Supplement*, January 24, 1997). At least Ringen discerns some progress in Britain; instead of an archaic society fully equipped with an aristocracy and a proletariat, we now just have rich and poor like everyone else. But Lord Bauer, in his essay 'Class on the Brain: the cost of a British Obsession' (1997), while joining Ringen in deploring the damage done by this obsession, prefers to point to continuities rather than transformations in our island story. What has always distinguished Britain from more rigid and hierarchical societies has been its relatively high class mobility and an admirable openness to change which flows from this mobility. Both observers agree that, to quote Ringen again, the British live in an open society but think they don't: 'Britain is a thoroughly modern society with thoroughly archaic institutions, conventions and beliefs' — which is what makes the British mentality so difficult to grasp for a stranger — and, I am tempted to add, for many British intellectuals too.

Of course, in certain respects Britain is still not as open as the more impatient reformers would like. Most judges are still educated at the more expensive schools, there are not many women chairing large public companies. And in some cases, policies designed to ensure equality of access and opportunity have not worked out as they were intended to. The huge expansion of higher education, for example, has mostly enabled the not-so-brilliant children of the middle class to attend university. The proportion of British graduates who come from the working classes has scarcely increased over the past half century (although their absolute numbers will have increased), because so many of the extra places are taken up by the 'green-welly brigade'.

In their huge survey of social mobility, *Origins and Destinations: Family, Class, and Education in Modern Britain* (1980), A.H. Halsey, A.F. Heath and J.M.Ridge looked back on nearly half a century of British education. Their conclusions were decidedly sobering. There had been some social mobility as a result of the huge expansion of State education, but not much.

In summary, school inequalities of opportunity have been remarkably stable over the forty years which our study covers. Throughout, the service class has had roughly three times the chance of the working class of getting some kind of selective secondary schooling. Only at 16 has there been any significant reduction in relative class chances, but even here the absolute gains have been greater for the service class. If the 'hereditary curse upon English education is its organisation upon lines of social class', that would seem to be as true in the 1960s as it was in 1931 when Tawney wrote. (p.205)

The class differences [in the age of leaving school and starting work] were the same in the 1960s as they had been in the 1920s, despite a relatively favourable demography, economic growth, and rising educational investment. Moreover, a class inequality with respect to the quality of education provided at all ages has persisted... In short, interpreting educational embourgeoisement to mean that, as education expanded, the typical educational careers of children from different social origins would converge, the result is disappointment. (p.207)

Halsey was writing just as the new comprehensive schools were getting into their stride, and he shared the hopes of other educationalists that this new universal system might change things for the better. But 20 years on, the verdict is little more encouraging.

In fact, Polly Toynbee in the *Guardian* (March 5 2003) reports that 'Research into children born in 1958 finds they were far more class mobile (up and down) than children born in 1970, who largely stayed in their father's social class.' She describes this as 'so counter-intuitive that people find these irrefutable truths hard to believe'. And so indeed they are if you expect comprehensive schooling and the huge increase in the numbers going to university to lubricate and accelerate social mobility as was the declared hope of the reformers. By now, it seems, that even lifelong enthusiasts for those reforms have to admit some disillusionment.

The Education and Child Poverty Report asserts that 'educational success in Britain is more determined by social class than in any other country'. The gap between poor and better-off children is evident by the age of two and widens throughout the school career, until school leavers from unskilled backgrounds are five times less likely to enter higher education than those from professional backgrounds (*Guardian*, March 25 2003).

David Bell, the Chief Inspector of Schools, told the Fabian Society that 'since 1996 the socio-economic attainment gap has widened in secondary schools'. Teachers were complaining that conditions had become tougher in the classroom over the past ten years and areas classified as 'disavantaged' had spread from inner-city areas to other parts of the country, notably coastal towns (*Times*, November 21, 2003). Shortly before she resigned in despair as Education Secretary, Estelle Morris, a former teacher, told the Labour Party conference of her disappointment and disenchantment with the comprehensive system:

> It hasn't achieved all that we campaigned for. I thought it would break the link between poverty and achievement. It hasn't. I hoped it would end the massive underachievement of ethnic minorities. It hasn't. (Blackpool, 2 October, 2002)

And both Estelle Morris and Tony Blair himself at the same conference chose to describe Britain as now being in the 'post-comprehensive era'.

By the middle of Tony Blair's second term, this disillusionment suddenly became widespread among his ministers and ex-ministers, especially those described as modernists. The loyalist Patricia Hewitt told the Fabian Society that the socialists of the 1930s would be horrified to see how little progress we had made in overturning poverty and inequality. Michael Meacher lamented that inequality was growing again under the government which he had served for six years before being discarded. And all in the same week, another ex-minister, Stephen Byers, talked about 'an environment in which disadvantage reinforces itself across generations, where underachievement leads to a spiral of decline' — just as Keith Joseph 25 years earlier had shocked his complacent audiences by talking about a cycle of social deprivation. In fact, Byers was the more shocking, since in his lecture to the Social Market Foundation (24 June, 2003) he indicated that things were actually worsening: 'We are witnessing a silent and secret revolution where, to a greater extent than before, those born into disadvantage and poverty will be condemned to it for the rest of their lives.' All this after half a century of the strongly redistributive taxation and thirty years of the comprehensive education that were supposed to flatten out inequalities and open up opportunities to the poorest.

Alan Milburn, former Health Secretary and another of Blair's modernisers, also declares that 'children born — as I was — in 1958 were far less dependent on the economic status of their parents than those born in later years. Birth not worth has become more key to life chances.' (*Guardian*, November 10, 2003)

Milburn argues for a huge extension of home ownership to the poor to narrow the gap. Similarly, Chris Holmes, former Director of Shelter, believes that 'housing inequalities are now much greater than they were 50 years ago'. Introducing his Housing Bill in 1949, Aneurin Bevan had argued that 'it is entirely undesirable that on modern housing estates only one type of citizen should live... we should try to introduce what was always the lovely feature of English and Welsh villages, where the doctor, the grocer, the butcher and the farm labourer all lived in the same street.' As a symbol of that aim, the Bill would sweep away all reference to 'the housing of the working class.' Yet as Holmes points out, far from that 'lovely feature' ushering in an era of social diversity in housing, it was instrumental in that long process of geographical social polarisation with which we are embarrassingly familiar (C. Holmes, *Housing, Equality and Choice*, IPPR 2003). In fact, Danny Dorling and Phil Rees of Leeds University argue in a paper for the Royal Geographical Society (*A Nation Still Dividing*, 2003) that the results of the 2001 census demonstrate that 'for key aspects of life in Britain, the nation has continued in the 1990s to divide socially and geographically often at a faster rate than was occurring in the 1980s and 1970s.'

Thus equality of opportunity in Britain today is neither such a new phenomenon nor in practice so fully achieved as we like to think. You can certainly find large areas of British life where someone from a poor background can find promotion and acceptance much more easily than a generation ago. The 'barrow boys' might not have quite taken over the City of London, but they certainly decimated the ranks of the Old Etonians in the Square Mile who used to swan through life without visible effort. But the picture of ever accelerating mobility is too brightly coloured to accord with reality.

What has changed emphatically and irredeemably is the universal acceptance of the *principle* of equal opportunity. As a slogan, an ideology, a political programme, equality of opportunity is now supreme. In practice, social mobility has stumbled along, always disappointing the progressives even more than it has alarmed the reactionaries.

But in *theory*, it has been an all-conquering *victor ludo-rum*. And we need to draw back from practice for a moment to consider the theory. Because when you think about it, equality of opportunity is an odd kind of equality. 'The equality to become unequal' — what sort of justice is that?

Society is to be organised, if necessary re-engineered in quite radical ways, but only to ensure a level starting-point. After that, you are on your own, every one of you. And if you at the back there should happen to lag behind, further and further as the years go by, then you have no one to blame but yourself.

Thoughtful people on the Left have been uncomfortable about this prospect for some time. To combat it, they have proposed that fresh opportunities should be available to the laggers, not just on moving from one school to the next, or even from school to college, but at every stage in life and every age. The Commission on Social Justice, set up by John Smith during his sadly curtailed period as Labour leader, declared that:

> Our vision is of a national Learning Bank which enables everybody to have access to lifelong learning. Expanding higher education is important — but lifelong learning is much broader and includes adult further education, current-ly the Cinderella of education and training policy. (*Social Justice*, Vintage, 1994, p. 141)

And as Chancellor of the Exchequer, Gordon Brown

maintained his own personal interest in lifelong learning, as a means to offer continuing hope to those who are otherwise left behind.

Even so, in what sense is this a *classless* society? Even if equality of opportunity is fully achieved, all that has happened is that each of us starts off on the same rung of the ladder. There is still a ladder, and for most of us what we shall be looking at most of our working lives are the perky bottoms of our betters climbing further and faster than we are capable of doing. Lifelong learning devices may offer renewed opportunities to alter our station in the pecking order, but they do not abolish the pecking order. In some senses, they may even increase our anxiety about our station, since the benign activities of the Learning Bank will have left us even less excuse for our failure. This raises the uncomfortable thought that there may not be any necessary connection between a classless society and a mobile society.

A classless society is not necessarily a mobile society. Think of a canton of mountain peasants all living the same kind of lives for generations. Or a tribe of South Sea islanders fishing and fruit-picking for centuries until they are invaded. Such ideal societies may be more or less classless, even egalitarian (although anthropologists often disagree as to how much), but we would certainly think of them as static societies, undisturbed by jealousy or ambition — which is why we love the idea of them. Conversely, a mobile society is not necessarily a classless one. The ambitions which drive its citizens on to achieve things their parents never dreamed of achieving are likely also to lead, willy-nilly, to the formation of new classes and new social distinctions.

Is this such an agreeable prospect? Among his many other achievements, that legendary British sociologist Michael Young published in 1958 a book called *The Rise of the Meritocracy*. It was automatically assumed by those who did not read the book that it must be a celebration of this new class. After all, it is so often the case that commentators who identify an emerging new class rather approve of it. If they do not themselves already belong to it, they would like to do so. Ever since, this new word 'meritocracy' which Young coined for the purposes of the book has been widely used, mostly with a sense of approval, even admiration. After all, other words deriving from the same root — 'meritorious' for example — had been terms of approval.

But *The Rise of the Meritocracy* is not like that at all. On the contrary, it is a satire, a slightly clumsy one perhaps (Young was not a creative writer by profession), but a satire that makes its point quite effectively. The book purports to be a history of English education between 1870-2003, told by a smug social historian of progressive views. In the latter year. he looks back on the steady advance of competition and promotion by merit in industry and in the civil service as a result of a stream of educational reforms, from the Forster Act of 1870 onwards. Over the course of the 20th century foreign competition demanded that we give up the old nepotism and promotion by seniority. In order to survive, we needed to reward and advance merit wherever it was found. As a result, a new elite was formed, and the lower classes were drained of their most talented members. In the old days, no class was homogeneous in brains: clever members of the upper classes had as much in common with clever members of the lower classes as they did with stupid members of their own. Now that people are classified by ability, the gap between the classes has inevitably become wider. The upper classes are, on the one hand, no longer weakened by self-doubt and self-criticism. Today the eminent know that success is just reward for their own capacity, for their own efforts, and for their own undeniable achievement. They deserve to belong to a superior class. They know, too, that not only are they of higher calibre to start with, but that a first-class education has been built upon their native gifts. (p.106)

... What can they have in common with people whose education stopped at sixteen or seventeen, leaving them with the merest smattering of dog-science? How can they carry on a two-sided conversation with the lower classes when they speak another, richer, and more exact language? Today, the elite know that, except for a grave error in administration, which should at once be corrected if brought to light, their social inferiors are inferiors in other ways as well — that is, in the two vital qualities, of intelligence and education, which are given pride of place in the more consistent value system of the 21st century. (p. 107)

And as a corollary:

As for the lower classes, their situation is different too. Today all persons, however humble, know they have had every chance. They are tested again and again. If on one occasion they are off-colour, they have a second, a third, and fourth opportunity to demonstrate their ability. But if they have been labelled 'dunce' repeatedly they cannot any longer pretend; their image of themselves is more nearly a true, unflattering, reflection. Are they not bound to recognise that they have an inferior status — not as in the past because they were denied opportunity; but because they are inferior. For the first time in human history the inferior man has no ready buttress for his self-regard. (pp. 107—8)

Nor apparently is there now, in 2003 AD, any way for the lower classes to remedy that inferiority. The ideal implicit in the comprehensive schools has been abandoned in favour of a revival of the old grammar schools. The historic mission of the Labour movement is exhausted. The trade unions have changed their names to less confrontational, more technical-sounding titles. The Mineworkers became the Mine Technicians, 'worker' being now a taboo word, as indeed is 'Labour'. The Labour Party has been reborn as the modern Technicians Party and co-opted into the rule of the meritocratic elite. Protest is useless, the fatuous narrator opines, and the new underground movements — the Populists and the Chelsea Manifesto of 2009 in favour of a classless tolerant society, for example, even the general strike which is about to happen — have no hope of success. The redistribution of ability between the classes in society has ensured that 'the lower classes no longer have the power to make revolt effective ... Without intelligence in their heads, the lower classes are never more menacing than a rabble, even if they are sometimes sullen, sometimes mercurial, not yet completely predictable.' (pp. 189—90).

The book ends with a footnote recording that 'since the author of this essay was himself killed at Peterloo, the publishers regret that they were not able to submit to him the proofs of his manuscript.' (p. 190)

Michael Young's warnings were not much heeded at the time and are not much heeded now. Yet quite a few of his prophecies have turned out pretty accurately: the trade unions have given themselves winsome new names like Amicus and Unison, the Labour Party has become New Labour, antique barriers to promotion by merit (such as the 'glass ceiling' keeping down women) have disappeared, comprehensive education is on the way out, at least in its unstreamed, idealistic form. Above all, we cannot help noticing that the old class system has been reconstituted into a more or less meritocratic upper tier and a lower tier which is defined principally by its failure to qualify for the upper tier. This is the new gap that we have to mind.

III

The Uppers and the Downers

In the spring of 1895, H.G. Wells published his first novel, *The Time Machine*. He had recently run away from his wife with Amy Robbins, whom he rechristened Jane and who was to become his second, even more betrayed wife. They were in lodgings with Amy's mother at Tusculum Villa, Eardley Road, Sevenoaks, and it was in these uncertain circumstances that, after several weeks of frantic rewriting, he produced the final, fictional version of a theme which had started life as a series of prophetic visions of the future, not as a coherent story. *The Time Machine* has remained one of Wells's most popular and most influential books — never out of print from that day to this. It has been rather firmly catalogued as science fiction, and as such has spawned a hundred imitations and developments of the idea of time travel.

Yet the science fiction element is not the original thing about this amazing short novel. In fact the technical details are rather lightly touched in. The time machine itself sounds more like an exquisite creation by Fabergé than something you could travel to the year AD 802,000-odd in. It has gleaming brass rails and levers. 'Parts were of nickel, parts of ivory, parts had certainly been filed or sawn out of rock crystal.' (*The Complete Short Stories of H.G. Wells*, 1927, p.17) As for time-travel, it is excessively unpleasant, 'a feeling exactly like that one has upon a switchback — of a helpless headlong motion.' (p.24) Just as you might expect in fact and not really so very remarkable.

The real brilliance of *The Time Machine* lies elsewhere. It is the first great modern dystopia, the heir of Plato's *Republic* and More's *Utopia* and the immediate forerunner of Huxley's *Brave New World* and Orwell's *Nineteen Eighty-Four*. Both his successors knew Wells's work. Huxley in fact described *Brave New World* as 'a novel of the future — Wells's *Utopia* realised, and the absolute horror of it' — although Wells was to dislike *Brave New World* (Aldous Huxley, Nicholas Murray, 2002, pp.249 and 262), and Huxley himself, like most of the Bloomsbury Group, detested Wells — 'that horrid, vulgar little man' he called him. Orwell, as you would expect, was more sympathetic to Wells both as a person and as a writer. He described a later fantasy story of Wells's, 'When the Sleeper Awakes', as 'a vision of a glittering sinister world in which society has hardened into a caste system and the workers are permanently enslaved.' What all these dystopias have in common, as does Plato's *Republic*, is a vision of a future society cruelly divided by class, a world in which the different sections of society have utterly failed to blend into a single undifferentiated species as Shelley envisaged,

Equal, unclassed, tribeless and nationless

On the contrary, the class divisions in these imagined societies have become unbreakable and dominant. In fact, class division seems to be the animating principle of the whole society: the Proles in *Nineteen Eighty Four* are there to serve the Party members; in *Brave New World* the Alphas direct and control the Betas and Gammas (the Deltas are too insignificant to be worth controlling). There is an important difference between the two dystopias. In *Nineteen Eighty-Four*, it is brutal state repression that extinguishes freedom. In *Brave New World*, it is by drugs and propaganda that the slaves have been conditioned to love their servitude. But in both dystopias the masses are brainwashed by the deliberate and sustained cunning of the masters — the Controller in *Brave New World*, Big Brother in *Nineteen Eighty-Four*. In both books the way things are is laid out as though in a manual of directions. Indeed, in *Brave New World* we are taken on a tour of the arrangements.

The Time Machine is different. For a start, it is more imaginative, less cut-and-dried, above all more frightening. Frightening in two ways. First because it faces, bleakly and without equivocation, the possibility, perhaps the probability, that human life on this planet is but a brief episode. Another million years or so and we shall be gone. Wells had not for nothing been a student of T.H. Huxley at what is now Imperial College. At the extremity of the Time Traveller's journey, there is nothing — a 'rayless obscurity. The sky was absolutely black.' Mankind has long disappeared from 'this remote and awful twilight'.

So the world of AD 802,000-odd is only a passing phase. But what the Time Traveller (the narrator who is never named) finds there is just as unnerving as the prospect of future extinction. David Lodge has described *The Time Machine* as 'one of the most desolating myths in Modern Literature'. (*Language of Fiction*, 1966, part 2, chapter 6). I remember how the Elois and the Morlocks made me shudder when I first read the story as a schoolboy. They make me shudder still, more so if anything, because on rereading the story I notice how explicitly Wells tells us that these two races have not arisen by accident. The Elois, the children of light who play and dance and twitter all day, and the Morlocks, the children of darkness who labour underground, are not simply random fancies. Wells sees them as the logical culmination of existing tendencies. Anthony West, Wells's son by Rebecca West, thought that in the dichotomy between the Elois and the Morlocks Wells was representing the gulf between the Upstairs and Downstairs worlds at Uppark, the great house in Sussex where his mother was housekeeper. But the Time Traveller tells us quite specifically that the division has much wider origins: 'The Upper-world people might once have been the favoured aristocracy, and the Morlocks their mechanical servants; but that had long since passed away. The two species that had resulted from the evolution of man were sliding down towards, or had already arrived at an altogether new relationship.' (p.60) These two species are nonetheless unmistakably descended from us. The Time Traveller tells us after he has had his first terrifying glimpse of a Morlock that 'this bleached, obscene, nocturnal Thing, which had flashed before me, was also heir to all the ages.' (p.50) The division had arisen out of the society of 1895: 'it seemed as clear as daylight to me that the gradual widening of the present merely temporary and social difference between the Capitalist and the Labourer was the key to the whole position.' (p.52) This, to quote the title of another of Wells's dystopias, was 'the shape of things to come'.

I must quote at length from the passage that follows:

There is a tendency to utilise underground space for the less ornamental purposes of civilisation; there is the Metropolitan Railway in London, for instance, there are new electric railways, there are subways, there are underground workrooms and restaurants, and they increase and multiply. Evidently, I thought, this tendency had increased till Industry had gradually lost its birthright in the sky. I mean that it had gone deeper and deeper into larger and ever larger underground factories, spending a still-increasing amount of its time therein, till, in the end —! Even now, does not an East-end worker live in such artificial conditions as practically to be cut off from the natural surface of the earth?

Again, the exclusive tendency of richer people — due, no doubt, to the increasing refinement of their education, and the widening gulf between them and the rude violence of the poor — is already leading to the closing, in their interest, of considerable portions of the surface of the land. About London, for instance, perhaps half the prettier country is shut in against intrusion. And this same widening gulf — which is due to the length and expense of the higher educational process and the increased facilities for and temptations towards refined habits on the part of the rich — will make that exchange between class and class, that promotion by intermarriage which at present retards the splitting of our species along lines of social stratification, less and less frequent. So, in the end, above ground you must have the Haves, pursuing pleasure and comfort, and beauty, and below ground the Have-nots, the Workers getting continually adapted to the conditions of their labour. (p.52)

What I think is so original here is Wells's insistence that the long-term result of this division is as disastrous for the Elois as for the Morlocks: 'the too-perfect security of the Upper-worlders had led them to a slow movement of degeneration, to a general dwindling in size, strength and intelligence.' (p.52)

The Upper-worlders spend all their time in playing gently, making love in a half-playful fashion. Their language is very simple. Far from 'being incredibly in front of us in knowledge, art, everything' as the Time Traveller expects, they ask him questions which show them to be 'on the intellectual level of one of our five-year-old children'. (p.29) Their children are extremely precocious physically, but mentally they never seem to grow up. 'All had the same form of costume, the same soft hairless visage, and the same girlish rotundity of limb.' (p.33) They are vegetarians and they have a short attention span, and virtually no curiosity at all.

A queer thing I soon discovered about my little hosts, and

that was their lack of interest. They would come to me with eager cries of astonishment, like children, but like children they would soon stop examining me and wander away after some other toy. (p.32)

The one emotion that these strange, pretty little creatures do seem to feel is fear. In particular they are terribly afraid of the dark. 'To come upon them after dark without a light was to put them in a tumult of apprehension.' (p.47) And it turns out that what they are afraid of are the Dark-dwellers, the Underworlders, the Morlocks, who in some terrifying not fully apprehended way are threatening the beautiful futility of the Upper-worlders' lives. 'The Nemesis of the delicate ones was creeping on apace.' (p.60) And suddenly there comes into the Time Traveller's head the memory of the red joint of meat he had seen in the Under-world. Perhaps the Morlocks have already started taking their revenge.

And what would the Time Traveller have found if he had pulled one of those little brass levers on his flight back to 1895 and come to rest at, say, 2010 AD? Are there not at the very least a few early indications that Wells's vision was not wholly fanciful? The early reports of the effects of the congestion charge in central London, for example, suggested that affluent motorists were purring happily through half-empty streets, while the proles who could not afford to pay £5 a day even if they had a car were jampacked into dirty unreliable underground trains. Elois and Morlocks, I thought at once.

Or again, as you come into a station concourse or an airport departure lounge early in the morning and see the sleepy-eyed night shift clocking off — the cleaners, maintenance staff, delivery men, baggage handlers — do we not catch a faint alarming sense of another world which only comes alive when we are asleep., an unregarded underworld of which we know little and, it has to be said, care less? In our time, the Morlocks wear saris and tracksuits, but they remain as mysterious as ever in their inconspicuous unpromising lives.

But what of the children of light? How do our 21st-century Elois live? To get a quick insight into the mindset of Elois Britain in the new millennium, the Time Traveller might, for example, glance at the *Daily Telegraph* for 27 January, 2003. He would know the *Daily Telegraph* well, of course. In his day (1895 or thereabouts), it provided the daily news service to the rapidly expanding middle classes. It was, in the famous phrase of the time, 'the paper of the man on the knifeboard of the Clapham omnibus'.

A century later, what are the first words that greet his eye, in the top left-hand corner of the front page? 'Kylie's bottom line, exclusive preview of her new underwear range, page 17'. These words are accompanied by a brightly coloured picture of a pouting girl with tousled long hair and a crumpled garment loosely held together with string across her breasts. Turning to page 17, we find the main headline: 'Kylie's bottom line – nice and naughty', with four pictures of the same girl in varied pieces of underwear, flouncing this way and that, most conspicuously with her pert bottom in sky-blue panties jutting towards the camera. The total effect is only nominally erotic, more playful in fact, kittenish, somehow bleached of anything sinful. The images owe a lot to the work of Hugh Hefner and the cameramen he used for his *Playboy* magazine, which overtly sought to remove any danger from sex and transform it into harmless, purposeless play with little connection either to passion or procreation.

Or consider that highly successful TV series, *Sex and the City*, with its glossy, skittish gang of girls and their naughty, never more than semi-serious but always sexually frolicsome affairs. The feminist author Naomi Wolf rightly, I think, asserts that 'The search for Mr Right is... merely a pretext, a plot device to keep the action moving. It gives the women who are watching — most of them married — the chance to re-enact at length the fantasy of singleness, of unpunished sexuality, of paramount female friendships and automony. It is about Neverland for women, about not growing up and becoming responsible' (*Sunday Times*, July 20, 2003).

Wolf diagnoses all this as a by-product of woman's new empowerment and, as such, no bad thing. But that harmless playfulness would have greatly puzzled the readers of 1895. They would obviously have been shocked by the salaciousness too, although this would not have been such a novelty to them. After all, the *Daily Telegraph* from its foundation in 1855 had been famous for its uninhibited reporting of scandalous court cases and found itself accused of 'dilating on the vices of the aristocracy'. But at the same time, like all Victorian newspapers, it claimed to be 'conducted with a high tone'. It was as deeply worried about any danger to public morality as about the latest threat to national security. And its readers would have found the brazen libertines of *Sex and the City* disturbing, not to say repellent.

The Time Traveller would not have to travel far through the media to find this playfulness a pervasive phenomenon. In *Hello!* magazine, for example, he would find a succession of pretty tableaux of today's celebrities lounging in their delightful sitting-rooms or gambolling in their beautiful gardens. These charming personages look as if they had never known a minute's trouble in their lives. Yet the text tells us of the traumas they have been through, often very recently: divorces, disastrous love affairs, life-threatening illnesses, financial collapses, desperately ill children. Even this information is comforting for the reader, since they seem to have swanned through it all without a scratch on them.

Our Time Traveller will not, of course, know who these celebrities are. In that ignorance he will be at one with many of their fellow-citizens who do not happen to have watched the particular TV soap they appeared in or have not kept up with the fashion world enough to be familiar with their designer label. The Time Traveller may be puzzled that they seem in fact to be celebrated for rather modest achievements — being famous for being famous, as the cynics say, or, as Malcolm Muggeridge's wife Kitty said of David Frost, that 'he has risen without trace.'

Yet this is precisely the point. Because their achievements are minimal, they are unthreatening. It is enough to have been seen and identified to qualify as a playmate of the imagination. One does not really wish to sit in on the home life of a Nobel Prizewinner or a ruthless tycoon or even a saint — unless these daunting figures can somehow be reduced and prettified to become playmates too. This may be possible, with a beautiful young singer or violinist — Cecilia Bartoli or Vanessa Mae, say — but it is a difficult trick to bring off with some forbidding titan. What matters, as it does in selecting a playmate for a child, is that the person should be compatible, of the right physical aspect and mental age for the readers and viewers.

The remarkable success of Reality TV and the *Pop Idol* programmes has two ingredients, both of which are relatively new not just to television but to public life generally. Or perhaps not entirely new but never before so openly displayed.

First, it is clearly understood by the programme-makers that what really matters is not the performance of the performers but the reaction of the audience. It is not simply that these programmes are 'interactive'. That is not such a novelty: in the music-hall or on the hustings, we have always had the liberty to heckle and throw rotten eggs and tomatoes. It is that the whole purpose, the entire success or failure of the programme, depends on our power to vote for or against this contestant or not; the size of the programme's audience and the enthusiasm with which we go on chattering about it for several days afterwards until the next one form part of the experience, ultimately the most important part.

And the other novel ingredient is that the 'real people' on the screen should be like ourselves. That also may not sound so new. An intimate medium like television has always demanded that its stars should be conversational, friendly, quiet-spoken, not alarming or too overtly formidable. Yet traditional television stars, by virtue of long experience on

72

the screen, do acquire a genuine aura, even if their initial talents were mediocre. We are, after all, accustomed to seeing them in charge — whether as newsreader, interviewer, game-show host, or soap star. But what we want now, what is the culmination of our hunger for the ordinary, is what might be called 'the Five-Minute Playmate'. And that really is a remarkable new twist in human curiosity.

The Five-Minute Playmate is someone *exactly* like our-selves. He or she stumbles on to the screen, is subjected to various comic or humiliating ordeals. For those five minutes each week he or she is intensely close to us. We discuss their looks, their clothes, their voices, their opinions, give them marks out of ten, rank them against other Five-Minute Playmates. And then imperiously, without a backward glance, we junk them. They are voted out of the semi-finals, ejected from the Big House. And we never give them another thought. Who was Lorraine, or Mark, or Greg? Once in a while, a Five-Minute Playmate is allowed, so to speak, to stay on, to become a full-time permanent pop star of the traditional sort, like Will Young from *Pop Idol*. But this crossover is the excep-tion that reminds us forcibly of the rule.

This playfulness is not simply a feature of our relations to those media which are after all expected to entertain us. It is merely an expression of the playfulness that pervades modern life for those who are comfortably off. Human relations, like clothes, decor, toiletries are to be reduced, as far as possible, to questions of lifestyle choice. I don't mean that these choices are not taken seriously. Indeed, they are discussed at great length. The Time Traveller would be much struck in

2010 as in 802,00 AD by the perpetual twittering of the pretty people. He would notice that the new technologies — the mobile phones and the Internet — were abuzz with pleasant conversation. Sometimes he would see two or three pretty people ambling along the street all with their phones glued to their ears talking to others of their tribe somewhere else, as though the present company could not slake their endless thirst for conversation. Twitter, that's the word for it. And in fact it's the word we now use for it, quite without any sense of shame or embarrassment.

The Time Traveller would be much more interested in this, I think, than in the technologies themselves, for these devices — hand-held speaking instruments without wires, typewriters which can transmit words and pictures all over the world — are just the kind of thing that visionaries in 1895 were always predicting, not least H.G. Wells himself.

What only Wells was genius enough to predict was how these devices and all the other modern conveniences would tend to hollow out the business of life, to slacken the muscles that the struggle for survival had kept in trim and so to induce an aversion from the serious and an insistence on *playmaking* in as many departments of life as possible.

Let us try to describe the pretty people, the Elois of our day, and attempt some sort of contrast with those people who are not so pretty and who are in various different ways left out of the game, yet still have to perform all the tasks that make the games possible — the dirty work, the heavy lifting — the people the logical culmination of whose destiny several thousand years later Wells found in the Morlocks.

To identify the particular aspect of these two tribes at the present stage in the process, we need new names for them. I suggest we call them the Uppers and the Downers. These terms are chosen for several reasons: first to remind us of the origins in the old class system of the gap we are minding; second, as a handy reference to the mood-altering drugs which, as Huxley in particular foresaw, have come to play such a serious part in our culture, replacing for many the old rituals of religion; and thirdly, because one of the most striking features is the gap in morale between those who are on the whole doing all right and those who are not.

The Uppers are up, upbeat, upwardly mobile, on the up, up for it. At every stage in life they test positive and they expect to do so. They feel good about themselves, and whenever they don't, they take action to put matters right: they hire a personal trainer, they take a course in some new physical or spiritual discipline, they pamper themselves with essential or inessential oils, they move into a new relationship. They are above all light on their feet. To be heavy in any respect is to be a loser. Mobility is the essence of being modern. It is the key both to success and to happiness.

Of course, success is not to be measured in material terms alone. Wealth and power are not the only things that count for the Uppers, though they are certainly legitimate targets to aim for. One can continue to be an Upper in good standing by downsizing and downshifting from a house in Holland Park to a cottage in mid-Wales, from £200,000 a year in the City to £10,000 a year as a carpenter or potter. But these downshifts do not bring you closer to full-time Downers, because they are voluntary moves which form a legitimate part of a self-chosen life project. You are still writing the script yourself.

Even on this first meeting, we notice striking differences between the Uppers of today and members of the upper, upper-middle and middle classes as traditionally understood and classified. Certainly the bourgeoisie have always wanted to 'make something of themselves'. The idea of 'life as a project' would be perfectly comprehensible to a midshipman in Nelson's Navy or a clerk sitting next to Mr Pooter in a City counting house in the 1890s. You start at the bottom, you work hard and/or show conspicuous daring or brilliance, and so you rise to wealth and honours and in due course retirement to a house much more desirable than the house you were born in.

The more straightforward, not to say crass, type of Upper these days will still be thinking in much the same way and hope to follow the same type of career path. During the Big Bang of the 1980s and the Telecoms bubble of the 1990s and the Banker's Boom of the 2000s, successful operators accumulated overnight fortunes and were able to retire to country estates in their late 40s and early 50s, as Victorian tycoons had done.

But the more sophisticated Upper would not be content with that sort of uncomplicated ascent. He or she will hope to explore his or her full potential in every way, not only materially, but culturally, sexually and spiritually. His or her notion of a full life encompasses, indeed insists on, what I would call 'maximum travel'. Travel, first of all, in the most literal sense to see as much of the world as possible, including and especially its most remote and exotic cultures. Foreign holidays at intervals throughout the year are seen not simply as a routine break but as part of the life project and a necessary refreshment of one's spirit. This kind of travel naturally extends to widen the range of experience available to Uppers at home, to include the dishes, perfumes and fabrics of those countries. The artefacts of other cultures become an essential part of the Upper's repertoire both in the kitchen and the wardrobe, a reflection of that cultural mobility which is the core value.

But 'maximum travel' also has a more profound implication for Uppers. They are under an obligation, too, to explore as many experiences as possible. This obligation is obscure, ill-defined, open to individual interpretation, but it is none the less there. As we say these days, 'it comes with the territory', the territory in this case includes parts of the globe that previous generations would have been content to leave undisturbed as 'terra incognita'.

Thus the Upper is not exactly compelled to try illegal drugs, even of the milder sort. At the same time, a refusal to sample cannabis at least a couple of times while at university will leave the nineteen-year-old Upper with a faint sensation of failure, of having uttered a fearful No to life. Is this so very different from a young milksop a century earlier who refuses to try a glass of wine? I think it is. That earlier refusal would simply be regarded as unmanly, a failure to be a sport — as it probably still is among Downers today — but in the modern world a refusal to try anything is seen as more generally life-denying.

The principle of maximum travel is most notorious when applied to sexual activity. The more daring Uppers will embark on a voyage of sexual discovery without claiming necessarily that it is in their nature to be unfaithful or gay or bisexual or inclined to sadomasochism. It is simply an experience that ought to be essayed. Such fantasies need to be explored. This 'ought' and this 'need' are not very strong imperatives, because strong commandments are uncool. Not every couple is compelled to experiment in wife-swapping — or 'swinging', the euphemism that was swiftly invented to make the pastime sound not only more acceptable but also, perhaps more importantly, less sexist. But the idea is lodged in the Upper mind to the extent of making it thinkable that people like us indulge in it. Indeed, it has been commonly stated that a lot of it goes on in the suburbs. Croydon is often mentioned as a hot-bed.

Much more genuinely common is the acceptance of promiscuity as a legitimate lifestyle choice. In theory, chastity is also recognised as a legitimate choice too, and every now and then is proclaimed as a new vogue. But only briefly, because any long-term commitment to chastity would infringe the overarching commitment to mobility. The commitment to be true to your own feelings trumps any commitment to a particular person.

I do not mean that all disapproval has been leached out of Upper attitudes to sexual activity. Adultery is now renamed 'cheating', which in a way desexualises the activity, as is intended. Cheating is bad because it generates an unhappy experience for the cheated-on partner. But this unhappiness can be dissolved if the partner also finds a fresh love and the cheating itself can be nullified by an eventual divorce. Bishop Spaceley Trellis, the fantasy trendy bishop imagined by the right-wing satirist Peter Simple, claimed that 'divorce is also a sacrament'. In fact, divorce is more like a papal indulgence of the medieval sort. Forgiveness can be purchased by undergoing certain clerical rituals, not least by making out large cheques to the clerisy.

I do not mean to imply that the break-up of marriages has in reality become painless. On the contrary. It is clearly one of the most agonising experiences that happens to people of any class at any time in their lives. Friends of mine going through a divorce have endured a wretchedness close to madness, regardless of whether the divorce is predominantly their own fault or whether they are what used to be called the innocent party. Those supposedly outmoded feelings of guilt and shame are by no means absent from the terrible rush of bewilderment and despair which overcomes most divorcing couples. The hard boiled customer who claims that the happiest day of his life was when his divorce came through is anything but typical.

What I am talking about really are third-party attitudes — how the outside world views the marital infidelity. The simplest examples are to be taken from British politics of the eighties. Before becoming Chancellor of the Exchequer, Nigel Lawson fell in love with a librarian in the House of Commons, left his wife and married the librarian. No blame attached to him. Cecil Parkinson, then Chairman of the Conservative Party, was found to have fathered a daughter by a colleague at

Central Office. He tried to rescue his career by ending the affair, making financial arrangements for the child and going back to his wife. But ever afterwards he was damaged goods. Robin Cook, then Foreign Secretary, was found to be having an affair. He, like Lawson, rescued his career by leaving his wife and swiftly marrying his mistress, it is said, on the orders of the Prime Minister's press spokesman Alastair Campbell.

In each case, the cheating had to stop, but it was forgiven if the man moved on to a fresh relationship. If like Parkinson he went back to the old relationship, namely his marriage, leaving his mistress high and dry with a baby (who, to make it worse, turned out to be quite badly handicapped), then he was felt, in some not fully defined sense, to have betrayed everyone, not least the truth of his own feelings, because surely his real desire must have been — ought to have been — to move on.

And this is radically different from the life project of a midshipman in Nelson's navy or a colleague of Mr Pooter's, because their life projects were enacted within a firm structure of conventional morality and settled ambitions. They were, or hoped to be, mobile only in an upward direction. They did not explore other fields or deviate from their chosen flight paths.

An Upper ought always to be on the look-out for a fresh challenge. Uppers who turn down a move to a new company, a new town, a new job, are thought, again in some not fully thought-out or openly expressed way, to have failed themselves, to have not made the best of themselves, explored their potential to the utmost.

In practice, large numbers of Uppers continue to live stable lives of the old sort, with little visible change from one year to the next. They cohabit with the same spouse, in the same town or village, working at the same trade or profession, quite often the same trade or profession as one of their parents pursued. And indeed their parents would have recognised the facts of their lives as comparable. Thousands of doctors, administrators, farmers, solicitors and surveyors and those following a dozen other callings would happily recognise themselves in this category. Many will even say with mock or real humility what boring, ordinary lives they lead.

Yet even these Uppers are well aware that, while the facts of their lives may not be all that different from those of their parents and even grandparents, the public estimation of those lives has changed quite dramatically. No longer are careers spent in one firm, or lives spent in one house with one partner, seen as the desirable norm. They are regarded as social residues, necessary perhaps from a practical point of view (we don't want to be operated on by a brain surgeon who has just taken up the profession because he felt he needed a change), but also stodgy, incomplete, not entirely fulfilling. And where the profession is not a life-saving one but merely a convenience to society — accountancy, let us say, or for that matter turf accountancy — then to do nothing else, to try no other way of life before you die is not to have lived to the full.

Uppers accordingly like to toy with ideas of life exchange. Wife-swapping may be too nerve-racking for most of us. But job-swapping and house-swapping are common exercises in the media and sometimes in reality too. If you live in another family's house for a couple of weeks or do someone else's job, you hope to be enriched by the experience, to learn a whole lot of new things about life. In practice, though, the experiment usually turns out to be strangely unrevealing; it may be fun — a change really can be as good as a rest — but you do not often find out anything very profound about your fellow swappers or the lives they lead.

That is because the lives they lead and indeed the way they are has been built up over time. You cannot gain access to other people's deep-lying habits of thought and feeling simply by cooking on their stoves and reclining on their sofas for a week or two. But this importance of the time dimension in the fashioning of a life is something that is not readily admitted by card-carrying Uppers. For it is an uncomfortable thought that a really satisfying life may be achieved by unremitting dedication in a single direction. I don't only mean dedication to a higher craft such as music or architecture but dedication to lives that are less glamorous and admired: the accountant's, let us say, or the housekeeper's. It would be more unsettling still to examine the possibility that the single-dedication life is not simply one way of achieving a satisfying life but the classic way, the model from which all other lives represent chancy deviations.

But then the word 'classic' will raise the Upper's hackles. It is now more often used in colloquial speech to mean the opposite of its traditional sense. 'That's classic' means 'that's cute, piquant, hilarious, and I'll forget it in half an hour's time.' Permanent standards of value which do not depend on the viewer are out of style.

Upper life today resembles the life of the traditional upper classes in that it is warm, well cushioned and full of amusing diversions. But unlike the traditional upper classes these home comforts are not constructed on the basis of certain values that are thought to be permanent and unchanging.

The Upper is anti-classic, because the Upper is essentially romantic. 'Happiness is a new idea in Europe,' declared the French revolutionary Saint-Just. Personal fulfilment is no longer part of some divine plan, or even dependent on overall social harmony. It exists in its own right, as the No.1 goal for Number One. The Romantic ego acknowledges no legitimate constraint on the pursuit of happiness. If social constraints are to be imposed, they can be defended only on the grounds that they will promote the greater happiness of the greatest number of individuals.

Throughout the eighteenth century, the sages of the Enlightenment had mocked all established religions and state rituals as mere encrusted superstitions which blocked men from achieving the happiness that was their due. That was the basis of the American Declaration of Independence and of declarations of the rights of man in subsequent revolutions all over the world. But it is only in the modern, post-war world that this pursuit of individual happiness has really become a practical proposition on a large scale. Only in the past half-century, first in the United States and then more recently in Western Europe and the old 'white Commonwealth', have prosperity and security been so entrenched and widespread as to make the pursuit of an interesting life available, not just to the artist and the aristocrat, but to the overwhelming majority of the upper and middle classes.

So far we have entered into this new world quite blithely. These new freedoms are entrancing, these limitless possibilities seem so innocent. What have we to fear? In fact we now enjoy all four of Franklin Roosevelt's four essential freedoms: freedom of speech, freedom to worship God as one pleases (or, more usually, not to worship at all), freedom from want and, yes, freedom from fear. What is there left to be afraid of?

There is a simple answer to that question. What the Uppers are afraid of is the Downers. Just as Wells prophesied, the children of light are afraid of the dark and of the tribes who live in the dark.

It is the Downers who burgle Upper houses and hold the house-owners at gunpoint. It is the Downers who abduct, rape and murder the children of the middle class. It is the Downers who shamble through the streets at closing time, noisy, foul-mouthed and vomiting.

Now in reality many of these unpleasant fates are visited not on Uppers but on other Downers. You are far more likely to get burgled in a poor area than in a middle-class one. Less than one per cent of households account for 42 per cent of burglaries, chief among them low-income and single-parent households. And as Ray Mawby, Professor of Criminology and Criminal Justice at Plymouth University, points out: 'Middle-class people are far less likely to be victims of burglary, and if they are burgled, they're more likely to respond by improving their security because they can afford to. And so you get a self-fulfilling prophecy: the inner-city, poorer homes are even more targeted because they can't afford the burglar alarm.' (*Guardian*, February 3, 2003)

But the Uppers neither know nor care about such things. To the readers of the *Daily Mail*, it is they who are the prime targets of a ruthless army of violent hoodlums which is inexhaustible and unstoppable. It has taken politicians thirty years to wake up to the fact that the poor are the principal victims of crime, and the Upper public has not woken up yet.

Nor is it possible to calm the Uppers' fears by producing statistics to prove that the crime rate is actually going down. Improved security both in homes and cars, the spread of alarms in particular, has produced a substantial decline in the rate of burglaries over the past few years. Yet the middle-class panic is as feverish as ever. The Downers are, after all, still out there, brooding, feral, mysterious. Mysterious especially, for the Uppers see so little of them these days.

In the old days, the classes lived side by side. I don't mean that they lived happily together. On the contrary, there was plenty of hauteur and resentment; condescension, apprehension and misapprehension abounded. But at least the lower classes still dwelled in the cottages between the vicarage and the manor house. As servants and employers, Uppers and Downers would be part of the same household. Before 1914, domestic service was the largest single category of occupation after farmworker. In the towns, too, poor dwellings might rub shoulders with the houses of the well-to-do, and for tradesmen and artisans alike the middle and upper classes were familiar neighbours, customers and employers.

One of the greatest changes of modern society has been

the geographical separation of the classes in Britain. The rise of council estates and the bourgeoisie's flight to suburbia have introduced an unintended social zoning into the cities. Only a handful of the upper-middle classes occupy their old positions in the civic life of the great cities. Most of them live out in their spick-and-span villages beyond the ring road, where they are surrounded by their own kind, while the poorer villagers are clustered in the village council estates. Other occasions of contact between the classes — such as military service or religious worship — happen only to a dedicated minority. It is indeed possible for a middle-class person to traverse the entire length of a blameless life without seriously engaging with a current member of the lower classes (although he or she may well meet plenty of upward achievers from modest origins). In some senses, the bottom class in England is more socially isolated than ever before in history. The exceptional visitations from the middle classes in a therapeutic role — as doctor or social worker or divorce lawyer — only serve to emphasise that isolation.

This separation is taken to its extreme in the appearance of 'the gated community' — an estate, usually covering several acres, with houses protected not only by their own gardens and often also by surrounding parkland or some stretch of water — lake, river or ocean — but also by a perimeter fence or wall. The electrically controlled gates are guarded and the roads within the estate patrolled by security men. These are scarcely an innovation in Britain. The St George's Hill estate in Surrey, for many decades a favoured retreat of the stars, was built in the early 20th century and many Georgian and Victorian squares had gatekeepers. But in the 21st century the fashion is really taking off. In the United States, nearly fifteen per cent of the population now live in gated communities (*Daily Telegraph*, November 27 2002). In Britain, many local planning authorities are resisting the growing demand for them. But private enclaves are creeping in, none the less. Indeed, it is only among planners confronting the problem of gated communities that I have seen any readiness to accept that, in the words of Louis Armstrong of the Royal Institute of Chartered Surveyors, 'there are indications that the upper and lower ends of our society are diverging further than ever before.' (*Sunday Telegraph*, March 2, 2003).

The residents of a charming little cul-de-sac not a cobble's throw from us in Islington applied a few years ago for permission from the council to buy the street and install an electric gate. Among the petitioners was a former trade union leader and Labour baroness. Various justifications are offered for these applications to be closed off from the rest of the world: children's safety, secure parking, preserving the environment, privacy (which is every Englishman's right), but the underlying reason is, I am afraid, fear of the Downers spilling out of the pub and creating mayhem in the shrubbery or the sitting-room.

It is impossible to remain entirely unaware of this separation which seems, contrary to the hopes and predictions of the bien-pensants, to be increasing rather than diminishing. And you will often hear Uppers voice their anxiety about the effects on the morale and temper of the Downers. In particular, it is often said how demoralising it must be for Downers to see the 'lavish lifestyles' of Uppers depicted in full colour on television. The advertisements are thought to inflame corrosive envy among Downers when they see glamorous models jetting off to exotic destinations, wearing clothes, scent and jewelry that would cost a dinner lady a year's wages. Nothing, we are told, could impress upon the Downers more forcefully the unfairness of present social arrangements than these crass ads. It is seldom suggested that Downers, like Uppers, may use the commercial breaks more profitably by fixing themselves a drink or, even when they do watch ads, regard them with a certain wry amusement rather than rancour or envy.

But the question that is seldom if ever raised is whether the Uppers are not themselves more corrupted by what television tells them about the lives of the Downers. For the consequences of social separation work both ways. And it is just as true of the Uppers that most of what they know about the home life of the Downers comes from television as it is the other way round.

All day long, the Downers may be largely invisible to the middle-class residents of British villages and suburbs, except as cleaners and deliverymen or when briefly glimpsed at the supermarket check-out. But after dark the Downers emerge from their obscurity to take dominant roles in the two leading dramatic television genres: the police drama and the soap. Sometimes indeed it seems as if television can offer nothing else. 'Cop shows' have come to dominate the drama schedules, so much so that even the occasional viewer may see an actor like Ross Kemp or Ken Stott figuring in a dozen gritty tales of mayhem and squalor over the course of a year. These tough, world-weary Detective Chief Inspectors walk down an endless succession of mean streets with their broken marriages behind them and nothing but violence, rancour and greed in front of them.

In these plays we see moral and physical degradation shown with a lurid relish that Dickens might have envied. The women are slags, either scrawny with straggly blonde hair, or grotesquely fat and bulging out of their tracksuit bottoms. The children are surly, whining, spoilt, wolfing down their junk food with no concept of manners and not much grasp of their native language. The men in the regulation get-up — T-shirt, earring, shaven head — are equally surly and incoherent, callous and faithless to their women, sentimental about their children but liable to forget to pick them up at school and prepared to leave home and abandon them if they meet a bit of skirt in the pub.

There is never any suggestion that the Downer men might be interested in anything except sex, drink, cars and football. I don't mean that they ought to be endowed with highbrow tastes — a fondness for Brahms, say, or the buildings of Hawksmoor. But they aren't given any individual traits or tastes at all, no interest in such things as Latin-American dancing or growing leeks which would have been plausible attributes in television fiction of an earlier generation. Downers are represented not merely as degraded and low but also in some awful sense as hollowed out, so that there is scarcely any human substance left in them.

Are people like that? Or is this some vile caricature invented by the media? Well, these characters appear on our screens, night in and night out, and nobody protests. Viewers do not jam the BBC switchboard to say that they live in Cardiff or South Shields and that people in their neighbourhood simply aren't like that. On the contrary, such pictures of bottom-class life are taken for granted. The television reviewer will refer to them, possibly with a sigh, as 'more gritty realism'. Nobody claims that they are not realistic.

As one critic remarks, turning to the soaps from his more usual viewing,

> If you switch on at any point during *EastEnders* you will nearly always find people arguing furiously. 'Dirty' Den Watts and his daughter Sharon spent large parts of the programme bawling because the fact that he got married while on the run had completely slipped his mind... About 12 million people watch *EastEnders*, and it's sometimes difficult to see why. Everybody in Albert Square seems to be having such a rotten time. Nobody really seems to like each other much. (Roland White, *Sunday Times*, May 16, 2004)

The National Family and Parenting Institute, a government-financed body, conducted an elaborate study of 'Soaps and the Family'. They concluded that in most of the series they examined, conflict was the norm. The only partial exception was *The Archers*, which had a much higher proportion of middle-class characters and contained more intact nuclear families:

In the episodes of *EastEnders* in the study, most scenes portrayed some kind of conflicting which was either directly or indirectly associated with relationships within the family, with the family's relationship to the outside world, with the relationship of one family to another or with relationships between couples.

Due to the combined facts that actions occurred in a close community and that almost all characters were strongly predisposed to negativity and showed very little restraint in giving vent to ill temper or in pursuing anti-social courses of action, conflicts proliferated, were constantly refuelled and frequently escalated into violence. Less frequent pro-social acts, when these did occur, tended to misfire or were shown to be misguided so that they, too, appeared to be almost as uncontrollable if not, at times, more uncontrollable than anti-social behaviour. While some conflicts did appear to be resolved, resolution was rarely complete or permanent. At the slightest hint of a 'happy ever after' ending, it was as though a bad fairy lurking in the workings gleefully sprang back to life and steered the warring families back to their customary game of 'unhappy families'. ('Soaps and the Family', p.40)

If *EastEnders* can be said to present models for behaviour, at first glance, this bad-mannered, ill-tempered, miserable bunch would scarcely seem likely to inspire confidence in the human race or, indeed, anything approaching joyful or noble sentiments... (ibid. p.41)

The authors of the study claimed to find subtler messages about human relationships within this bleak emotional landscape and consoled themselves with the reflection that soaps 'can represent very diverse families, have the potential to stimulate valuable debate and can have a very positive role to play in increasing public awareness of the needs of people in a wide range of situations.' Yet surely one of the effects of portraying lower-class families as existing in a morass of failed relationships and a constant state of resentment and ill temper must be to suggest that lower-class families habitually fail in the most intimate and precious aspects of life as well as in the more material struggles to survive.

It is not until 1955 that the *Oxford English Dictionary* records the first British use of 'loser' to mean an unsuccessful or incompetent person, a failure in life. This notion that there is a whole category of people who are doomed to flop in all significant departments of existence was originally American. Over here we would once have felt it indecent to brand people in this way. Not any more.

Soaps are in this context a sign of the times. They do, after all, occupy a special position in the lives of those who are addicted to them and in some sense are taken to depict normality. They are not perceived at all in the same light as, say, *Macbeth* or *King Lear* or a thriller in which exceptional unpleasantness may be expected. They are a running companion to the lives of their fans and the characters may become as familiar as the real people who are closest to them. It is not at all surprising, for example, that another survey, 'Is Britain Dumbing Down?' (*Whitaker's*, September

2002), found that 46 per cent of adults in Great Britain could name at least five *EastEnders* characters, while only ten per cent could name five members of the current Labour Cabinet. If their fans come to regard soap characters as if they were real people, so they are likely to regard life in soaps as a reasonable representation of real life.

Yet in the early postwar years, soaps presented a very different picture of family life, exaggerating no doubt the stability and contentment. And TV serials such as *When the Boat Comes In* and the many screen re-creations of the Welsh Valleys between the wars depicted working-class life of an earlier generation as prone to violence, drunkenness and occasionally squalor but essentially governed by stoicism, self-discipline, solidarity and good humour. Now the exaggeration is in the other direction. In all the soaps under investigation, the family with two parents (which still represents 75 per cent of all families in the real Britain) 'did not feature highly in any of the television programmes'. But neither the viewers nor the authors of the study seem to object very strongly to this distorted representation. It is accepted that lower-class family life is overwhelmingly a disaster area and that only a Pollyanna would linger too long on happy two-parent families or even two-parent families who are rubbing along.

Thus you do not have to leave your armchair to be given a vivid and scarcely varying picture of how millions of our fellow citizens presently live. It is taken for granted in hospital dramas, for example, that representatives of the bottom class will be ill-shaven, surly and chaotic, needing to be managed tactfully by doctors and nurses. Their family lives will be revealed as swamps of brutality, neglect and desertion, larded with lacrimose sentimentality. Yet the popular media once represented the lower classes as sturdy, indomitable, responding to misfortune and hardship with a chirpy stoicism — 'Mustn't grumble,' 'It's a great life if you don't weaken,' 'Don't let the buggers get you down.' Now the worst-off are shown as sour, whingeing and defeatist. Documentaries tell the same story and rouse even the most moderate commentators to passionate indignation. Richard Morrison, for example, of the *Times*, reviews in a state of mounting fury *Out of Control*, a BBC programme on the failures of the youth justice system:

> Do you recognise the Government that was going to be 'tough on crime, tough on the causes of crime'? Oh yes, we are coming down like a ton of bricks on pre-pubescent shoplifters. We are building more and more prisons, as fast as we can.
>
> But the causes of crime? They have barely been addressed. On any inner-city estate you will find an underclass of teenage boys — thousands of them — who have nothing to fear because they have nothing to lose. No training, no job, no instilled sense of morality, no loving family, no prospects, no self-esteem. And our one strategy for dealing with them is to use the criminal justice system like some big, scruffy carpet under which we can sweep all of society's losers — out of sight, out of mind. (*Times*, September 19, 2002)

These reports and reactions come from all political quarters. Dr Theodore Dalrymple, the pseudonym of an experienced prison doctor, describes in his long-running columns in the *Spectator* and the *City Journal* the foul-mouthed whingeing of the chain-smoking drunks whom he comes across in his work, all tattooed and pierced, and all complaining how the system has screwed them, how they never had a chance, how their wives and girlfriends deserve to be beaten up, and how they need their drugs. Dalyrmple has been accused (by that great medical historian the late Roy Porter, for example) of lacking compassion. Yet I do not think you have to be very alert to hear the anguish behind his acerbic descriptions of the feckless, callous, demoralised prisoners he has to treat.

No accusation of heartlessness could be launched against the reports in the *Guardian* by Nick Davies or against the writings of Jeremy Seabrook. There the failures of modern Britain are faced with an unflinching grimness and unstinted sympathy. Davies was the only reporter with the moral stamina to sit through the entire length of the North Wales inquiry into the abuse of children in council homes. The catalogue of depravity and neglect he reported was so endless and so awful that it dwarfed the imaginations of most novelists.

In *Dark Heart: The shocking truth about hidden Britain* (Chatto 1997), Davies presents horrific accounts of the child prostitution, violence, crime and drug addiction which accompany family breakdown in the poorest areas of Britain's cities and towns. His case histories come mostly from the back streets of Nottingham and Paddington, but he presents convincing evidence to demonstrate that the same scenes of anarchy and despair can be found anywhere in Britain. It is a tremendous polemic, as full of passion, empathy and anecdote as anything ever compiled by Mayhew or Rowntree. All the same, it is possible to argue with or at least to qualify the stark simplicity of Davies's conclusion: that these ghastly conditions can all be blamed on Margaret Thatcher's deliberate cuts in the Welfare State and creation of mass unemployment. Family breakdown is, after all, by no means confined to the very poor, the Downest of the Downers; nor are the worst horrors of drug addiction. The number of children in care — who represent so many of Davies's tragic victims — has actually declined in recent decades. Nor have the years since publication dealt kindly with his prophecy that Labour could not hope to bring down unemployment so long as Gordon Brown kept to Tory expenditure targets. Unemployment fell sharply under Tony Blair and has only soared again under Gordon Brown because of the Credit Crunch, not so far because of any cuts in government expenditure. Whatever the causes of social damage, they seem to have been active for quite a long time and while poverty may be the overarching cause, it cannot be the only one. This is a question to which we shall inevitably return.

In *What Went Wrong?*, published in 1979 (thus before Mrs Thatcher could have done any damage), Seabrook travelled round Britain finding pain and resentment among working-class communities, both in the older industrial areas such as the Rhondda and Wigan and in the newer southern towns of Milton Keynes and Northampton. Old Labour activists in all trades confessed their disappointments and shattered hopes, while young people, angry and frustrated in the midst of relative material abundance, turned away from socialism and towards violence. Like the people he talks to, Seabrook mourns the loss of community and yearns for its rebirth. The possibility of an alternative future 'has been slowly extinguished by the events of the past 30 or 40 years' (p.276). Remorseless economic change has swept aside the old trades, like the shoemakers of Northampton. New towns aren't the answer; something else is needed 'to mend the sense of belonging that has been broken by uprooting people and flinging them arbitrarily across the countryside like seeds scattered on the wind' (p.280).

I don't want to spend much time examining the analysis or motives of those who investigate the underside of British society and report on the despair and degradation they so often find there. Nor do I want to dwell on their diagnoses and remedies. No doubt the motives may have flaws and so may their remedies.

All I want to point out, rather emphatically, is that even their critics don't question the accuracy of their findings. Just as people do not deny the reality of Downer life as portrayed on television, so readers of Dalrymple, Davies and Seabrook don't say, 'No, the criminal classes — or the underclass or the deprived — are not like that.' They may hurriedly explain away the disaster areas of every big city (and small towns too) as the result of poverty or inequality. But they do not deny the reality. Nor do they attempt to argue that these benighted people are somehow exceptional among the worst-off members of British society. On the contrary, it is accepted, tacitly at least, that these miserable, demoralised loungers and spongers grow quite naturally out of a scarcely less miserable social landscape.

It is not only the campaigning journalists, the sociologists and the popular media who paint a grim picture of life at the bottom. Modern literary fiction, too, accepts this picture of the Downers. The slobs and yobs of Martin Amis, the foul-mouthed, aimless, treacherous drunks and junkies of James Kelman and Irvine Welsh, these are only the most lurid visions of the lower depths of today. Writers like these find that the stunted incoherent existence such people lead can be expressed only through a stylised argot peppered with four-letter words or with entirely invented terms. And the brutality and hopelessness they describe are not restricted to the very poor, but rather as seeping upward like some mephitic gas.

The films of Mike Leigh and Ken Loach have a kinder undertow in which all possibility of redemption is not excluded, but they don't flinch from portraying the squalor, both physical and moral, in which their characters are mired. Leigh is funny; Loach is angry; but neither offers us any illusions. Again you won't find much fashionable writing or film-making that describes the traditional stoicism, patience and good humour of the 'British working man'. Even the New Towns which were supposed to liberate the old working class from their squalid environments and release a new self-confident spirit are now routinely described as peeling and down-at-heel, places where youngsters are just as listless and demoralised as in the older towns and cities. It must be nearly twenty years since I was struck by Robert Chesshyre's dismal description of how Skelmersdale had gone downhill. At last even a committee of MPs has noticed and published a damning report on the state of the New Towns, prompting Jason Cowley, later editor of the *New Statesman*, to return to Harlow where he was brought up and find the same dismal atmosphere there as Chesshyre had found in Skelmersdale a decade earlier. This decay is usually blamed on poverty and unemployment and sometimes on a lack of facilities for young people. Politicians may argue about who is to blame for these things or whether in relative historical terms the citizens of these New Towns are so badly off. But inescapably the impression is left that the Downers will mess up any opportunity of building a new life, because they are simply so inadequate. If they don't keep coal in the bath any more, it is only because the dwellings provided by the New Town corporations tend to have central heating.

How do Uppers react to the spectacle of so much apparently intractable misery? It is surely a sight for embarrassment and guilt, as well as terror. Can it be possible for persons who are so very much *alive*, as Uppers believe themselves to be, to remain indifferent and pretend to be unseeing? How do Uppers appease these feelings of guilt and apprehension (I am not talking here about the large number of less sensitive Uppers who seem to experience no such feelings)?

Well, one route, predominantly taken by younger Uppers, is to ape their inferiors, to play Caliban in the mirror.

Never have young people of the middle classes been keener to imitate the clothing, accent and manners of their lower-class peers. Such imitation is necessary for street cred.

Tattooing and body-piercing are the badges of initiation into the ranks of the cool. Only thus can you indicate your solidarity with the underprivileged and demonstrate your indifference to the privileges you are burdened with.

Dalrymple argues that this is a deeply insincere strategy:

> No bourgeois really wants to let go of his money or his position any more than Marie Antoinette really wanted to be a shepherdess. Hell, we should always remember, hath no fury like a bourgeois taxed. Nowadays he wants to be both a man of the people, and better off than the people. From my point of view, working in the lower depths of society, this insincere flattery of the underclass and its ways by the middle classes has disastrous and devastating effects. It persuades the underclass that there is something truly worthy of imitation in their way of life, and that consequently there is nothing better in life to aim for. (*Times*, September 11, 2002)

Dalrymple declares that there is no way of life so utterly without redeeming features, so completely lacking in emotional, aesthetic, spiritual or cultural sustenance, so devoid of charm, as that of people in the lower depths of British society. And to imitate them is a cruel act, because it merely helps to enclose them in that way of life.

But I wonder if the imitation is entirely insincere. The Uppers do, I think, find something worthy of imitation in the Downers' way of life, even if they can't or won't articulate very well what it is. What they seek in working-class life is precisely what the Uppers don't have: namely, that stuck, immobile, rooted substantiality. Working-class families seem somehow more real, partly because there appears to be no escape from belonging to them. They may be warm and spontaneous, or bad tempered and foul-mouthed, or both. But they are not pretending. In their very lack of aspirations they are genuine. Solidarity is the word for it — or at any rate the word that middle-class ideologues have devised for it.

We shall argue later on that this notion is far from accurate or complete. From the Industrial Revolution to the present, the poorest classes of British society have included the ambitious, the pretentious and the conscientious in the proportions to be found in most classes and societies.

Older members of the Upper tribe who may feel themselves too old for earrings and baseball caps often adopt a different tactic for dealing with the embarrassing gap. They jump class. That is to say, they make the bold leap of claiming to be members of the socioeconomic class which in fact they no longer belong to or never did belong to.

Some public figures are not shy of ascribing themselves to the class to which sociologists would say they do actually belong. Charles Clarke, then Chairman of the Labour Party, claimed recently that all politicians were upper-middle-class, including the party's Deputy Leader John Prescott, the son of a railway signaller and a former steward in the Merchant Navy. Prescott himself had said a few years earlier that he had become middle-class, which much annoyed his old father who publicly relegated his son to the working class again, prompting a rift between them which lasted years.

But many other people claim to belong to a class which

bears no relation to the observable facts of their lives. In one opinion poll, more than two-thirds of British adults considered themselves to be 'working-class'. A startling 55 per cent of those classified as belonging to the ABC1 social groups refused to admit to their true place on the social scale. They preferred to claim that they had resisted the charms of embourgeoisement and still stood shoulder to shoulder with the fellow toilers from whom they or their parents had sprung.

Such downward mobility of the mind may be seen as an endearing moral gesture, or by the less forgiving as humbug. But it remains only a gesture. Such people do not, on the whole, move back to the streets from which they claim to spring. It is only as a gesture, if at all, that they pop round to their old local now and then and stand a round. Even those Uppers who do go so far as to attempt to send their children to the same schools as the Downers find themselves conveniently baulked by the geographical apartheid which has made it quite hard for the well-to-do to send their children to a really bad comprehensive. This is described, in the no-fault language of modernity, as 'the post-code lottery'. But there is nothing in the least accidental about the outcome, since the Uppers are ready to pay tens of thousands extra for a house in a neighbourhood where the schools are known to be good. Thus belonging in your mind to the working class does not entail living alongside them or indeed having much contact with them.

The Uppers have often made prolonged, passionate and usually successful efforts to prevent Downers from living too close to them. As far back as 1927, there was the extraordinary affair of the 'Downham Wall'. In order to minimise contact with the tenants of an overspill London County Council estate, the respectable residents of a Bromley estate built a wall to prevent their access. It took years before the LCC defeated Bromley council and managed to get the wall removed. There was a similar affair in Oxford some years later — the Cutteslowe Walls. It took the combative energies of R.H.S. Crossman and Sir Stafford Cripps to gain the right of council tenants to walk through a private housing estate to reach the main road, saving a detour of half a mile to the schools, shops and buses of the Banbury Road (Holmes, p. 19). And of course in a more general sense suburban and rural home-owners have, through their representatives on the local planning authorities, sternly — and again usually with success — resisted all efforts to plant social undesirables in their midst — whether prisoners, asylum-seekers or ordinary Downers. The so-called 'battle for the countryside' is, as often as not, a battle to preserve the delicate terrain for the better-off from contact with their inferiors.

Many middle-class people, it seems, would like to minimise that contact still further, by living in another country altogether. In the same week that one opinion poll found that most of us considered ourselves working-class, another opinion poll (*Daily Telegraph*, August 26, 2002) reported that 54 per cent of the adult population would prefer to settle abroad if they could, even in a country like France or Spain where most of them couldn't speak the language (an even better method of avoiding serious contact with the lower classes).

This figure of would-be emigrants has steadily increased over the past half-century, years during which this country has become steadily richer, the salmon have returned to the rivers which used to be industrial sewers, there are more trees growing than at any time since the Iron Age, the food in restaurants has improved beyond recognition, and, according to the theorists of global warming, even the weather has got better. There is very little apparent social or industrial conflict, and we are supposed to be living in a more or less classless society. And yet, it seems, a growing number of us — many belonging to those 'working-class' ABC1s — find life in this country somehow unsatisfying and would prefer to live somewhere else.

So there is something peculiar about the British attitude to class, some contradiction or unease. On the one hand, we say that class is a thing of the past or rapidly becoming so. Those divisions belong to the bad old days, and even if we haven't achieved anything resembling economic or social equality, anyone can now pass so freely from one part of society to another that the barriers, such as they are, are no longer to be taken seriously. They are like the hedges in a decayed maze. You can peer between the bushes, step through them right to the heart of the labyrinth or make a quick exit if you prefer. The whole construction may amuse us. It may strike visiting foreigners as quaint. But we claim that it is no longer a serious constraint on our assertions and actions.

On the other hand, we continue to 'mind the gap'. The subject has not lost its power to provoke and wound and illuminate. We still talk quite a bit about it in various ways:

journalistic-facetious, or pretend-anthropological, or even old-fashioned snobbish. But that does not mean that we are at all comfortable with the subject. On the contrary, we are often decidedly uneasy when it is brought up, and we do not care for it when the question of class is described in such terms as 'Britain's dirty little secret'. We tend to be especially resentful when the Americans or the French describe Britain as uniquely class-divided. Don't they have their own class divisions too? Anyone who has been snubbed by a French Marquis or patronised by a Boston Brahmin may complain that there are double standards at work here. Don't American cities have their own absurd Social Registers? In what way is *Debrett's* a more disgraceful publication than the *Almanach de Gotha*? Don't the Americans talk quite casually about someone being 'from the wrong side of the tracks' or as 'having the dirt of Indiana between her toes'? And don't Parisians talk about being 'bien' or 'BCBG' in the most flagrantly class conscious way?

So they do, but the difference precisely is that they say these things so flagrantly, without shame or discomfort. They seem unfussed by the contradiction between the divided social reality and the promise of the American Declaration of Independence or the French Republic's ideal of citizenship — both of which insist on a full-hearted equality. Is there something different about the history or the present reality of class in Britain which prevents us from being just as blithe? Is there something which has gone wrong here and which so far we have not discovered how to put right, or even to identify and define to our own satisfaction? Are the Downers in this country somehow worse off than people at the bottom of the heap elsewhere?

I believe that they are. But it is, I think, hard to see why exactly, unless we attempt to go back to the origins of the problem, to track how it got progressively worse and to describe our difficulties in facing it, let alone in fumbling our way towards any sort of solution. What I shall attempt to describe is a long process of deprivation. The word 'deprivation' is often used rather loosely these days to mean not much more than 'poverty' or 'being badly off'. In this essay, it will be used (where it is used at all) in its classic original sense to mean 'the action of depriving or fact of being deprived; dispossession, loss' (*Shorter Oxford English Dictionary*). To put it more exactly still, I mean 'taking away from people something they once had, something they needed and cherished.'

The English working class is, I think, uniquely disinherited, and the most important ways in which it is disinherited are the more crippling because they are largely hidden from us. We are fairly well aware of how little the worst off have had in the way of independent material resources throughout the past two centuries of our history: until recently scarcely any savings to speak of, not much in the way of valuable chattels, and for the most part no financial stake in their own home. But there are other sorts of capital to which they have also had little or no access — social, cultural and spiritual. And it is because the rest of us are so uneasily conscious of this other poverty without being able or willing fully to articulate it that our attitude towards 'them' oscillates between

106

pity and disdain. Above all, it is difficult to show or feel respect towards people who are so embarrassingly impoverished.

We are often told that deference has disappeared from modern Britain. Yet the adulation of the rich and famous is surely as fulsome as ever. In hotels, restaurants and aircraft — the sites of modern luxury — the new upper crust is fawned on as egregiously as old money in its Edwardian heyday. All that has happened is that the composition of the upper class has changed, as it has done roughly once a century since the Norman Conquest. The pop stars and IT tycoons are the equivalent of the upwardly mobile merchants and lawyers of Tudor times and the cottonocracy and beerage of the eighteenth and nineteenth centuries. What has almost disappeared is deference towards the lower classes. Throughout the two world wars and the decades following both of them, the lower classes were widely revered for their courage in battle and their stoicism in peace. Values such as solidarity, thrift, cleanliness and self-discipline were regularly identified as characteristic of them.

That is no longer the case. By a remarkable shift in public discourse, the middle classes have come to regard most of these virtues as characteristic of their own behaviour, indeed as largely confined to themselves. For the ultimate deprivation that the English working class has suffered — in fact the consequence of all the other deprivations — is the deprivation of respect.

It may be a little difficult to explain what I mean to an audience which is so accustomed to think of deprivation in more down-to-earth terms: access or the lack of it to easily identifiable things like central heating and literacy. Perhaps the best way of explaining my argument is to point to certain kinds of respect which the worst-off enjoy in other cultures. My remarks here may be loosely based and easily contested by suspicious scholars or historians. My only hope is that these examples may provoke readers to stop and think.

In Wales, Ireland and Scotland, the local languages which are regarded as the bedrock of the national culture are or were the languages of the people, not of the elite. Welsh has survived the best largely because it was the language in which the Bible came to the people and a Welsh-speaking clergy continued to be needed to preach the gospel. It is in the humblest cottages and cabins that the language has clung on most tenaciously in Cardiganshire and North Wales as it has to a lesser extent in the Western Isles and the westernmost counties and islands of Ireland. And it is to these cottages and cabins that the intellectual elite over the past century and more have made their pilgrimage, to collect folksongs and folk stories before their singers and tellers die out and also to participate in a way of life that seems to the pilgrims more authentic than the lives they live back in modernity.

Of course there were pilgrims in England, too, who sought to record or copy the songs and ways of smock-frocked yokels. But these ventures have always been treated with a certain embarrasment by intellectuals in England. They seem to us artificial, even bogus exercises in archaism. Cecil Sharp is a joke to us in a way which, say, J.M. Synge is not in Ireland. When asked by an admirer whether he had been influenced by English folk tunes, Sir Edward Elgar is said to have replied: 'Madam, I write the folk tunes of England.' It is almost impossible to imagine a great composer in any other country making such a retort.

In Germany and Russia, too, the elite of the *ancien régime* would speak among themselves a language that was not the language of the people — French for the most part, or in the Western duchies of the Russian empire occasionally German. The vulgar tongue had to struggle to achieve dominance in the affairs of state and church — as it had had to do centuries earlier in England, France and Italy. In Germany especially, the language of the Volk was deeply intertwined with the struggle to build a German nation state. Volk-song and Volk-tale enjoyed a supreme authenticity and would be lifted by the greatest composers and writers to give their work a kind of electricity that musical themes invented by themselves could not hope to rival. The Volk thus became endowed with a kind of basic moral, aesthetic and spiritual value which subsequent upheavals, even of the most terrible kind, have never managed to obliterate. All this is absent from English culture.

And a good thing too, it may be said. These days we do not think back much to those pursuits of tribal authenticity except as an awful warning. For it is true that, taken to extremes — and there is always a strong urge to take it to extremes — the quest for national authenticity swells and festers into the most poisonous form of nationalism, infecting intelligentsia, bourgeoisie and proletariat alike. Nazi Germany remains the most terrifying instance in human history. There the belief in the simple but heroic virtues of the old German tribes completely took hold of the most brilliant and profound minds, such as that of Martin Heidegger, no less than of the dullest Bavarian peasant. Much milder versions of the same infection have poisoned the history of modern Ireland. The sturdy lads and romping maidens of de Valera's dream of the Gael uncontaminated by modern materialism issue forth in the horrific deeds of the Provisional IRA.

So it is not surprising that we should not wish to examine too closely the consequence of the opposite extreme: a nation in which Marx's categorisation of 'the idiocy of rural life' is taken more or less literally. We English pay remarkably little respect to the lives and traditions of our poorer rural ancestors, or even to those of the underclass of the eighteenth and nineteenth centuries as they migrated in their millions to the growing industrial towns. Or rather we are interested in what was about to happen to them, in the historical process rather than in the folk — for Volk when translated into English becomes a strictly comic word.

It will be argued that there does exist a culture of the poor which has achieved legitimacy among English artists and intellectuals and it is the culture of the industrial working class. Indeed, that is the burden of E.P. Thompson's famous book, *The Making of the English Working Class*, to which we shall return later. For the moment, it is enough to note that this industrial working class was conceived of not for its own sake, but as a weapon in the political battle. The forging of the proletariat was a process worthy of study and admiration mostly because it was to lead to a social upturning in which the last would become first. So those actual elements in proletarian culture which looked unlikely to contribute to this social revolution were ignored or actively ridiculed — most noticeably the rise of the dissenting churches, the movement for working-class self-improvement and the strong sense of a morality which elsewhere would be described as 'bourgeois'. We were not supposed to learn much from the way the independent working classes actually lived. Their value to us was that their traditions of collective agitation would remake society on more just and communalised lines. Since that has not happened — or not happened in quite the way that socialists thought and hoped it would — the civilisation of the English proletariat is now not much more than a curiosity in our discourse, a moment in social history that is fast fading from our memories.

In most Continental countries, by contrast, the life of the peasant remains an active exemplar. When striking farmers in France blockade the streets with their tractors, this is not regarded by the public as nothing but a bloody-minded nuisance, it is a legitimate act of self-assertion. In all countries where land holdings are typically small, sometimes no more than a couple of stony fields, the scratch farmer enjoys a certain dignity. And this dignity, I think, spreads to encompass the poor as a whole. England's record on Ireland may be stained with crime and neglect, but the land reforms of the nineteenth century underpin an equality of respect in Ireland, both North and South, which the English, accustomed as we are since the Enclosures to large landowners and landless workers, find hard to grasp.

In the same way, we find it hard to grasp that strange equality of respect which even the serfs in Russia seem to have enjoyed. Here we are not talking, as in Western Europe, of small peasant proprietors but of a communal tradition of village landholding in which each *moujik*, however poor and drunk, however beaten and abused, had his share.

Of course, a 'free-born Englishman' had infinitely more rights at law and enjoyed a much better standard of living. But he enjoyed them as an individual — as a non-English visitor would enjoy them too, even an involuntary visitor like a slave, for as the famous judgment of Lord Mansfield instructed us, there can be no slavery in England. The fact that the individual enjoyed these rights did not, however, make him a member of a community in which mutual respect might be expected.

Perhaps I can make this rule clearer by pointing to the one huge exception to it: the two world wars of the 20th century. People in England — like almost nowhere else in the world — look back to wartime with acute nostalgia. We believe now that we were together then in some sense we find it awkward to identify with any precision. Dogmatic socialists may look back fondly to the state control of almost everything, the rationing, the free orange juice. But non-political people have something more personal in mind: the feeling that everyone was doing his or her bit — bits which added up to a whole — and that this feeling legitimated an equality of respect which trumped the continuing inequalities of wealth and power. Naturally this equality of respect included the poor, too, who were 'for the duration' endowed with qualities of stoicism and good humour of which they were to be progressively stripped in the postwar period. Queen Elizabeth was pleased when Buckingham Palace was bombed because now she felt she 'could look the East End in the face'.

The actual behaviour of the poor might not always live up to the heroic stereotype. There was panic in the Blitz, there were scrounging and spivvery, there were strikes in the coalmines. But for that brief period we like to think there was mutuality of respect. And the rich thought that the poor belonged to the same nation. The ultimate confirmation of this is to be found on the war memorial in every town and village. The names on those memorials will often, though not always, mention title and military rank. Sometimes the names of officers will be placed before those of other ranks. More often, though, the order will be straightforwardly alphabetical. What we see in those Celtic crosses is not only an embodiment of collective gratitude and memory but also an act of communal solidarity, one which has been rehearsed at rare moments since in those manifestations or celebrations that are designed to encompass the entire nation, such as the Queen's Jubilees, and in the extraordinary revival of Remembrance Day half a century after the end of World War Two, a revival which was quite unexpected by the intelligentsia who preferred to talk of 'moving on', assuming that these unhappy things and battles long ago had no resonance for the young, especially the working-class young.

But with the apparently indelible exception of the two world wars, the dismal divide continues. Sometimes we pretend that it isn't there or at least that it is not as bad as it was.

Most of us do not care to contemplate the possibility that it may be as deeply entrenched as ever and may indeed be more difficult to bridge now than it was in the past.

How and why and when did the divide begin? What forces unique to this country or, if not unique, experienced here with a uniquely shattering and long-lasting impact, brought it about? Why are the English different?

IV
The Invention of the Masses

One hundred and fifty years ago, there was no doubt about the great social question of the hour. To us looking back, the most striking thing is how instinctive and how wide was the agreement about the nature of the problem. Tories, Socialists and Marxists alike, Liberals too, throughout Europe and beyond, spoke the same language. Even when most hotly objecting to one another's answers, they assumed that there was only one social question worth answering. Marx says in the *Communist Manifesto* (1848):

> Our epoch, the epoch of the bourgeoisie, possesses, however, this distinctive feature: it has simplified the class antagonisms. Society as a whole is more and more splitting up into two great hostile camps, into two great classes directly facing each other: Bourgeoisie and Proletariat. (Penguin ed.1967, p.80)

Disraeli's no-less-celebrated passage in *Sybil* (1845) deserves to be quoted again and more fully:

'Well, society may be in its infancy,' said Egremont slightly smiling; 'but, say what you like, our Queen reigns over the greatest nation that ever existed.'

'Which nation?' asked the younger stranger, 'for she reigns over two.'

The stranger paused; Egremont was silent, but looked inquiringly.

'Yes,' resumed the younger stranger after a moment's interval. 'Two nations; between whom there is no intercourse and no sympathy; who are as ignorant of each other's habits, thought and feelings, as if they were dwellers in different zones, or inhabitants of different planets; who are formed by a different breeding, are fed by a different food, are ordered by different manners, and are not governed by the same laws.'

'You speak of —' said Egremont, hesitatingly.

'THE RICH AND THE POOR.'

Cobbett a little earlier declared: 'We are daily advancing to the state in which there are but two classes of men, *masters* and *abject dependants*.'

Mr Hale, the soft Southern clergyman in Mrs Gaskell's *North and South*, asks Mr Thornton, the hard Northern manufacturer:

Is there any necessity for calling it a battle between the two classes?... I know, from your using the term, it is one which gives a true idea of the real state of things to your mind...

[Thornton insists:] It is true; and I believe it to be as

much a necessity as that prudent wisdom and good conduct are always opposed to, and doing battle with ignorance and improvidence. It is one of the great beauties of our system, that a working-man may raise himself into the power and position of a master by his own exertions and behaviour; that, in fact, everyone who rules himself to decency and sobriety of conduct, and attention to his duties, comes over to our ranks; it may not be always as a master, but as an over-looker, a cashier, a book-keeper, a clerk, one on the side of authority and order.

Formerly, we were told, the class structure had been intri-cate and many-layered; not merely had there been a middle class to soften the harshness of the contrast between rich and poor; there had been fine gradations between and within each class. Now — and *now* is the word that matters — all these mitigations were being swept away.

There was no doubt in anybody's mind of the cause. It was the Industrial Revolution and the crowding together of the hitherto scattered and geographically isolated rural poor into the great manufactories. W. Cooke Taylor wrote in *Notes of a Tour in the Manufacturing Districts of Lancashire* (1842):

As a stranger passes through the masses of human beings which have accumulated round the mills and print works... he cannot contemplate these 'crowded hives' without feelings of anxiety and apprehension almost amounting to dismay. The population, like the system to which it belongs, is NEW; but it is increasing in breadth and strength. It is an aggregate of

117

masses, our conceptions of which clothe themselves in terms that express something portentous and fearful... as of the slow rising and gradual swelling of an ocean which must, at some future and no distant time, bear all the elements of society aloft upon its bosom, and float them Heaven knows whither. There are mighty energies slumbering in these masses... The manufacturing population is not new in its formation alone: it is new in its habits of thought and action, which have been formed by the circumstances of its condition, with little instruction, and less guidance, from external sources.

The above passage is quoted (Pelican ed. 1968, pp.208-9) in that extraordinary, mesmerising work, E.P. Thompson's *The Making of the English Working Class* (1963). Here in the mills, Thompson argues, the working class was made. As the ultimate Mancunian arbiter, Frederick Engels, wrote in the *Condition of the Working Class in England* in 1844: 'The first proletarians were connected with manufacture, were engendered by it.' Those who were appalled by the consequences of the Industrial Revolution were no less certain than those who rejoiced in what they saw as progress that the new system of production had given birth to a new class and a new simplified class division. Revolutionaries and reactionaries were equally convinced that the factories were the heart and soul of the matter. Thompson shows beyond a doubt how Sherwin, Thelwall and all the more sensitive reformers placed much of their trust and hope in the *crowding effect* of the factories.

For a working man, Sherwin argued, 'the nature of his

calling forces him into the society of his fellow men.' In a manufacturing district, political discussion was inevitable and the workers could organise themselves by clubbing their pennies together. Numbers brought self-confidence and an absence of deference.

Even now, we may underestimate how devastating and horrific was the sight of the first factories. What struck observers on approaching them was their sheer size, then the incessant noise, the clanking and whirring, the smoke and the smell, of chemicals, of industrial waste and then, of course, and alas, of the blackened ragged specimens of humanity who worked in them, above all of the children, as young as five or six years old toiling away at repetitive tasks without any of the relief or variety of the equally tiring work traditionally performed in the fields for even fewer pennies.

And the first factories were English — or at least that was what the English felt. The silk factories of the Rhône Valley, the glass factories of the Venetian lagoon, the ironworks and silver mines of Bohemia were industrial sites too, but they did not dominate the national debate, since they formed so small a part of their predominantly agricultural economies. Other countries had other political questions looming over them with far greater menace: the nature of the political regime, for example, and, outside the few long-established nation states such as Britain and France, the question of nationhood. Only in England did industrialisation pose itself as the question of the day with quite such overwhelming force. Only Britain had the masses.

For this unprecedented *massing* of people led, naturally,

almost unthinkingly, to the concept of 'the masses'. The experiences of men, women and children in the new factories were so horrific, so alien to genteel observers that they assumed that these people must be transformed by experiences into a new all-embracing class, welded together into a vast terrifying force, untrammelled by custom or religion, with huge appetites for power, money and revenge; in short, the masses.

Observers and later historians acknowledged that the creation of the masses was a little more complicated than that. E.P. Thompson's argument is characteristic:

> The working-class did not rise like the sun at an appointed time. It was present at its own making. *Class*, rather than classes, for reasons which it is one purpose of this book to examine. There is, of course, a difference. "Working classes" is a descriptive term, which evades as much as it defines. It ties loosely together a bundle of discrete phenomena. There were tailors here and weavers there, and together they make up the working classes. By class I understand a historical phenomenon, unifying a number of disparate and seemingly unconnected events, both in the raw material of experience and in consciousness. I emphasise that this is a *historical* phenomenon. I do not see class as a "structure". nor even as a "category", but as something which in fact happens (and can be shown to have happened) in human relationships. (p.9)

More concretely, he puts it a few pages later:

In the years between 1780 and 1832 most English working

people came to feel an identity of interests as between themselves, and as against their rulers and employers. This ruling class was itself much divided, and in fact only gained in cohesion over the same years because certain antagonisms were resolved (or faded into relative insignificance) in the face of an insurgent working class. Thus the working-class presence was, in 1832, the most significant factor in British political life. (p.12)

The dividing of the nations into two and only two classes was not quite as novel as all that. We may look as far back as Gregory King's *General Account* of the 1690s to see something similar. King was a herald by trade — a rather successful one, who rose to the post of Lancaster Herald. He was also perhaps the first reliable sociologist in English history — an achievement which you may take as progressive or dismal, according to your taste. At any rate, his table of the structure of English society for the year 1688 is described by Peter Laslett in *The World We Have Lost* as the only such table ever worked out by a contemporary for a European society in pre-industrial times, and where its figures can be cross checked against other evidence, it seems remarkably accurate.

Gregory King lists every category of society by rank or occupation, estimates their number and the number of their dependants and their incomes and outgoings. At the top of the list come lords, temporal and spiritual; then baronets, knights, esquires and gentlemen; then persons in greater and less offices and places, merchants and traders, lawyers, clergymen and freeholders, farmers, persons in liberal arts and scientists, shopkeepers and tradesmen, artisans and handicrafters, and naval and military officers. All these — 'above the line', so to speak — are described as 'increasing the wealth of the Kingdom'.

Then below the line come the others: common seamen, labouring people and servants, cottagers and paupers, common soldiers and finally 'Vagrants; as Gipsies, Thieves, Beggars etc'. All these are described as 'Decreasing the Wealth of the Kingdom' — 849,000 of them as opposed to the 500,586 who are said to be increasing England's wealth.

Three centuries later, John Goldthorpe and others in *Social Mobility and Class Structure in Modern Britain* (1980) divided the country up into seven occupational classes, these seven representing an aggregation from the authors' original scale — the 'Hope-Goldthorpe occupational scale' — which divided people up into 36 categories. Gregory King, by contrast, has 26 categories.

Goldthorpe's Class I comprises higher-grade professionals, whether salaried or self-employed, top administrators and proprietors. Class II includes lower-grade professionals and administrators, higher-grade technicians and supervisors. Class III is mostly clerical employees and sales personnel and other rank-and-file employees in services. Class IV comprises farmers, smallholders, self-employed artisans and other small independent workers. Class V includes lower-grade technicians and supervisors of manual workers — 'a latter-day aristocracy of labour or blue-collar elite', whose earnings may approach those of Class II. Class VI includes all skilled manual workers, while Class VII comprises all unskilled manual workers and agricultural workers.

Now one may feel that these divisions are, if anything, more arbitrary than those of Gregory King three centuries earlier. The distinction between, for example, self-employed artisans (Class IV), lower-grade technicians (Class V) and skilled manual workers (Class VI) is far from easy to draw in any permanent sense. A plumber, for example, might oscillate between any of the three, depending on how he chooses to organise his working arrangements.

But what strikes us forcibly is that, although Goldthorpe genially admits that there is 'a good deal of overlap' in many of his categories, he determinedly identifies Classes VI and VII together as 'the working class' — with Classes III, IV and V as the 'three intermediate classes'. Which corresponds more or less to Gregory King's Increasers and Decreasers — except that the modern sociologists would be more inclined to call King's Decreasers the real Increasers of wealth.

So running through the whole experience of modernity there seems to be an almost irresistible urge, even among the most careful observers, to define society in terms of the two classes. Stanislav Ossowski in his *Class Structure in the Social Consciousness* (Eng. tr. Sheila Patterson, 1963), a secret classic among sociologists, points out that there are three, and really only three ways in which you can divide up society. As we have been seeing, you can split it into two opposing camps. During periods of intense class struggle, Ossowski points out, this approach, ignoring any intermediate positions between the two contending groups, 'becomes an important propaganda factor for those whose strategy is best suited by the stressing of a single front line' (p.36). In this scheme of things, the middle class is dismissed as a less important or less permanent element in society. When sharp conflicts arise, we are told, people in the middle class join up with one or other of the two opposing classes. This way of slicing up society is what Marx is most famous for, although, as we shall see, Marx's writings are not quite straightforward on this question.

For Aristotle, by contrast, it is the middle class which constitutes the basic class, from which the rich and the poor are deviations. 'It is not the middle class but the extreme classes which are in some sense marginal' (pp.38-39). For Aristotle, the most perfect society is that in which the middle classes predominate. In fact, what Aristotle describes as perfection is nothing other than the 'diamond' shape that has finally emerged in Western industrial societies two-and-a-half millennia later, as opposed to the earlier pyramid, in which the poorer classes at the bottom are easily the most numerous and the numbers in each class dwindle as you approach the peak.

So a second way of slicing up society — the one preferred by many sociologists — is by strata or *grades*: upper, upper-middle, middle, lower-middle and so on. This is different again from Ossowski's third approach — dividing society up by *function*. For example, Aristotle also divided society up into warriors, statesmen, farmers and labourers. The medieval Church divided its flock up into prayers, defenders and toilers, also known as priests, knights and workers — the Three Estates, as they came to be known. Adam Smith in *The*

Wealth of Nations has an updated version: rentiers, 'profiteers' (that is, entrepreneurs) and wage-earners.

But the original thing about Ossowski's analysis — and perhaps only a Polish sociologist amid the acute turmoil of Eastern Europe in the late 50s could have been so sensitive to this — is to show us how Marx himself actually uses all three methods. In *The Class Struggle in France*, Marx could not and does not overlook the 'mass of the nation standing between the proletariat and the bourgeoisie'. He also refers to 'intermediate strata' and to the liberal German middle class, with its 'professors, its capitalists, its aldermen and its penmen' (pp.75-76). Most remarkable of all is the fact that nowhere in all his voluminous writings does Marx define precisely what he means by 'social class'. Indeed, the manuscript of the third volume of his magnum opus *Das Kapital* breaks off dramatically at the moment when he was about to answer this central question: 'What constitutes a social class?' And even this chapter — interrupted by Marx's death — opens with the following sentence: 'Wage labourers, capitalists and landowners constitute the three big classes of modern society based upon the capitalist mode of production' (Ossowski, p.80) — which sounds much more like Adam Smith than Karl Marx.

Why these apparent ambiguities and confusions in discussing something which is so central to Marx and the whole Marxist tradition?

For the simple reason, I think, that Marx *needs* all three approaches, and so do his followers. As an *economist*, he needs the functional approach to describe how the modern capitalist economy actually works and the relationship in which each class stands to the productive process. As a *social scientist*, he needs the gradational approach to produce a plausible picture of the social differentiations in a modern society. But as a *revolutionary warrior*, he can tolerate only two classes, *Us* and *Them*, the proletariat and the bourgeoisie, the winners who have history on their side and the losers whose day will soon be over. Marx the economist and Marx the historian don't really believe that last bit. They are too mesmerised by the huge transforming achievements of the bourgeoisie to imagine that they will be so easily superseded. Indeed, the economist Lord Desai argues that, with one part of his brain at least, Marx thought that the bourgeoisie would never be superseded.

But I am not trying here to establish what exactly pure Marxism is or was — or how intellectually dishonest or muddled Marx himself might have been. All I want to point out here is that, however he might have had to distort social and historical realities to achieve it, the trick worked.

By his ferocious rhetoric, his thundering certainties and his air of scientific infallibility, Marx succeeded in persuading not only his own immediate followers but a large part of mankind that two irreconcilable classes faced each other with a huge no-man's-land between them. In modern industrial societies, there were effectively only two classes and this division was the crucial fact about these societies, a fact which was bound to animate and permeate their politics. And not just their politics, but their whole life too — society, family, morality. If you wished to understand the world, you could not separate politics from society; even if such a separation might once have been possible in the old world, it was certainly impossible in the new industrial world.

Ineluctably, every man was pushed to one side or the other of the great class divide, whether or not he himself was conscious of being so pushed. And what's more, he was pushed with increasing abruptness, rudely shoved into his historically determined position. For history had suddenly speeded up. The Industrial Revolution had administered a shock to settled patterns of life which was more violent than anything previously experienced in human history. It had brought a new world into being, the modern world, but at a terrible cost. Beliefs, occupations and even whole communities, which seemed to their inhabitants to have lasted since the beginning of recorded time, were wiped out overnight; no longer could men expect to live in the same village, tilling the same fields with the same tools as their fathers and grandfathers. With one brutal wrench they were uprooted. Not merely were millions driven off the land to seek fresh work, usually in wretched conditions, in inhuman cities; this fresh work was itself insecure and might become obsolete in a handful of years. Men were at the mercy of violent impersonal and incessantly *active* forces. History, capitalism, technology, secularisation — however these forces might be described, it was agreed that they brought into being a new class, however *that* might be described — the urban poor, the industrial working class, the proletariat. The elaborate class structure of previous centuries had rusted and collapsed, leaving only one great stark simple division between haves and have-nots. No longer were there three or four or even more estates whose rights, privileges and duties might be the subject of subtle debate for politicians, lawyers and historians. To those observers who looked through to the realities, there were now Two Nations and only Two Nations.

Industrial society might refine and subdivide the tasks by which men earned their living; but in social terms, it coarsened and simplified. Subdivisions of class — such as the petty bourgeoisie — were of use only to the professional analyst seeking to explain how the two classes came to be formed. For practical purposes, there were only two sides — the victims and those who, whether consciously or not, were the victimisers. For observers, the distinction was between those who had the power to shape society and those who were powerless — between agents and patients.

Now this simplifying aspect tends to be taken as read, to be treated as the precondition of any theory of class *conflict*. What interests us today is the way in which Victorians mostly came to dread or to welcome the prospect of class conflict; for Lord Salisbury or Karl Marx, the most crucial question was if and when and how these two classes would come into violent collision with one another. Yet from the perspective of most other centuries, that question would not seem particularly fresh. Classes were, after all, always quarrelling; sometimes in alliances, sometimes in single combat; on occasion, the clergy would ally with the merchants against the aristocracy, or the merchants with the peasants against a combination of the clergy and aristocracy, and so on. This was nothing new, nor indeed was it surprising, a class tended to become conscious of itself only when its members felt their interests to be threatened by a shared adversary. But the notion that there were only two classes was much less usual. It was class *simplification*, not class conflict, that seems to me to have been the distinguishing mark of Victorian debate (I use the word 'Victorian' not to restrict the argument to Britain or the British Empire, but simply to denote the period between 1840 and 1900).

To remind ourselves how unusual this was, we need only glance at the extraordinary complexity and subtlety of the class divisions in many ancient and primitive societies, or at the social intricacies of the *ancien régime* in France.

Or again we could look at a tiny and quite newly formed society, like Philadelphia in the 1770s on the eve of the American Revolution. That city was dominated by the wealthy merchants who had carriages and mahogany furniture and owned half the wealth. Below them came the artisans, themselves subdivided into skilled master craftsmen and their wage-earning journeymen; the journeymen might side with the masters on matters of price control and protection against foreign competition; but they were capable of striking against the masters for higher wages. Below the journeymen came the indentured servants, the apprentices and the black slaves — each a distinct form of unfree labour. Below these again came a free-floating population of sailors, dockworkers and unskilled labourers, scorned by and scornful of the large artisan classes. This rich variety of class identification existed within a city of not much more than 30,000 people, moreover a city which contained no hereditary landed nobility, no established clerical hierarchy and no real large-scale industrial enterprises.

Now the Victorian explanation — explicit in the case of Marxists, implicit for others — is that the terrible force of the Industrial Revolution 'sharpened' class consciousness and class conflict. People became aware that their interests must lie on one or other of the two sides; they were forced to become aware by the pressure of economic change. Smallholders, artisans, shopkeepers and other independent operators became hired hands; the last remnants of feudal relations crumbled; everything and everyone could be bought and sold; the complex intimacy of community was replaced by the cold simplicity of the market. In the Middle Ages, for all the poverty and ignorance, there had at least been stability and a sense of community. The Chartist leaders in *Sybil* argue:

> There were yeomen then, sir; the country was not divided into two classes, masters and slaves... As for community... with the monasteries expired the only type that we ever had in England of such an intercourse. There is no community in England; there is aggregation, but aggregation under circumstances which make it rather a dissociating than a uniting principle... It is a community of purpose that constitutes society... without that men may be drawn into contiguity, but they still continue virtually isolated... In great cities men are brought together by the desire of gain. They are not in a state of co-operation, but of isolation. (p.71-76)

How much historical truth was there in this argument?

While old forms of property and independence might be destroyed, particularly in the country, were there not new forms of urban independence coming to birth — small businesses, shops, new leaseholds and freeholds? And where were we to place the other new classes or sub-classes — the armies of clerks and bureaucrats, the practitioners of the new professions and so on? The spectacle of the mills and manufactories in Lancashire and the Black Country, horrific though it might be, was not sufficiently overwhelming evidence to prove that the Industrial Revolution simplified society. One obvious factor left out of account was the rapid growth of the State apparatus in most industrial societies; surely government grew big mainly in order to cope with the *complexity* of industrial society. Furthermore, even in comparing the early Victorian age with the eighteenth century, let alone with the Middle Ages, the simplifiers tended to exaggerate the advantages of agricultural society; in most times, after all, your security was at risk not only of bad harvests or low corn prices but also of bad landlords. Rural poverty could be abysmal too. It is still debatable whether the working-class standard of living rose or fell or stagnated during the early years of the Industrial Revolution. But by the time we come to the mid-Victorian years there is no doubt about it. The workers were better off, so much so that Marx himself doubted whether they might lose the stomach for revolution.

At all events, by then the masses had been invented; society had been divided into two great opposing forces. And these two facts were to dominate British politics for a century and more.

It is the conventional wisdom now that those days are over. Technology has done away with the old heavy industry and the horrors of early factory life. Prosperity and the Welfare State have turned the working class into members of the bourgeoisie, insecure members sometimes but members none the less. We are a one-culture society; we all wear blue jeans and listen to the same pop songs and watch the same television programmes. We have seen off the old dinosaurs like Arthur Scargill who kept on telling us that 'in a capitalist society it is inevitable that there will be class conflict. There are only two classes in Britain. The ruling class which arms and controls the means of production, and the working class which provides the labour. There is no such thing as a middle class. How do you become a member of it? A building worker may earn more money than a man in pinstripes. Does this make the building worker middle class? It is an illusion.' (*Sunday Mirror*, September 7, 1980)

How idiotic such views sound in affluent, free-and-easy Britain. And if you consider the present-day economic facts alone, they are idiotic. Indeed, even in the 1980s, the two-classes model was already a crude and imperfect picture of Britain.

But the impact of the two-classes model was never simply economic. From the outset it had a devastating effect, not so much upon the mindset of those who were grouped together in 'the working class' as upon the attitudes and assumptions of those who weren't. It was in the mind of the upper and middle classes that the idea of the masses really took hold — and with effects that were to prove baleful.

V
Looking into the Abyss

The experience of factory life seemed so alien, so barbaric to those who saw it for the first time that they could only assume that it must alter people in some profound irrevocable way. Even the most charitable observer could not help thinking that factory workers must be degraded and demoralised. Torn from their families and from the peaceful country life they and their forebears had supposedly enjoyed for centuries, they could hardly help falling prey to every kind of depravity. In such bewildering surroundings, how could they keep hold of their self-respect and their sense of individuality and responsibility?

Once again, it is Disraeli's *Sybil* that sets the terms of the argument. 'There is more serfdom in England now than at any time since the Conquest,' declares Gerard, the Chartist sympathiser: 'There are great bodies of the working classes of this country nearer the conditions of brutes than they have been at any time since the Conquest. Indeed, I see nothing to distinguish them from brutes except that their morals are inferior. Incest and infanticide are as common among them as among the lower animals. The domestic principle wanes weaker and weaker every year in England.' (p.200)

Egremont, the enquiring hero of the novel, responds with the economist's argument, one taken up a century later by R.M. Hartwell and others in the long debate about the effect of the Industrial Revolution on the workers' standard of living: 'I was reading a work the other day... that statistically proved that the general condition of the people was much better at this moment than it had been at any known period of history' (ibid). Gerard sweeps this counter-argument away: people had been better clothed, better lodged and better fed just before the Wars of the Roses; average life expectancy in the local towns in their own day was now no more than seventeen. He takes it for granted that such appalling social conditions must lead to moral degradation.

And Disraeli himself makes it clear that we are not to regard Gerard's remarks as those of a wild extremist. For it is the author who describes Wodgate (a Black Country town derived from the real-life Willenhall, Staffs) in these terms:

On Monday and Tuesday the whole population of Wodgate is drunk; of all stations, ages, and sexes; even babies who should be at the breast; for they are drammed with Godfrey's Cordial. Here is relaxation, excitement; if less vice otherwise than might be at first anticipated, we must remember that excesses are checked by poverty of blood and constant exhaustion. Scanty food and hard labour are in their way, if not exactly moralists, a tolerably good police.

There are no others at Wodgate to preach or to control. It is not that the people are immoral, for immorality implies some forethought; or ignorant, for ignorance is relative; but they are animals; unconscious; their minds a blank; and their worst actions only the impulse of a gross or savage instinct. There are many in this town who are ignorant of their very names; very few who can spell them. It is rare that you meet with a young person who knows his own age; rarer to find the boy who has seen a book, or the girl who has seen a flower. Ask them the name of their sovereign, and they will give you an unmeaning stare; ask them the name of their religion, and they will laugh: who rules them on earth, or who can save them in heaven, are alike mysteries to them. (*Sybil*, pp.190-1)

There is more than an echo here of Marx's description of the alienated worker under capitalism:

We arrive at the result that man (the worker) feels himself to be freely active only in his animal function — eating, drinking and procreating, or at most also in his dwelling and in personal adornment — while in human functions he is reduced to an animal. The animal becomes human and the human animal. (*Early Writings*, pp.124-5, quoted Shlomo Avineri, *The Social and Political Thought of Karl Marx*, p.106)

This animal existence naturally knows nothing of social and moral institutions such as marriage. Under capitalism, the *Communist Manifesto* tells us, the family is based on private gain: 'In its completely developed form this family exists only among the bourgeoisie. But this state of things finds its complement in the practical absence of the family among the proletarians and in public prostitution... by the action of Modern Industry, all family ties among the proletarians are torn asunder, and their children transformed into simple articles of commerce and instruments of labour.' (pp. 100-1)

Even middle-class observers who did not share Marx's bitter view of the bourgeoisie often shared his view of the moral degradation of the lower classes. Walter Bagehot, for example, that witty, worldly-wise banker and political commentator, was the most modern-minded of Victorian Whigs. Yet he took fright at the effects of the 1867 Reform Bill, because he thought the new voters lacked the sense and judgment of their betters. More particularly, they lacked the moral sensibility:

If men differ in anything they differ in the fineness and the delicacy of their moral intuitions, however we may suppose those feelings to have been acquired. We need not go as far as savages to learn that lesson; we need only talk to the English poor or to our own servants and we shall be taught it very completely. The lower classes in civilised countries, like all classes in uncivilised countries, are clearly wanting in the nicer part of those feelings which, taken together, we call the *sense* of morality. (*Physics and Politics*, Ivan R. Dee ed., Chicago, 1999, p.106)

Bagehot did not care for the idea of universal adult suffrage: 'Upon this theory each man is to have one twelve-millionth share in electing a Parliament; the rich and wise are not to have, by explicit law, more votes than the poor and stupid.' (*The English Constitution* p. 130) And in his gloomy Introduction to the Second Edition (1872) of his masterpiece *The English Constitution*, after the 1867 Act had so widened the franchise, he declared:

> As a theoretical writer I can venture to say, what no elected member of Parliament, Conservative or Liberal, can venture to say, that I am exceedingly afraid of the ignorant multitude of the new constituencies (Oxford World's Classics ed., 1968, p.276)

On the Tory side, the young Lord Salisbury in the *Quarterly Review* reflected with equal gloom:

> The transfer of power has been complete... Many are sanguine that a great and salutary change in our legislation is at hand: many more affect a hopefulness which they are far from feeling. Few care by injudicious frankness to incur the wrath of the new masters, whose rule is inevitable now. (*Lord Salisbury on Politics*, ed. Paul Smith, Cambridge, 1972, p.257)

The ignorance of the working classes was taken for granted then, and, with a few significant exceptions, historians have continued to take it for granted. The celebrated labour historians J.L. and Barbara Hammond claimed that in the new manufacturing towns,

> all diversions were regarded as wrong, because it was believed that successful production demanded long hours, a bare life, a mind without temptation to think or remember, to look before or behind... The ruling class argued... that with the new method of specialisation, industry could not spare a single hour for the needs of the man who served it. In such a system education had no place. (*The Rise of Modern Industry*, 1937, p.239)

The most popular and influential of all social historians of nineteenth-century England, G.M. Trevelyan, wrote that 'only about half the children in the country were educated at all and most of these very indifferently.' (*British History in the Nineteenth Century*, p.354)

More recently even, Richard Altick writes in *The English Common Reader* (Chicago, 1957) in terms which the young Disraeli would have applauded a century earlier:

The occupational and geographical relocation of the people — the total disruption of their old way of life, their conversion into machine-slaves, living a hand-to-mouth existence at the mercy of their employers and of uncertain economic circumstances; their concentration in cities *totally* unprepared to accommodate them, not least in respect to education; the resultant moral and physical degradation — these, as we shall see, had significant consequences in the history of the reading public. (Quoted E.G. West,

The intensity with which these views were put across to a nervous and bewildered public left a lasting, seemingly indelible mark, not just upon British politics but upon British culture in the widest sense. The impact upon politics is well-known. To rescue the working classes, the State had to step in. It was assumed that the poor were incapable of fending for themselves, educationally and morally as well as economically. There must therefore be a national system of education, a state system of welfare, public housing schemes and, later on, a state system of hospitals, a comprehensive system of National Insurance and much else besides.

We shall come back to the question of how far the facts justified the erection of these huge structures. For the moment, all I want to emphasise is how their being erected helped to embed in our consciousness the idea that the working classes were in all essential respects *helpless*. In terms of political power, they might be, as Salisbury grimly asserted, 'the new masters'. But they were not to be masters of their own fate. They never had been in the past, and now even less than ever could they be expected to undertake their own moral, educational and economic regeneration.

And naturally, as these great new state edifices grew in reach, splendour and cost, they had to justify their existence. Like all institutions, they wrote their own history, which was designed to prove that it was vitally necessary and indeed almost inevitable that they should have come into existence in the way that they did and at the time that they did, and should go on to develop further in response to the pressing needs of each successive period. From Trevelyan's *History of England* onwards, it is taken for granted not only that the past century and a half has seen huge and unprecedented progress but that this progress could have been achieved in no other way than by the State first taking a lead and then gradually assuming the operation of all the relevant services. That indeed is the social element in what we call the Whig view of history, just as the growth in the power of Parliament, and of the House of Commons in particular, provides the political element. In all of this, the working classes are firmly tagged as the patients, never the agents, and it is not a tag they are expected to shake off.

Of course, welfare states and state systems of education were growing up in other countries at much the same time or a few decades later. But there are, I think, crucial differences between the British experience and the experience of the leading Continental countries on the one hand and of the United States on the other. On the Continent, industrialisation came later and was for the most part not nearly so intense. The new manufacturing towns were not so large, and the vast majority of the poor still lived on the land, enjoying – if that is the word – a measure of independence as peasantry which English farm workers had already lost in the Enclosures. The horrors of Coketown were not so overwhelming in France or Germany, and nor was the sense of the working class as a helpless, demoralised, yet at the same time terrifying force. It was on the basis of the English experience, after all, that Marx and Engels built their analyses of deprivation and exploitation.

Besides, the ruling classes in Britain had other preoccupations which distracted them from the toiling masses beyond the park gates. We must not forget how close at hand the masses were for some of the great magnates of the Midlands and North. The pits which were the source of their wealth were often just over the hill, from the Sitwells at Renishaw, for example, or the Londonderrys at Wynyard. Sometimes, as in the case of the Lambtons in Co. Durham, there were actually mineshafts in the park. Small wonder that they should raise their eyes from these distressing prospects and look further afield — to the enormous enterprise which marked out Britain from the other great powers: the Empire. Britain was not the only European nation to possess an ever-expanding Empire, but Britain's was the biggest, and its protection and expansion were the principal anxieties of her rulers throughout the latter half of the nineteenth century. New public schools such as Haileybury and Bradfield came into being with the prime aim of providing servants for the Imperial administration, while the younger sons of the upper classes served in the Imperial wars. Take, for example, the younger brothers of the 4th Earl of Durham: Admiral Sir Meux Lambton served in the Egyptian and South African wars, commanding the naval battalion throughout the Siege of Ladysmith and was later C-in-C of the China Squadron. Brigadier Charles Lambton served in the Nile Expedition and in the Boer War. So did General Sir William Lambton. You would find the same pattern in many a great house built on an industrial fortune.

At the same time, the most ingenious minds were set to work on devising schemes of social improvement for the Empire: the Macaulays and the Trevelyans reformed the laws and the bureaucracy of the Raj. Many modern devices — such as PAYE income tax — were tried out first in India. Many of the founders of our own Welfare State in a later generation were themselves children of the Raj, such as Sir William Beveridge, R.A. Butler, Sir Robert Birley and R.H. Tawney.

Small wonder that this concentration of energies, both physical and mental, should have helped to give rise to what we might call 'domestic imperialism'. When political attention did finally turn to the British working classes, it is not so surprising that something of the same attitudes should be imported as had directed the treatment of the 'natives'. It was difficult to forget Kipling's indelible appeal:

Take up the White man's burden —
    Send forth the best ye breed —
Go, bind your sons to exile
    To serve your captives' need;
To wait in heavy harness
    On fluttered folk and wild —
Your new-caught, sullen peoples,
    Half-devil and half-child.

When 'the best ye breed' returned from such long and arduous exile, you could not be surprised if they took much the same view of the sullen people they found back home. They were dangerous and so must be curbed and flattered; they were undeveloped and so must be harried and regulated and, of course, educated.

But could they be educated? Politicians might propose schemes for bringing learning and taste to the most benighted rookeries. Disraeli might, as the *Times* wrote of him after his death, discern in the inarticulate mass of the English populace 'the Conservative working man as the sculptor perceives the angel prisoned in a block of marble'. But was there anything of value in there? Wasn't that what the working man really was, a blockhead?

You could teach them to read *Paradise Lost*, but still, according to George Gissing, it could not conceal 'the depth of the gulf which lies between the educated and the uneducated'. It was impossible to take up a newspaper without noting the 'extending and deepening vulgarity of the great mass of people'. 'The gulf between the really refined and the masses grows and will grow constantly wider.' For Gissing, 'education is a thing of which only the few are capable.' As John Carey shows so brilliantly in *The Intellectuals and the Masses* (from which I have lifted many of the quotations in the next few pages), this horror of vulgarity runs through every one of Gissing's novels, along with a terrible sense of the fragility of the refinement he himself so passionately seeks. Nancy, the heroine of *In the Year of Jubilee* (1894), has only to mingle with the crowds celebrating Queen Victoria's Golden Jubilee (1887) and the worst happens:

Nancy forgot her identity, lost sight of herself as an

individual. She did not think, and her emotions differed little from those of any shop-girl let loose. The 'culture', to which she laid claim, evanesced in this atmosphere of exhalations. Could she have seen her face, its look of vulgar abandonment would have horrified her. (Dover ed. 1982, p.62)

Even to flip through the titles of Gissing's novels (all highly readable today, I must concede) is to be aware of a mind terrified of slipping down into the abyss: *The Nether World*, *The Whirlpool*, *New Grub Street*. It is important to note here that Gissing's fear and contempt cover both absolute poverty with its physical and moral squalor and threadbare lower-middle-classdom with its painful pretensions and worthless gentility.

You will find exactly the same double disdain in many of the modernist writers after the First World War. Thirty years after Victoria's Golden Jubilee, for example, Virginia Woolf described in a letter to her sister Vanessa her experiences on Armistice Night in terms which are eerily similar to Gissing's:

... everyone seemed half drunk — beer bottles were passed round — every wounded soldier was kissed, by women; nobody had any notion where to go or what to do; it poured steadily; crowds drifted up and down the pavements waving flags and jumping into omnibuses, but in such a disorganised, half hearted, sordid state that I felt more and more melancholy and hopeless of the human race. The London poor, half drunk and very sentimental or completely stolid with their hideous voices and clothes and

144

bad teeth, make one doubt whether any decent life will ever be possible, or whether it matters if we're at war or at peace. But I suppose the poor wretches haven't much notion how to express their feelings. (*Congenial Spirits, The Selected Letters of Virginia Woolf*, pp.106-7)

No question here, even for an avowed socialist, of finding any fellow-feeling with the common people at a moment of high national emotion after so many years of shared suffering.

Crowds terrify intellectuals. They see in them a new, specifically modern threat to civilisation. For Gissing, the Jubilee crowd suggests 'some huge beast purring to itself in stupid contentment'. But the beast could snarl and roar as often as it purred. And whatever noises it made, it was so confoundedly *there*. In *The Revolt of the Masses* (1932), an inordinately popular book among intellectuals between the wars, Ortega y Gasset begins by lamenting 'the fact of agglomeration, of plenitude. Towns are full of people, houses full of tenants, hotels full of guests, trains full of travellers, cafes full of customers, parks full of promenaders, consulting-rooms of famous doctors full of patients, theatres full of spectators and beaches full of bathers.' (pp.11-12).

Everywhere you look, your eyes meet with the multitudes — 'not just in any direction but precisely in the best places, the relatively refined creation of human culture, previously reserved to minorities' (p.13). By 'masses', Ortega tells us, he doesn't mean exclusively the 'working masses' but the average, vulgar sort of person, 'the mass man who might be found in any class'. But he cannot help adding that there is much more likelihood of finding worthwhile men and women among the upper classes, 'whereas the "lower" classes normally comprise individuals of minus quality'. (p.16)

These views came to be commonplace among some of the most admired intellectuals of the period. Aldous Huxley, for example, claimed that 'universal education has created an immense class of what I may call the New Stupid.' He believed that 'the gulf between the populace and those engaged in any intelligent occupation of whatever kind steadily widens. In 20 years time a man of science or a serious artist will need an interpreter in order to talk to a cinema proprietor or a member of his audience.' Characteristically, as Stefan Collini points out (*TLS*, May 10, 2002), Huxley does not seem to allow that the person engaged in an intelligent occupation might also be a member of that audience. Like Ortega, Huxley was repelled by the 'hot smelly crowds' who had invaded his precious South of France. 'It's sad,' he lamented, 'that all the things one believes in — such as democracy, economic equality etc — should turn out in practice to be so repulsively unpleasant.'

Aldous Huxley was one of those many intellectuals in the 1920s and 1930s whose thoughts drifted from loathing of the masses to some active consideration as to how they might be got rid of. How nice it would be if the Downers no longer bred like rabbits and if the stupid, the criminal, the insane, the mental and physical defectives found in such huge numbers among the Downers were prevented from breeding at all, by forcible sterilisation if need be. Half-wits were on the increase, Aldous wrote in an article for *Nash's Magazine* in 1934, and the only remedy lay in encouraging the normal and super-normal members of the population to have larger families and in preventing the sub-normal from having any families at all (Murray, p.275). Aldous and his brother Julian were pillars of the Eugenics Society. W.B. Yeats, also a member, declared 'sooner or later we must limit the families of the unintelligent classes' (Carey, p.14). He feared the decay of European civilisation through 'the triumph of their gangrel stocks'. In his later verse, he was more vituperative still, lamenting the fate of

We Irish, born into that ancient sect
But thrown upon this filthy modern tide
And by its formless, spawning fury wrecked.

Other writers like Shaw, Wells and D.H. Lawrence in one form or another deplored the overbreeding of the underbred and hoped in one way or another to correct the process and produce a new race of healthy intelligent beings on the Nietzschean model.

Later historians have of course deplored these diatribes and wondered that they should have united intellectuals of Left and Right. Charitably they have pointed out that in many cases these horrific views, although bearing a close resemblance to both the views and actions of Adolf Hitler, did not include anti-Semitism. This seems to me poor comfort. The extraordinary thing remains that so many of the finest talents of their generation should have found the mere existence of millions of their fellow countrymen loathsome to the point of being intolerable.

As to this strange and repellent belief infecting intellectuals of differing political persuasions, there is really no mystery about it, since the loathing of the lower classes, as we have seen, seems to have been common among all writers since the mid-nineteenth century if not earlier.

Nor is it unknown among those writers who thought of themselves as bearers of a new sensitivity, and as destined to raise our consciousness of oppressed classes, such as women or colonial peoples.

Virginia Woolf, for example, muses in her letters on a verger with an impediment in his speech (who has incidentally rescued her little dogs from police custody): 'Do you think all the lower classes are naturally idiotic?' (*Congenial Spirits, Selected Letters*, p.46).

Staying at Manorbier, Pembrokeshire, she complains of having to make conversation with the locals: 'One has to be so cheerful with the lower classes, or they think one diseased' (ibid. p.48). The lower classes couldn't win. Either they appalled her, as on Armistice Night, by being loud and drunk, or they were too respectable:

What rather appals me (I'm writing in a hurry, and cant spell, and dont please take my words altogether literally) is the terrific conventionality of the workers. That's why — if you want explanations — I dont think they will be poets or novelists for another hundred years or so. If they can't face the fact that Lilian [Harris] smokes a pipe and reads detective

148

novels, and cant be told that they weigh on an average twelve stone — which is largely because they scrub so hard and have so many children — and are shocked by the word 'impure' how can you say that they face 'reality'? (I never know what 'reality' means: but Lilian smoking a pipe to me is real, and Lilian merely coffee coloured and discreet is not nearly so real). What depresses me is that the workers seem to have taken on all the middle class respectabilities which we — at any rate if we are any good at writing or painting — have faced and thrown out. (ibid. p.273)

One can multiply such examples from Mrs Woolf's voluminous letters and her equally voluminous diaries. Her comments on the lower classes range from the sour and gloomy to the manic and vicious. And, as we have seen, how she hates any popular manifestations of patriotic feeling, especially anything resembling affection for the monarchy. She wrote to her nephew and subsequent biographer Julian Bell on the death of King George V:

We have been, as everyone will tell you, deluged in tears and muffled in crape for the past ten days. The British public has had a fit of grief which surpasses all ever known. It was a curious survival of barbarism, emotionalism, heraldry, ecclesiasticism, sheer sentimentality, snobbery and some feeling for the very commonplace man who was so like ourselves. But it's over today thank God. (ibid. p.369)

As Carey makes clear in his magnificent essay, virtually all

149

the great modernist writers of the first half of the 20th century followed Gissing in his fear and loathing of the masses: E.M. Forster, Virginia Woolf, D.H. Lawrence, and, not least, T.S. Eliot.

For sheer revulsion it might seem hard to beat Gissing's description of a Bank Holiday crowd at the Crystal Palace in *The Nether World* (1889):

Hours yet before the fireworks begin. Never mind; here by good luck we find seats where we can watch the throng passing and repassing. It is a great review of the People. On the whole how respectable they are, how sober, how deadly dull! See how worn-out the poor girls are becoming, how they gape, what listless eyes most of them have! The stoop in the shoulders so universal among them merely means over-toil in the workroom. Not one in a thousand shows the elements of taste in dress; vulgarity and worse glares in all but every costume. Observe the middle-aged women; it would be small surprise that their good looks had vanished, but whence comes it they are animal, repulsive, absolutely vicious in ugliness? Mark the men in their turn: four in every six have visages so deformed by ill-health that they excite disgust; their hair is cut down to within half an inch of the scalp; their legs are twisted out of shape by evil conditions of life from birth upwards. Whenever a youth and a girl comes along arm-in-arm, how flagrantly shows the man's coarseness! They are pretty, so many of these girls, delicate of feature, graceful did but their slavery allow them natural development: and the heart sinks as one sees them side by side with the men

150

who are to be their husbands...

A great review of the People. Since man came into being did the world ever exhibit a sadder spectacle? (*The Nether World*, Oxford World's Classics ed., 1992, pp.109-110)

But is this any more fastidious or repellent than the passage from *The Waste Land* in which Tiresias, the old man with wrinkled dugs, watches the typist return home at teatime? She clears her breakfast, being too sluttish to have washed up before going off to work. Her combinations are hung out of the window to dry. Her stockings, slippers, camisoles and stays are heaped up on the divan that doubles as her bed. Into this dispiriting dishevelled scene comes a spotty young man. He is a house agent's clerk but with the cockiness of a Bradford millionaire. He picks his moment to seduce her after they have eaten the tinned food she has laid out, engaging her in caresses which she does not fend off even if she does not actively desire them. She is bored and tired and his exploring hands meet no resistance:

His vanity requires no response
And makes a welcome of indifference.

What blistering class disdain reeks from these lines. Copulation among the lower middle classes is a mere mechanical procedure, we are given to understand, a listless slaking of lust as squalid and commonplace as the surroundings in which it is carried out. Eliot's anti-Semitism is notorious, undeniable and inexcusable, but is his snobbery much better?

Do not duchesses wear lingerie which has now and then to be washed and dried (by somebody else of course)? Are poets free from carbuncles?Are not distinguished female novelists occasionally seduced by men they don't much care for? Observe here how easily the hatred of the masses transmutes up a notch to a special hatred of the lower middle classes, the petit bourgeoisie, the clerks and typists who have been the target of intellectuals from Marx onwards. Leonard Bast, the insurance clerk in *Howards End*, also eats food in tins and, Forster tells us quite plainly, is inferior. 'He was not as courteous as the average rich man, nor as intelligent, nor as healthy, nor as lovable.' And above all he cannot be forgiven for his pathetic attempts to acquire culture, which ought to remain reserved for those who have it, as it were, by natural inheritance, such as the Schlegels.

There is nothing to be said for the lower middle classes. They lack the noble vigour of the peasant. Their efforts to imitate the refinement of the civilised classes are vain and repellent. And, worst of all, they will insist on polluting the countryside with their suburbs.

From Nietzsche to Graham Greene, writers have been scornful of suburbia and the dull, mean lives that its residents are presumed to lead there. Poets and artist cannot breathe in such places. They must decamp to sunnier climes where there are no licensing laws and no inhibitions. Civilised people may live in the heart of great cities, or on remote islands, or deep in the country — anywhere except in those rows of little boxes within easy commuting reach of the City.

And these ghastly people insisted on spreading their little

boxes all over the unpolluted globe D.H. Lawrence in *Kangaroo* describes, with a brilliant disdain, the suburbs of Sydney, which in fact he had only known for not much more than a fortnight:

> Murdoch Street was an old sort of suburb, little squat bungalows with corrugated iron roofs, painted red. Each little bungalow was set in its own hand-breadth of ground, surrounded by a little wooden palisade fence. And there went the long street, like a child's drawing, the little square bungalows dot-dot dot, close together and yet apart, like modern democracy, each one fenced round with a square rail fence. The street was wide, and strips of worn grass took the place of kerb-stones. The stretch of macadam in the middle seemed as forsaken as a desert, as the hansom clock-clocked along it.
>
> Fifty-one had its name painted by the door. Somers had been watching these names. He had passed 'Elite', and 'Très Bon' and 'The Angels Roost' and 'The Better 'Ole'. He rather hoped for one of the Australian names, Wallamby or Wagga-Wagga. When he had looked at the house and agreed to take it for three months, it had been dusk, and he had not noticed the name. He hoped it would not be U-an-Me, or even Stella Maris. (*Kangaroo*, Penguin ed., p.5)

It was not simply that these bungalows were trite, vulgar things. It was also that no worthwhile life was possible in such a place:

The *vacancy* of this freedom is almost terrifying. In the openness and the freedom this new chaos, this litter of bungalows and tin cans scattered for miles and miles, this Englishness all crumbled out into formlessness and chaos. Even the heart of Sydney itself — an imitation of London and New York, without any core or pith of meaning. Business going on full speed: but only because it is the other end of English and American business.

The absence of any inner meaning: and at the same time the great sense of vacant spaces. The sense of irresponsible freedom. The sense of do-as-you-please liberty. And all utterly uninteresting. What is more hopelessly uninteresting than accomplished liberty? Great swarming, teeming Sydney flowing out into these myriads of bungalows, like shallow waters spreading, undyked. And what then? Nothing. No inner life, no high command, no interest in anything, finally. (ibid. p.24)

Across the other side of the globe, at about the same time, the travel writer Robert Byron was flying over upstate New York, and the kind of early executive homes which were to drive the radical folk singer Pete Seeger to such heights of derision: 'Little boxes on the hillside,/ Little boxes made of ticky-tacky,/ Little boxes, little boxes,/ Little boxes, all the same.' Byron's reaction was more violent:

I can't tell you how loathesome [*sic*], how inconceivably disgusting, the landscape is here. Even from the air it almost made me feel sick... Everything is under snow, which adds to the squalor of the millions of little detached houses sitting by themselves. (John Carey, *The Intellectuals and the Masses*, p.50)

In a recent collection of essays, *Town and Country*, Roger Scruton laments that

The wastelands of exurbia — such as those which spread from Detroit for fifty miles in every direction — are places where past and future generations have been disregarded, places where the voices of the dead and the unborn are no longer heard. They are places of vociferous impermanence, where present generations live without belonging — where there is no belonging, since belonging is a relationship in *history*, a relationship which binds both present and absent generations, and which depends upon the perception of a place as home. (*Town and Country*, ed. Anthony Barnett and Roger Scruton, 1998, p.321)

...What disturbs people in those suburbs dropped from nowhere is not the environmental damage but the sense of these buildings as apart from the landscape, shelters for nomads who are not dwelling but passing through.
...The commuter suburbs violate the landscape partly because they violate the sense of rural time. Even if they remain there for ever, people feel, it will be with a stagnant impermanence. (ibid. pp.322-3)

But when precisely did suburban development begin to acquire these noxious characteristics? Surely not in those charming pioneers of villadom, such as classical Tivoli or

Renaissance Fiesole, or the heights of Hampstead and Highgate, or the delightful riverside developments at Chelsea and Twickenham? No, a suburb is only a social disaster when it is invaded by the more mobile members of the lower middle class.

Town and country unite in loathing of the suburbs. When a public committee is set up to look into the housing shortage — such as that recently headed by the architect Richard Rogers — it seldom recommends more suburbs as the solution. On the contrary, suburbia needs no bien-pensant approval to flourish. It is the solution that the masses choose of their own free will. Their betters would like to wish upon them the tightly knit community of the traditional village or of the urban skyscrapers. For most people these offer neither liberty nor space, and they don't see why they should not live where and how they please. I like to trace this English cussedness back to Tacitus, who described how the German tribes preferred to live in separate houses, but even if this may be fanciful, there is no doubt that the preference for the nuclear family and the separate dwelling house can be traced back a very long way, as the work of Peter Laslett, Alan Macfarlane and the Cambridge Group for the History of Population and Social Structure demonstrated over a long period, shattering the *marxisant* illusions about our forefathers living all together in one great tumbling tribal horde. Suburban life is in our blood, and all the disapproval of the intellectuals will not wean us from it.

This hatred of the suburbs is relatively recent. For the Romans, the suburbs could have pleasant and civilised associations, as a resort of villas and gardens, free from the filth and smoke of the city. And this tradition continued throughout the revival of classical learning in the Renaissance and beyond. In *Paradise Regained*, Milton hymns

> Athens the eye of Greece, Mother of Arts
> And Eloquence, native to famous wits
> Or hospitable, in her sweet recess,
> City or Suburban, studious walks and shades.
> (IV. 240-4)

And for many these positive vibrations continued to resound throughout the eighteenth century and even into the nineteenth. An unknown poet wrote in William Hone's *Table Book* (1827) of the district where I live:

> You who are anxious for a country seat
> Pure air, green meadows and suburban views;
> Rooms snug and light — not overlarge but neat,
> And gardens water'd with refreshing dews,
> May find a spot adapted to your taste,
> Near Barnsbury Park, or rather Barnsbury Town
> Where everything looks elegant and chaste,
> And Wealth reposes on a bed of down.
> (quoted in Pieter Zwart, *Islington*, 1973, p.128)

People were queuing up to buy the new stucco villas mushrooming around London and other great cities. But that was just the trouble. There were too many of them. It was all right for Pope and Horace Walpole to build their delicious villas among the strawberry fields along the Thames. But when the masses started imitating them, it was a disaster. Even before the unknown poet had been praising Barnsbury in terms reminiscent of a property developer's ad, Byron in *Beppo* had described an ill-dressed woman at the carnival in Venice as looking 'vulgar, dowdyish and suburban' (LXVI). And was not Byron the greatest style guru in history? From Lord Byron to Robert Byron a century later, the intellectual hatred of suburbia was unwavering, culminating perhaps in T.S. Eliot's declaration that his new periodical, the *Criterion* would be directed against 'suburban democracy'. To quote John Carey:

The massive expansion of suburbia, and the antagonisms, divisions and sense of irrecoverable loss it generated, were major shaping factors in 20th-century English culture. They exacerbated the intellectual's feeling of isolation from what he conceived of as philistine hordes, variously designated the middle classes or the bourgeoisie, whose dullness and small-mindedness the intellectual delights in portraying (that is, inventing). Hostility to the suburbs as ecologically destructive quickly fused with contempt for those who lived in them. The supposed low quality of life encouraged by suburban conditions became a favourite theme for intellectual ridicule or censure. Mrs Leavis in *Fiction and the Reading Public* stigmatised the 'emptiness and meaningless iteration of suburban people, ascribable to newspapers and radio'. Life for the suburban dweller is, she reported, 'a series of frivolous stimuli'. Cyril Connolly in *The Unquiet Grave* considered suburbs worse than slums. 'Slums may well be breeding-grounds of crime, but the middle-class suburbs are incubators of apathy and delirium.' Graham Greene in *The Lawless Roads* described suburbia as 'a sinless, empty, graceless chromium world'. (*The Intellectuals and the Masses*, pp.50-51)

Carey forbears to mention that in *The Unquiet Grave* the passage he quotes concludes with an asterisk referring the reader to a passage from Norman Douglas's *Siren Land* — that sensuous classic of intellectual travel literature:

We are not yet ripe for growing up in the streets... has any good ever come out of the foul-clustering town-proletariat, beloved of humanitarians? Nothing — never; they are only waiting for a leader, some 'inspired idiot' to rend to pieces our poor civilisation. (*The Unquiet Grave*, Penguin ed. 1967, p.57)

So the lower classes can't get it right. They can continue to belong, along with Alfred Doolittle, the dustman in Shaw's *Pygmalion*, to the 'undeserving poor' and they will be reviled for their fecklessness and immorality. Or they can give in to 'middle class morality' and become part of the deserving poor and climb into the lower-middle class and they will be reviled all the more. After all, as George Mikes put it in *How to be an Alien*: 'The one class you *do* not belong to and are not proud of at all is the lower-middle class. No one ever describes himself as belonging to the lower-middle class.' Not quite true today perhaps. People are quite happy to describe

themselves as having been born into the lower-middle class —
but only if they have climbed out of it.

But climbing *into* the lower-middle class is nothing to be
proud of. So for those born somewhere near the bottom, the
going is tough. In fact the problem is more or less insoluble.
If they are loud and drunk and fornicate like rabbits, they are
little better than animals. But if they are quiet and respectable
and well-behaved, they are worse still. Either way, the intellectuals will continue to loathe and despise them.

There is something weird and disordered in this volley of
abuse directed downwards by those who regard themselves as
the heirs and protectors of civilisation. For their comments,
as often as not, lack those very qualities of refinement and
discrimination on which they so pride themselves. They are
violent, lurid caricatures, in tone not unlike, say, the anti-
Semitic ravings of Julius Streicher in *Der Stürmer* (and perhaps it may be no coincidence that so many of the writers we
are dealing with have had a weakness for anti-Semitism).

The one thing in modernist writers and intellectuals —
except for Joyce — that you seldom get is any sense of close
observation of the lower classes, let alone any sympathy with
their endeavours and anxieties. The depictions of lower-class
speech that you find in Eliot or Virginia Woolf are plain
embarrassing. How much truth therefore can we expect to
find in their descriptions of lower-class life and behaviour?
How closely does the elite account match the reality? Has any
good ever come out of the 'foul-clustering proletariat'?

VI

A Hidden Civilisation

Immoral, godless, ignorant, feckless, infantile. And hence unable to sustain family life, utterly heathen, incapable of absorbing education, unable to look after themselves economically, and unfit to take part in politics and government. These are only some of the accusations that have been repeatedly flung against the lower classes. Let us take them in turn and see how much truth there is in them.

(i) Morality and the Family

It is commonly assumed that one of the most horrific effects of the early factories was to break up families. So grim and inhuman were the conditions of work that the moral hazards must surely have been as fearful as the damage to physical health. No longer could parents and grandparents keep a kindly eye on children within the security of the traditional village in which everyone had known each other from childhood. Children as young as four or five years old were torn from their mothers and set to work in the hellish noise and danger of the pit or furnace or mill. No wonder that morality and family life collapsed under the strain.

These are natural inferences to draw, and those who have never had to work in such horrible places have always been quick to draw them. Yet the historical reality seems to have been rather different. I too found it hard to believe when, 20 years ago, I began reading for an earlier book on the history of the family, but almost everything in the conventional picture of the social effects of the Industrial Revolution seems to be only partially true and for the most part not true at all. Subsequent research mostly confirms what I wrote in *The Subversive Family* (1982): that, contrary to the conventional wisdom, it is only *since* the Industrial Revolution and pre-eminently in industrial towns that married couples have started living with their parents in any great numbers. The extended family, in Western Europe at least, is a *modern* development in as much as it exists at all. Michael Anderson in his studies of industrial Lancashire, the heartland of the Industrial Revolution, suggests that this startling increase in parents and grandparents living together occurred for strictly economic reasons. For the first time, parents who both worked at the mill were earning enough to feed the grandparents; in return, the grandparents could act as babyminders for them or their neighbours and perhaps perform a few odd jobs as well. Moreover, the children could remain at home longer than they had in rural pre-industrial England because their earnings would contribute towards the household expenses — whereas in the country, there would be enough work on the farm for only a small minority to stay at home until they married. Despite its barbarities and deprivations, one thing that the Industrial Revolution did *not* do was break up families.

The rate of illegitimacy is one of the indicators most frequently taken by historians to show the quality of family life. In particular, the proportion of children born illegitimate is supposed to demonstrate how living in cities and working in factories tend to corrupt the morals of the young, destroy parental control and lead to a general sense of aimlessness and lawlessness, or 'anomie', which can only result in sexual license.

Unfortunately, as Peter Laslett points out, 'It is simply not true, in fact, that living in towns or cities, or migrating to such population centres, has always been directly and positively correlated with illegitimacy, during the so-called sexual revolution, or at any other time' (*Bastardy and Its Comparative History*, P. Laslett et al, 1980, p.27).

In Scotland, Germany and England at least, the rate of illegitimacy was always higher *in the country* — most remarkably so in some parts of rural Scotland, where the strict morality of the kirk seems to have gone almost unheeded. And in many other European countries — Austria, Belgium, Denmark, Germany, Italy, the Netherlands, Sweden and Switzerland — the rate of illegitimacy actually fell, often quite sharply, throughout the period of maximum industrialisation, the late nineteenth and early 20th centuries.

In 1845, when bastardy in England and Wales was at its highest point before the 20th century, most London districts were among the least bastard-prone in the land; the highest rates of illegitimacy were often to be found in the remotest parts of Cumberland and Wales. Even the new industrial cities, so notorious in Victorian fiction for the looseness of moral behaviour, cities such as Manchester, Liverpool and Newcastle, were well down the Registrar-General's list. Whitechapel and Bethnal Green, the direst of the East End's slums, were below the national average for illegitimacy throughout the nineteenth century. Up to 1930, rural districts had far higher bastardy rates than the cities. Thereafter the loss of rural population and the growth of suburbia make the comparisons less valuable.

Here at least there is no evidence for assuming that moving to industrial cities weakened family life or sexual morality, contrary to the automatic assumptions of novelists such as Dickens and Disraeli and sociologists such as Marx and Engels. Marx may have had a child by his maid, Engels may have seduced the girls in his father's mill, but the great majority of urban courtships and pregnancies ended in marriage between young people of equal social station.

By contrast, in pre-industrial society, the classic case of the unmarried mother was of the girl in domestic service, living away from home, made pregnant by the young farmhand, also living away from home in service, the couple being prevented from marrying by poverty and perhaps also by their conditions of service. Wage labour in the factory, whatever its other horrors, did not suffer from those constraints.

The freedom to marry was a genuine freedom and one which came to many young people only after moving to the city. It was this new freedom which contemporary moralists, though not the most acute observers such as Mrs Gaskell, were all too ready to confuse with immorality, suffering as they did from the naive illusion of the well-to-do that physical squalor is bound to breed moral squalor.

In reality, it would be truer to say that such records as we have of life in Lancashire mill-towns and the like bear witness to a moral tenacity in the face of continuous hardship which is as poignant as any record of heroism in war or captivity. And the principal object of that tenacity was to keep the family together through thick and thin.

These moral restraints strengthened, if anything, as the years went by, so that by the beginning of the 20th century, standards of behaviour in industrial towns were strict to the point of being stifling — just as Virginia Woolf complained. From Arnold Bennett to Alan Bennett, those who have had first-hand experience of life in industrial towns and cities have borne witness — rueful, satirical, admiring — to the strenuous ethic that was born out of those communities — an ethic that in some aspects could be harsh and unforgiving and in others pernickety and excessively genteel but could never be accused of slackness or indifference. Yet in between the interstices of the stern moral framework, certain human accommodations could be made: for example, the tradition that the child of an unmarried mother might be brought up as a brother or sister of its parent, or as the child of an absent aunt.

What are the images of the working-class home that have come down to us in books and films? The housewife polishing the front step and the front room or parlour that is only used for funerals — images of a cleanliness and a formality that are utterly at odds with the kind of upper-class propaganda which claims that the lower classes keep coal in the bath and hens in the kitchen. Once again, as we shall see so often in our ramblings, the upper-middle class pursues its war against the lower-middle class by trying to separate the petit bourgeoisie off from the true proletarians, miners and factory workers — who are depicted as uninhibited, good-hearted *bon vivants*, scornful of respectability and inhibition. Such a distinction is in reality not so easy to make, since the desire to keep up standards seems to have burned just as strongly in mining villages and mill towns as in the suburbs, as a million gleaming front steps and a thousand chapels and temperance lodges witness.

(ii) Heathen hordes?
For if the new industrial towns were not predominantly amoral, they certainly were not godless either. Indeed, the strong religious ethos of every industrial community from the South Wales valleys to the cotton towns of the North was profoundly interlinked with and underpinned by that intense morality.

The history of the Nonconformist churches is one of the least fashionable subjects you can imagine. All that most people remember about the history of religion amongst the lower classes in the nineteenth century is that the Church of England never made much headway and soon turned its back on the working classes, leaving the immigrant Irish priests as the only suppliers of salvation in the poorer districts.

Now it is true that the Church of England always found it difficult to reach into the new industrial districts and, as the nineteenth century went on, became increasingly conscious of and anxious about that failure. But what made the Established Church so uneasy was its awareness that the Nonconformist churches were making such huge advances in those districts and elsewhere too. They filled in the gaps where the ministers of the Church of England were too snobbish or slothful or simply absent: Methodists in the Midlands and Yorkshire, Baptists in the Home Counties and Wessex and Wales, Congregationalists in much the same areas, Plymouth and other more or less 'exclusive' Brethren in the West Country. Above all, Dissenters were concentrated in the North and in Wales. The 1851 census revealed that Dissenters actually formed the majority of worshippers in Halifax, Huddersfield, Manchester, Bolton, Newcastle-upon-Tyne, Hull, Birmingham, Bradford, Leeds and the whole of Wales. In the late 1850s it is reckoned that one chapel a week was being opened in Wales.

This remarkable census formed part of the general census of that year and was organised by Horace Mann. His enumerators drew up lists of every church and chapel in the country and asked their ministers to return the numbers attending divine service on Sunday March 30, 1851. The results were startling and acted as an alarm to the Church of England. First, the census revealed the overall level of attendance as 52 per cent of the population — to us today a hugely impressive statistic but by the expectations of the Victorians themselves a deeply worrying indication of popular apathy. But more worrying still to the Anglican authorities was the fact that half of those attending church did not belong to their own flocks.

On that March Sunday, 5,292,551 people attended 14,077 Anglican places of worship (the figures are not wholly reliable, because they do not take account of those who attended church more than once on that day, but for comparative purposes they are serviceable enough). By comparison, 1,214,059 Congregationalists attended 3,244 of their chapels; 939,190 Baptists went to 3,890 of theirs; no less than 2,416,153 Wesleyan Methodists of various types attended 11,007 Methodist fanes; the smaller, more austere Calvinistic Methodists mustered 308,754 at their 937 chapels. If you include Quakers, Unitarians and an assortment of other, smaller sects, this reaches a total of 5,175,454 Dissenters — only a whisker behind the total of practising Anglicans. If you add in the 383,630 Catholics — a number which was destined to grow at an ever increasing rate for the next century as Irish emigration gathered pace after the Famine — then the Anglicans were already in a minority of practising Christians.

This worrying news led to fresh spurts of enthusiasm among Anglican Evangelicals, who stepped up their efforts to convert the nation in the most impressive fashion. But for us the even more impressive fact is the amazing progress of Dissent, especially the newer Dissenting churches such as the varieties of Methodism. From modest beginnings, barely a century earlier, they had swept through the nation like wildfire — to use one of their own favourite similes. They had no influence in politics or society, no legal support, no money. And they were alternately persecuted, sneered at and ignored, a fact which they gloried in, quoting with relish Acts xxviii.22: 'But we desire to hear of thee what thou thinkest: for as concerning this sect we know that everywhere it is spoken against' — the words of the Jews of Rome to St Paul. In his brilliant book which takes its title from that text — *Everywhere Spoken Against* (1975) — Valentine Cunningham explores the overwhelmingly hostile attitudes of Anglican writers to Dissent, including the most celebrated authors of the age — Dickens, Thackeray and Trollope. We shall return in greater detail to the attack on Dissent, but for the moment all we need to record is the stupendous achievement.

The evangelical Anglicans did their best for the poor. But, as E.P. Thompson, no friend of the Methodists, points out,

> the Methodists — or many of them — *were* the poor. Many of their tracts were confessions of redeemed sinners from among the poor; many of their local preachers were humble men who found their figures of speech (as one said) "behind my spinning-jenny". And the great expansion after 1790 was in mining and manufacturing districts. Alongside older Salems and Bethels new-brick Brunswick and Hanover chapels proclaimed the Methodist loyalty. (*The Making of the English Working Class,* pp.386-7)

Many Dissenting meetings didn't even take place in such chapels which were at least dedicated to the purpose. An 1879 attack on the statistics produced by Nonconformists alleged that many so-called chapels were in fact secular premises and shabby premises at that:

> 'A dwelling-house in the occupation of John Poor, Labourer'; 'Nos. 75 and 76 Railway Arches, under Eastern Counties Railway, North Street, Bethnal Green'; ...'Room over a stable, Hoyle Mill'; 'Chamber of a building in the occupation of Abraham Sykes, coal-miner, Littletown, Liversedge'. (Valentine Cunningham, *Everywhere Spoken Against*, p.30)

The Dissenters gloried in this too. For were not such meeting-rooms like the modest upper rooms where the early Christians met? And it was the practice of the founders of the Church that the Dissenters earnestly hoped to recreate and refresh. In their language, the language of the Bible, of Bunyan and Wesley, they hoped to reopen the wellsprings of Divine Grace. In their hymns and hallelujahs they offered up praise to the Creator with a fervour and joy which the rituals of the Established Church could not begin to rival.

And even today their chapels speak for them, in their plainness, their modesty, their passion. As John Betjeman wrote, the most interesting phase of Nonconformist architecture

> shows more surely than any Victorian Established church, whether high, low, broad, Gothic, Romanesque or Classic, what was the true architecture of the people. Not since medieval days had the people clubbed together to adorn a

place of worship and this time it was not a shrine but a preaching house. In mining districts and lonely villages of Wales, among the gleaming granite and slate of Cornwall, down the brick-red streets of Leeds, Belfast, Liverpool and Manchester, in almost every city and corrugated suburb of Great Britain and the Six Counties Area, wedged in on the common land beside country houses and red and blue among the thatched roofs of southern villages or the stone roofs of northern ones, stand the chapels of the mid-nineteenth century. Despised by architects, ignored by guide books, too briefly mentioned by directories, these variegated conventicles are witnesses of the taste of industrial Britain. They try to ape nothing. They were anxious not to look like the church, which held them in contempt; nor like a house, for they were sacred piles. They succeeded in looking like what they are — chapels, so that the most unobservant traveller can tell a chapel from any other building in the street. (*First and Last Loves*, 1952, pp. 102-4)

Subsequent historians, most of them hostile to Nonconformity, have tried to devalue the achievement of the Dissenters by pointing to the fact that half the population did not go to any church. But Horace Mann's census did not restrict itself to church attendance by adults. It revealed also that over two million children were enrolled in Sunday school. The explosive growth of Sunday schools had been noted since the previous century. John Wesley wrote in his *Journal* for 18 July, 1784, 'I find these schools springing up wherever I go.' Originally these schools — designed almost exclusively for lower-class children, the better-off having other means of instruction — were largely set up by Anglicans. But the Dissenters soon got going and by the time of the 1851 census had overhauled the Church of England. In 1801, the total percentage of working-class children enrolled in Sunday schools was 13.8 per cent. By 1851, it had reached the astounding level of 75.4 per cent. (*Religion and Respectability: Sunday Schools and Working Class Culture 1780-1850*, T.W. Laqueur, 1976, p.44)

T.W. Laqueur argues in his massive survey of the subject that 'the magnitude of enrolment was such that very few working-class children after 1830 could have escaped at least a few years in Sunday school' (Laqueur, p.45). Nor is it true that Sunday schools were predominantly set up by the bourgeoisie to buy social peace and political tranquillity. This may have been true in a few large cities or on great country estates. But the great majority of Sunday schools were financed out of contributions from working-class congregations, and many of the teachers were ordinary working men and women. 'The bulk of our teachers, as well as our scholars, belong to the lower — some of the best of them to the lowest — classes of society,' the *Sunday School Magazine* claimed in 1839 (Laqueur, p.92). In fact, the *Evangelical Magazine*, a year earlier, had condemned 'the too prevalent habit of more educated and genteel classes excusing themselves, on various pretexts, from the work' (ibid).

Now and then there were complaints about the education provided in the Sunday schools. Horace Mann's introduction to the 1851 census praises their moral efficacy but dismisses their educational efforts (Laqueur, p. 96 fn) But then moral and spiritual teaching was their prime purpose, and in any case many children did learn to read and write in Sunday school. For most students, Sunday schools added three, four or five years of part-time schooling to supplement their more limited period of weekday schooling.

Nor were the years at Sunday school the only contact that non-attenders at Sunday service had with their local church. All the rites of passage continued to be celebrated in church, almost universally so until the end of the nineteenth century. In particular, almost all marriages were solemnised in an Anglican church (which by virtue of Establishment dispensed with the need for a civil ceremony as well). In 1851, for example, of the 154,206 marriages celebrated in England and Wales, 147,393 were conducted in a religious ceremony and 130,958 by the Church of England. By 1901, of the 259,400 weddings, 218,333 were religious ceremonies and 172,679 of those Anglican. Other denominations and civil ceremonies continued to creep up, until by 1972 of the 426,241 weddings, only 272,107 were religious and 194,134 civil — with the Church of England down to 155,538. (*Churches and Churchgoing*, Robert Currie, Alan Gilbert & Lee Horsley, 1977, pp.223-4)

Thus throughout the nineteenth century, far from being untouched by religion, the great majority of the lower classes were cradled in a complex hammock of religious education, controversy and ritual, more intensely so perhaps than ever before or since.

What is interesting is how keen the middle-class intelligentsia was to prove that this was not the case and that the working classes were godless and deprived of all religious influence or enthusiasm. Sheila Smith has shown how unscrupulously Disraeli distorted the evidence of the Government Blue Books on which he drew when writing *Sybil*. In Dizzy's Wodgate there is no church, and 'even the conventicle scarcely dares show its humbler front in some obscure corner'. In fact we are later told that there are no churches *or* chapels. Yet in Willenhall, Staffs, the basis for Wodgate, according to R.H. Horne's report for the Children's Employment Commission of 1843, there were in reality one Anglican Sunday school, one Wesleyan, one Baptist, one Primitive Methodist and another Wesleyan one two miles away at Short Heath — most of them taught by working men — locksmiths and coal-miners. (*Review of English Studies*, 1962, pp.368-84, quoted *Everywhere Spoken Against*, pp.102-3)

The point of denying the existence of religious education in Willenhall/Wodgate is, of course, to allow the high-minded Morley to sigh, 'Ah me, and could not they spare one Missionary from Tahiti for their fellow countrymen at Wodgate!'

Valentine Cunningham quotes at length from the biography of Travers Madge, a Sunday school teacher and friend of Mrs Gaskell's who had left the Unitarian ministry and in 1859 organised meetings in a room in Crown Street, Hulme. The passage is so vivid and says so much about the motives and practices of lower-class Nonconformity that I cannot resist following his example:

Religious life in our great cities takes more varied forms than most people are aware of. Not even the divergent types of the Anglican church, with the varieties of Baptist and Independent Nonconformity, and the multiform sections of the great Methodist family, can satisfy the restless individuality of the human soul. New offshoots from existing religious communities are growing up every year, which never find any place in the formal catalogue of sects. Probably there is no large town but has, here and there in its great wilderness of absorbed and busy life, some half dozen of these little sporadic churches, that, most in little upper rooms in back streets, are carrying on their humble work and worship, and aiming at something nearer to their ideal of what a church of Christ should be, than their members have been able to find in the larger ecclesiasticisms of the religious world. The little sketch of 'The Church of God in Lantern Yard' which forms one of the quaintest parts of George Eliot's story of humble life, 'Silas Marner', is true, almost to the letter, of humble religious communities, which may be met with by the curious in such matters in London, or Manchester, or Liverpool. Some of these have come out from existing churches, because they can find none rigid enough in Calvinistic doctrine or Puritan discipline; others, in search of simpler, homelier, religious communion, and greater scope for evangelistic work; others again, from love of doctrinal freedom and dislike of sectarianism.

Such a little church of humble, earnest folk, was there in 1859, meeting in a room in Crown Street, in Hulme, one

175

of those densely-populated suburbs which have sprung up about Manchester during the last quarter of a century. Here, a few tradespeople and a goodly number of working-folk met together, Sunday by Sunday, carrying on a Sunday school, and holding religious services and prayer meetings. Not bound together by any rigid orthodoxy, and eschewing any sectarian name, they were what would ordinarily be called strongly evangelical. Some of them had come from the Plymouth Brethren, some had been Baptists, some Independents, a good many Methodists. A few were old friends of Travers's at Lower Mosley Street, who like him, partly by his influence, had become dissatisfied with Unitarianism. They had no minister; — if they had any strong cardinal dogma, it was perhaps dislike of what they called the 'one-man system'. As near as might be, they conformed to the habits of the early church; and when they came together, every one had 'a psalm, a doctrine, a tongue, an interpretation'; and so, striving to edify each other, they lived an obscure, but simple, happy, useful, religious life. (*Everywhere Spoken Against*, pp.31-2)

I would only add that something of the same spirit was still to be found nearly a century later when as a child I was taken to services in the Baptist chapel in our fairly remote village on Salisbury Plain. As a family, we usually attended the local parish church, along with the Lieutenant-Colonel, the Wing-Commander, the parish clerk, the farmers, the carpenter, blacksmith and electrician (the last three all brothers). The rest of the village, the farmworkers and domestic servants, crowded into a much smaller red-brick chapel up the lane. When my parents were away, Mrs Herrington, who walked two miles each way every day to cook our meals, sometimes took my sister and me there. I remember to this day the fervour of the hymn-singing, the sermons by Mr Maidment, the lay preacher, who kept the sub-post office next door, the hallelujahs and the quiet intensity of it all. And I have been reminded of Chitterne Baptist Chapel whenever in subsequent years I have attended Protestant services in other countries: Lutheran churches in Germany, Dutch Reformed in Holland, Baptists in Virginia. The crucial difference is that in those other countries the congregations are not restricted to one class or another (though in Virginia in the 1960s they were, shockingly, selected by colour). Unlike the British Nonconformist churches, these overseas Protestant denominations basked in the approval and often the patronage of the local upper classes. They were as much part of the national religious tradition as the American Episcopalians or the Continental Catholics.

(iii) Education, education, education

But if the Industrial Revolution produced an explosion of religious activity, what effect did it have upon the secular education of the lower classes? Did the hard-hearted mill owners succeed in depriving their workers of the opportunity to learn the rudiments, assuming they had any energy left to do so after their back-breaking labours? The conventional picture is of an uneducated, largely illiterate proletariat sitting in moronic torpor until the beginnings of state education were unleashed by W.E. Forster's Education Act of 1870. Sir Arthur Bryant, for example, claimed, like G.M. Trevelyan that 'in 1869 only one British child in two was receiving any education at all' (quoted E.G. West, *Education and the Industrial Revolution*, 1975, p.4)

The extraordinary thing is that this description runs so counter to the fears of upper-class pessimists of the time, such as T.R. Malthus. whose apprehensions were that the working classes read *too much* and too dangerously. It has been claimed that Tom Paine sold one and a half million copies of *The Rights of Man*. Samuel Bamford, the 'weaver-poet', claimed that the writings of Cobbett 'were read on nearly every cottage hearth in the manufacturing districts of South Lancashire.' Cobbett sold 200,000 copies of his *Address to the Journeymen and Labourers* in only two months (see E.G. West, *Education and the State*, Revised edition, 1970, p.127). More detailed studies at the time suggest a high level of literacy among the poorest. The Poor Law Commission in 1841 found that 87 per cent of workhouse children in Norfolk and Suffolk between the ages of nine and sixteen could read and more than half of them could write. The Committee of the Council on Education in the same year was told that 79 per cent of miners in Northumberland and Durham miners could read and — again a lagging skill — more than half of them could write. Of the population of Hull in 1839, 14,109 out of 14,526 adults had attended day or evening school and over 92 per cent of them could read. Most of these adults must have left school *before* the first modest State subsidies to education began in 1833 (West, p.150).

Some of this schooling was paid for by philanthropists and the Church. But ordinary people played a larger part, either through their church subscriptions which went to support the new local schools or directly through the payment of modest fees.

In Leeds, for example, in 1869, of the £18,776 spent on day schools for 'the poorer Classes of Children', £9,098 came from fees of payments by scholars, £2,291 from voluntary subscription and only £6,036 from taxes and government grants. Forster himself calculated that school fees by parents added up to £420,000 per annum for the whole country and that 'generally speaking, the enormous majority of them are able, and will continue to be able, to pay these fees'. That certainly was the view of Henry Brougham when in the House of Lords in 1835 he argued that the doubling of the school population over the past ten years was not exactly an argument for State interference:

And surely this leads to the irresistible conclusion that, where we have such a number of schools and such means of education *furnished by the parents themselves from their own earnings*, and by the contributions of well-disposed individuals in aid of those whose earnings were insufficient, it behoves us to take the greatest care how we interfere with a system which prospers so well of itself; to think well and long and anxiously, and with all circumspection and all foresight, before we thrust our hands into a machinery which is now in such a steady, constant, and rapid movement; for if we do so in the least degree incautiously, we may occasion ourselves no little mischief, and may stop that movement which it is our wish to accelerate. (E.G.West, *Education and the State*, p.138)

Even enthusiasts for the 1870 Act stopped short of claiming that it hastened the spread of literacy. After all, if you take the traditional test of literacy — who signs a marriage register rather than makes his mark — the Registrar-General's returns show the leap in adult male literacy came before much of the 1870 Act could take effect, from 67.3 per cent in 1841 to 81 per cent in 1871.

This increase in private schooling was observable even before Waterloo. James Mill in the *Edinburgh Review* of October 1813 remarked that:

From observation and inquiry assiduously directed to that object, we can ourselves speak decidedly as to the rapid progress which the love of education is making among the lower classes in England. Even around London, in a circle of fifty miles radius, which is far from the most instructed and virtuous part of the kingdom, there is hardly a village that has not something of a school; and not many children of either sex who are not taught more or less, reading and writing. We have met with families in which, for weeks together, not an article of sustenance but potatoes had been used; yet for every child the hard-earned sum was provided to send them to school. (E.G.West, *Education and the State*, p.136)

By the time of the Newcastle Commission on Popular Education, set up in 1858 following on the 1851 census, the Assistant Commissioners reported that schooling of some sort was almost universal. All over the country, the story was the same. With the exception of recent immigrants from Ireland, there were very few children who had not been at some school for some length of time — and a great number of these had attended the private, fee-paying schools which were multiplying at an amazing rate, many of them refusing to accept government grants, not wishing to have the bother of government inspection. The number of private day scholars had increased from 674,883 in 1818 to 2,535,462 in 1858, from one in seventeen of the population to one in 7.7.

And if we can chalk this up as very largely an achievement of the working classes themselves, we must not leave out the basic educational contribution of the Sunday schools. Laqueur concludes that 'within the context of a working-class childhood, three to five hours of instruction each week for an average of four years, using specialised textbooks in small classes graded according to scholastic ability, had a significant impact on the creation of mass literacy in nineteenth-century England' (p.123). *The Morning Chronicle* of 15 November, 1849, claimed not only that many of the richest men in Manchester owed their ability to read and write to the Sunday schools, but also that:

Long before educational committees of the Privy Council and British and Foreign Societies were heard of, long previous to the era of Institutes, and Athenaeum, the Sunday-schools were sedulously at work, impregnating the people with the rudiments of an education which, though always rude and often narrow and fanatical in its teachings, was yet preserving a glow of moral and religious sentiment, and keeping alive a degree of popular intelligence which otherwise would assuredly have perished in the rush and clatter with which a vast manufacturing population came surging up upon the land. (Laqueur, p.136)

Some schools continued to forbid the teaching of writing on the Sabbath, but others became increasingly liberal in their curriculum. Robert Milhouse, the poet who began employment on a stocking loom at the age of ten, learnt to read, write and do arithmetic at Sunday school. Roland Detrosier, a working-class radical who became superintendent of the Swedenborgian Sunday school in Hulme, wanted Sunday schools to become 'the Universities of the Poor' and taught himself, and hence his students, the rudiments of astronomy, mechanics and natural history. Laqueur advances many other such examples and indeed goes on to argue, contrary to Horace Mann, that Sunday schools were more successful in inculcating the thirst for secular knowledge than in implanting religious belief and the habit of going to church.

Going to university was still, of course, largely out of the question, especially for Dissenters who could not matriculate at Oxford or take a degree at Cambridge and who, even after the University of London began in 1828, might be suspicious of the secular intellectuals and philanthropists associated with it. John Bright, for example, the son of a leading Quaker

mill owner in Rochdale, did not think of a university education and, even after he became perhaps England's leading
orator, still 'stood outside the classically based culture of the
Victorian upper-middle classes.' (*John Bright*, Keith Robbins,
1979, p.8). 'If all existing Greek and Latin books were
destroyed,' he concluded towards the end of his life, 'is there
not in our English classics sufficient material to build a future
of which our posterity need not be ashamed?'

But many working-class enthusiasts for self-improvement
were more broad-minded. They wanted to read the best of
everything that had been thought and written. By the time the
Great Reform Bill was passed in 1832, the mechanics' institutes, the working men's schools and the mutual improvement
societies were to be found in almost every industrial district.
In Carlisle, at least 24 reading rooms were founded between
1836 and 1854 with a total of almost 1,400 members and
4,000 volumes. Such reading rooms typically offered classes in
reading, writing and mathematics, taught either by the members themselves or by professional teachers who volunteered
their services. The mechanics' institutes were often founded
by middle-class philanthropists and could be forbiddingly
genteel, but some of them — for example at Bradford,
Keighley and Halifax — began as small mutual improvement
societies, with the members clubbing together a penny or two
a week to rent a room and buy books.

Autodidacts like these were the true heroes of Samuel
Smiles's *Self-Help* (1859), which sold a quarter of a million
copies by the end of the century and was widely translated.
This notorious work has been caricatured as a manual for

material success in life. In fact, Smiles condemned unmitigated economic individualism as empty and selfish and believed in universal suffrage and many of the Chartist ideals, and *Self-Help* was much admired by early trade union leaders.

Jonathan Rose in his superb survey, *The Intellectual Life of the British Working Classes* (2001), demonstrates over and over again how broad and lofty were the ambitions and appetites of the working-class self-improvers. The Chartist Robert Lowery found among the miners of Northumberland and Durham:

> many superior mathematicians, and the booksellers of Newcastle were known to sell, chiefly among the workmen of the north, a larger number of works on that science than were sold in any other similar district of the country. Some of these men were excellent horticulturalists and florists... I was acquainted with one... as he walked among his flower beds he would sound their scientific names in his provincial tones, intermingling his conversation with remarks on the philosophy of Locke, or quoting passages from Milton, Byron, Shelley, or Burns. (Rose, p.71)

Manny Shinwell (b.1884), the Labour firebrand and Cabinet Minister, built up from rubbish heaps and second-hand bookstalls a library of 250 volumes, including Dickens, Meredith, Hardy, Keats, Hume, Darwin, Huxley, Kant and Spinoza. The father of the folk singer Euan MacColl, an ironfounder by trade, deluged his son with second-hand books. By the age of eight, MacColl had read Darwin, by fifteen Gogol, Dostoevsky and the entire *Human Comedy*. Rose recalls many such instances of entirely self-taught readers attempting the most varied and abstruse works, never deterred by the intellectual difficulty or the esoteric quality of the subject.

At the age of 14, the Durham collier Jack Lawson (b. 1881) had found emancipation at the Boldon Miners' Institute:

> which was then nothing more than two pit-houses knocked into one. And didn't I follow the literary trail, once I found it! Like a Fenimore Cooper Indian, I was tireless and silent once I started. Scott; Charles Reade; George Eliot; the Brontes; later on, Hardy; Hugo; Dumas, and scores of others. Then came Shakespeare; the Bible; Milton and the line of poets generally. I was hardly sixteen when I picked up James Thomson's *Seasons*, in Stead's 'Penny Poets'... I wept for the shepherd who died in the snow (Rose, p.52)

In other words, he was seeking education as a form of enrichment, as a means to the good life, in terms which would have been recognised as kindred by Cardinal Newman or Michael Oakeshott.

Such experiences could be duplicated from the memoirs of dozens of the leaders of the trade unions and of the Labour Party through its first half-century of existence: Shinwell, J.R. Clynes, Emrys Hughes, George Lansbury, Keir Hardie, Will Crooks, Ben Tillett.

What was absorbed in the Mechanics' Institute was very far from mechanical. Behind those dignified buildings which went up all over the Welsh valleys, in the mill towns of Yorkshire and Lancashire and behind the shipyards of the Tyne, the Clyde and Mersey lay a cultural upsurge of the most uninhibited, energetic, idealistic kind. But it was only an intensification, a heightened version of the general thirst for education which united the clerical lower-middle classes and the industrial working class throughout the period.

(iv) Welfare before the Welfare State

It may seem remarkable enough that the lower classes in the early and mid-nineteenth century could spare enough pennies from their modest wages to buy some sort of education for their children and themselves. It is more remarkable still that on top of that they should manage to save something to provide for their sickness and old age. Long before the welfare acts of the Asquith and Lloyd George governments, let alone the stream of subsequent legislation under both Labour and Conservative governments, the poor were making provision for their own hard times. The establishment of the National Health Service and the National Insurance scheme by the Attlee government in the late 1940s was greeted by such a fanfare of publicity as to drown out the more modest efforts that working people had made for themselves and their families throughout the preceding century.

The principal agency for this self-insurance was the friendly society. The membership of friendly societies had made great strides during the eighteenth century. The Poor Law return of 1803 estimated that there were already 9,672 societies with 704,350 members in England and Wales. By the time Lloyd George introduced compulsory social insurance in 1911, there were 6.6 million members of registered friendly societies (plenty more were not registered).

The societies began, as their name suggests, as associations of friends and workmates who met regularly and paid regular contributions into a kitty to be drawn on when a member fell ill. These small groups rapidly found that federation increased strength and solvency. By the time of the Royal Commission on the Friendly Societies of 1874, there were 34 such federations which each had at least 1,000 members. The largest federation, the Manchester Unity of Oddfellows, had just over half a million (*Before Beveridge*, David G. Green ed, 1999, p.21).

Thus the friendly societies were not charities but systems of mutual aid, in which members came together as equals and friends. Their purpose was to create both solidarity and independence by providing all the services that enabled individuals to be self-supporting. If illness or injury struck, the societies provided both a cash benefit and medical care, usually through the society's own doctor, who was typically paid a capitation fee per member. If the breadwinner died young, the society ensured that widow and orphan were provided for. Towards the end of the century, the system was elaborated to offer something in the nature of a retirement pension, which the original friendly society had not offered. The Deposit and Holloway Societies, as they were called, enabled the member to build up a savings account which, provided it was not depleted by repeated ill-health, might secure him a tolerable income in old age.

Between 1912 and 1946, the societies could become 'approved' societies under Lloyd George's compulsory National Health Insurance Scheme, along with industrial insurance companies and several trade unions. These societies administered benefits and paid the 'panel' doctors and dispensaries. Some societies offered additional benefits, such as ophthalmic and dental care, to attract new members. It was also possible to top up your publicly approved policy with a private policy, and this was where the industrial insurance companies looked to make their money. At all events, the number of working people covered by the scheme expanded from 11.5 million in 1912 to over 20 million in 1938. In theory, this sounds as if the voluntary principle was being allowed to survive under benevolent government supervision. In practice, ever-increasing government regulation throttled much hope of popular participation, and the contributions were paid through stamps which you bought from the GPO, so the money was filtered through the Ministry, and when the government was short of cash — as in 1922, the notorious 'Geddes axe' on public expenditure, and again in 1925 and during the public expenditure cuts forced by the economy crisis of 1932 — the Exchequer did not hesitate to slash its own financial support for the system. 'Society profits were transformed into savings for the Treasury, not better benefits for the public, as the scheme's founders had originally intended' (Noel Whiteside in *Before Beveridge*, p.31). By the time Beveridge came along, the world recession and repeated government raids on the kitty had left the approved societies unable to grow and flourish into a system that would provide the scale of health care and pension provision that people expected after the war.

But despite its faults, the old system was mourned, not least by Labour MPs. Even in its government-dominated form, it kept alive some memory of mutuality, and even the profit-making industrial insurance companies offered more personal service than the centralised bureaucracies of later years. But Beveridge was adamant. Compulsory standardised contributions and central administration were more economical and efficient.

Could the friendly societies have survived with more tactful reinforcement by government aid? Could the insurance principle have been built on to provide a comprehensive service with high standards and no queues for treatment, such as we are told is what happens in Germany and in the HMOs in the United States? It is not my purpose here to argue whether this was or was not possible at the time or whether it is today necessary or desirable to transform the NHS into a social insurance system of either sort. Over the past few years we have been watching a controlled experiment in the other approach, as Gordon Brown's large increases in public expenditure on health care have come on stream and we are seeing whether or not it is possible to finance the health service of our dreams entirely out of taxation. It can certainly be argued that some at least of the deficiencies of the old Lloyd George scheme were simply due to poverty — the poverty not only of the workers contributing to it but to the relative poverty of the nation as a whole.

All I want to point out here is the massive advance of voluntary self-financed provision for sickness and old age among the poor from the end of the nineteenth century until the coming of Lloyd George, and then of Beveridge. The friendly societies were huge enterprises that deserve to be remembered not only for the services they provided with so little fuss but for the solidarity and pride they inspired amongst their members.

(v) 'Go out and govern New South Wales'

But then the friendly societies were by no means the only working-class institutions that were 'godly and quietly governed'. A whole raft of societies and organisations were set up by the poorer classes with little or no encouragement — and often a good deal of discouragement — from the well-to-do. We have already mentioned the chapels and their Sunday schools, the private schools financed entirely and often largely staffed by the lower classes, the mechanics' institutes and the working-men's schools and reading rooms. And to the friendly societies themselves we must add the trade unions to which they were closely allied and whose organisation, manners and customs were often so alike.

As E.P. Thompson somewhat sourly remarks, 'the discipline essential for the safekeeping of funds, the orderly conduct of meetings and the determination of disputed cases involved an effort of self-rule as great as the new disciplines of work' (*Making of the Working Class*, p.458). There were fines for drunkenness, for insulting fellow members, for reflecting adversely upon the character of members receiving sick money, for failing to attend meetings, for refusing to take one's turn in the rota of officers, for disclosing secrets to outsiders.

Anyone who has attended the conference of any trade union, or of the TUC or the Labour Party, will be familiar with the meticulous, often nit-picking adherence to the rules of procedure and the severe intolerance of those who break those rules. By comparison, the rules of the Conservative Party conference are conspicuous by their shameless manipulation or to a large extent their total absence. The Constitution of the Conservative National Union is regularly changed at the whim of the party's leadership. In contrast, it took the efforts of a whole generation, from Gaitskell to Blair, to alter the Constitution of the Labour Party so as to remove the commitment to nationalisation of the commanding heights of the economy — a piece of socialist dogma which, it should be noted, was originally inserted not by working-class Labour leaders but by middle-class intellectuals such as Harold Laski and Sidney Webb.

I do not mean to romanticise the almost religious adherence to rules of procedure. It can be pettifogging to the point of madness, and those who are most adept in working the rules are often up to no good. But anything less headstrong and erratic than the British Labour movement would be hard to imagine. These are people soaked in traditions of democratic debate and parliamentary procedure. When their leaders came to sit at Westminster, they took to the life of the Commons as though they had been born to it and found no greater difficulty in heading a government ministry than in acting as general secretary, or even a branch secretary in the trade union that sent them there — the powers and limits of the two tasks being not entirely dissimilar.

Nor need we make a distinction here between the respectable working class (whom we might assume to have been influenced by 'middle-class morality') and the rougher sort. Many trade union leaders have been great boozers and have liked to stay up all night, but this did not damage their mastery of the procedures, nor, except in a few freak cases such as that of Arthur Scargill, rob them of common sense. All but a minority of ideologically driven Hard Left leaders have retained most of the time a reasonable understanding of how far their members could be pushed and of when to settle with the employers in their members' best interests. The damage done to British industry through restrictive practices and the encrusted conservatism of the membership is an almost inevitable consequence of any militant trade union activity. But the political *manners* of British trade unionism have always owed more to the friendly society than to the revolutionary mob.

If you want a supreme example of the political maturity that could be displayed by the 'lowest of the low', you have only to consider the history of Australia — that distant society sneered at as so suburban and thoughtless by D.H. Lawrence. Here, after all, were the ultimate rejects of British society. The men and women transported on the first fleet in 1787 were not the 'notorious felons' of popular imagination. Nor were they political exiles as fondly imagined by later

Australians — rick-burners, trade unionists and the like (*The Fatal Shore*, Robert Hughes, Pan ed., 1988, p.71). They were mostly petty criminals convicted of theft, highway robbery, fencing, swindling and forgery. The articles they had stolen included one live hen, twelve pounds of Gloucester cheese, ten yards of ribbon and a pair of silk stockings. Some had used violence or the threat of violence, but on the whole they were a random selection of the desperately poor, the deviant and the dodgy. Those who sent them had only the most modest expectations of their rehabilitation at the other end of the world; the principal motives for transportation had been to remove the offenders from the scene of their crimes and to deter others who might be tempted to imitate them. Yet within a generation all the penal colonies had developed a flourishing civil society; within two generations, they had developed into self-governing states; after little more than a century, these states, by now fully democratic, had federated into a nation. Throughout this period, the crime rate fell steadily. In New South Wales, for example, the rate of convictions fell from nearly 1,100 per 100,000 inhabitants in 1835 to 122 in 1861, nearly a tenth of the earlier level. The conviction rate for New South Wales in 1835 had been about ten times that of England. By 1861, it was only twice as large (Hughes, p.587). And it should be remembered that transportation continued throughout most of the first century of British settlement. The last convict ship, to Western Australia, docked as late as 1868. So fresh supplies of Britain's rejects were constantly arriving to menace the development of civil peace in the new land.

Except that they did not menace it, or not to any serious extent. Despite the efforts of some historians such as Manning Clark to inflate the occasional episodes of lawlessness and labour disputes into a history of turbulence and violence, Australia has remained one of the most peaceful countries known to history. And, as Hughes somewhat reluctantly concedes in his massive history of transportation,

> it may be that more people were reformed in Australia — in the sense that they came out of bondage meaning to work for their living and obey the law, and were not convicted again — than were ever 'deterred' from crime in England. This was due to the assignment system. Assignment did give its 'objects' a chance...
>
> For all its flaws (and one cannot imagine a prison system without defects) the assignment system in Australia was by far the most successful form of penal rehabilitation that had ever been tried in English, American or European history. (Hughes, p.586)

Under the assignment system (Hughes, pp 283-4), convicts were lent out as labourers by the government to private settlers, until either they had served their sentence and were emancipated or were granted a ticket-of-leave, equivalent to parole, which allowed the convict to work where he wished as long as he did not misbehave or attempt to leave the colony.

In Hilaire Belloc's *Cautionary Verses* the ineffective lachrymose Lord Lundy, who had been expected to be 'the next Prime Minister but three', is sent out to govern New South

Wales. But New South Wales, like the rest of Australia, was already being self-governed in impressive style by the descendants of the convicts who had been dispatched there.

The history of public order in Australia may have been less eventful than its equivalent in the Mother Country — but not by much. Again and again, throughout the nineteenth and early 20th century, the authorities in Britain trembled at the prospect of large public protests turning into violent insurrections: the Luddites and the Blanketeers in the early years, then the Chartists, and the dock strikes and suffragette agitations of the later nineteenth century and the Edwardian years.

For the most part, though, there turned out to be remarkably little violence. The great Chartist demonstration on Kennington Common in 1848 — the year of revolutions in Europe — produced mass panic among the ruling classes. The Queen and the royal family left for Osborne; many middle-class families also decamped. The 80-year-old Duke of Wellington was recalled for his last command. 200,000 people — including Sir Robert Peel himself — enrolled as special constables. By the time the 30,000 demonstrators, superbly organised, converged on Kennington Common on the morning of April 10, they were accompanied by several times as many special constables and policemen, not to mention the Iron Duke's troops, who were kept carefully concealed in the Tower, the Bank and elsewhere with steamers on call to ferry them up river should the need arise.

In the event, what happened? A Commissioner of Police, Richard Mayne, met the Chartist leader Feargus O'Connor.

Mayne gave his word that the Chartists' petition would be allowed to reach the House of Commons but said that the crowd would not be permitted to pass the bridges. O'Connor promised that the procession would not attempt to cross the river, so long as the petition was sent across in cabs. Two cabs duly trundled across Westminster Bridge with the petition (which Parliament, not for the first time, rejected). The Chartist crowd dispersed. The middle classes sang *God Save the Queen*. The soldiers and special constables went home, and the Queen returned to London. And as T.A. Critchley records in *The Conquest of Violence* (1970, p.140), Palmerston crowed. It was, he said, 'a glorious day, the Waterloo of peace and order.'

Such, predominantly, has been the subsequent history of protests and demonstrations in this country: careful preparation on both sides, self-restraint and discipline by the leadership, and a process of negotiation between fellow citizens, underpinned by Peel's conception of his new policemen as civilians in uniform, unarmed except with wooden truncheons and enjoying no special protection from the law, and enjoined in the code of instructions which every police recruit was and still is expected to learn by heart to be 'civil and obliging to all people of every rank and class' and 'not to form false notions of their duties and powers.' (Critchley, p.120).

This admirable 'mission statement' rested on an unspoken corollary, that the lower classes would, as a rule, themselves be civil and obliging in return. Such a reciprocal understanding was broken now and then in moments of passion and desperation — during the Captain Swing riots of 1830, for example, when the agricultural workers were in dire straits, both from low wages and the threat of the new threshing machines. But England did get through all the political turmoil of the 1830s and 1840s, despite the fact that as the French historian Elie Halévy remarked, outside London, England was still:

> a country without officials and without police, where the executive was weaker than in any other country in Europe, and where the justices of the peace, members of the nobility and gentry, in whose hands the local government of England lay, were obliged to trust for the maintenance of order to the voluntary obedience of the people. (Critchley, p.120) (E. Halévy, *A History of the English People*, 1815—1830, 1926, p v)

This obedience was not born of apathy or social contentment among the lower classes, nor of their indifference to the possibilities of social and political reforms. On the contrary, there was a strong and steady current of lower-class opinion demanding democratic institutions and the relief of poverty and injustice. But equally strong and steady was the understanding that these reforms could be secured through Parliament and by peaceful protest and the expectation that they would ultimately be so secured.

This understanding rested on a highly sophisticated grasp of democratic process and its possibilities — much more so than that possessed by many upper-class politicians, with the exception of men like Gladstone and Peel. And it was no accident that these two giants could draw huge working-class audiences and win such popular affection. When Peel fell from his horse on Constitution Hill and lay dying in Whitehall Gardens, great crowds of working men and women thronged the streets for days on end. (*Sir Robert Peel*, Norman Gash, 1972, pp. 704-5). 'He fell from official power into the arms of the people,' wrote *Chambers' Papers for the People*. And Gladstone, too, enjoyed that same trust. The title 'the People's William' might be ironically bestowed by jealous rivals, but the thousands who flocked to hear him were confident that the great man shared both their principles and their aspirations, that he was as capable of appreciating their achievements as they of his.

For all their great personal wealth, these two sober, pious, ponderous statesmen seemed epitomes of the Victorian ideal, an ideal which appealed as strongly to the lower classes as to their supposed superiors, and which in the struggles of the lower classes to overcome poverty and ignorance received a peculiar force of its own. It is not too much to say that the lower classes in Britain between 1800 and 1940 had created a remarkable civilisation of their own which it is hard to parallel in human history: narrow-minded perhaps, prudish certainly, occasionally pharisaical, but steadfast, industrious, honourable, idealistic, peaceable and purposeful.

A dedicated rearguard continued to celebrate that lower-class civilisation. George Orwell in *The Road to Wigan Pier* and in many of his wonderful essays and Richard Hoggart in *The Uses of Literacy* reminded us of its steadfast virtues. But the prevailing culture preferred to move on, enjoying these reminders but treating them essentially as excursions into nostalgia which had nothing much to teach modern-minded people.

As a result, for most of us today the civilisation of the working classes is largely hidden from view, buried under the ideology of social progress which is our orthodoxy and which has been drummed into us by schoolteachers, historians and self-congratulatory politicians ever since. Just how and why so much of that civilisation came to be lost is the story of the next chapter.

VII
Abodes of Desolation

(i) How the institutions of the lower classes were destroyed

If this civilisation of the lower classes was at one time so energetic and so remarkable, why then do we remember it so little? Why in fact are most of us scarcely aware of it at all? In my own case, I must confess that I have stumbled upon it almost by accident, in the works of only a handful of authors many of whom I have pillaged shamelessly. The traces of the institutions of the poor in Britain today are vestigial. Not the least remarkable fact about this whole episode in British history is how the memory of it has been so successfully erased. Those who seek its remains cannot help feeling like the murderer in the story by the marvellous Czech writer Bohumil Hrabal. The murderer is released from jail at the end of the war, gets drunk, then stumbles all the way back in the dark to his home village, hoping to surprise his mother, but can find no trace of it at all because the occupying forces have erased the buildings and grassed the site over, seeking to remove all evidence of the atrocities they have committed. I have visited the real-life site of the story, a few miles outside Prague. It is called Lidice and it is an eerie spot.

Now and then I experience something of the same uneasiness in revisiting the sites where the institutions of the lower classes in England once flourished — working men's institutes with their windows smashed and graffiti on the walls, Baptist chapels turned into bingo halls — in Bolton even into a casino — or converted into private houses, or left to the ragwort and the buddleia until the developer comes to put them out of their misery. On my way to have the car serviced in Islington, I pass a bare mission hall with a stone panel over the windows bearing the inscription (from Psalm 127), 'Except the Lord keep the city the watchman waketh but in vain'. The hall is now a studio for a Communications Design Group — no doubt turning out new 'mission statements' to replace the old one. The inscription is all that remains of its former ambition to bring the lower classes to God.

If one chapel a week was being opened in Wales in the late 1850s, by the 1990s it is reckoned that one chapel a week was being closed. Anthony Jones, former Rector of the Royal College of Art, records in his pioneering work, *Welsh Chapels* (revised edition 1996), that, as well as domestic residences, chapels have been converted into furniture showrooms, a strip club, agricultural feed stores, bingo halls, recording studios, clubs for squash, boxing and climbing and even into mosques. The decline has not only been as precipitate as the ascent. It has been a dismal, degrading affair. The fate of these central social and spiritual sites of the lower classes demonstrates in the most visible and painful fashion that society today sets little or no value on them and regards their disposal as a matter of indifference. While the closure and conversion of any Anglican church has always aroused local and sometimes national concern, chapels can go down like ninepins and nobody in authority cares.

This is no accident. The final closure of so many working-class institutions is only the culmination of a long and bitter campaign to deride and eclipse them.

It is, of course, grossly unfair to bracket the rewriting of British lower-class history and the appalling deeds of the Nazis. Yet we do need some sort of violent metaphor to bring home the length, ferocity and success of the campaign. Not all of it was conscious or deliberate. But a good deal of it was. And those who sought to replace independent lower-class initiatives and institutions by the hand of the State mostly knew what they were about.

From the moment that those lower-class institutions began to blossom, they were under unremitting attack from the guardians of the Established culture. The most famous and perhaps the most influential of such attacks was Matthew Arnold's essay *Culture and Anarchy*. When I first read this formidable polemic some 30 years ago, I could not really get the hang of it. Who were these Barbarians and Philistines whom Arnold inveighed against so vehemently? Against whom were the 'dreaming spires of Oxford' to be protected? And what was it exactly that his famous recipe of 'Sweetness and light' was to replace?

Rereading *Culture and Anarchy* today, I find it a vicious, snobbish and panicky assault on two targets: Nonconformists and Evangelicals on the one hand, and on the other, the pretensions of the lower orders to run their own affairs without the aid of the State. Arnold exclaims for example:

> Look at the life imaged in such a newspaper as the *Nonconformist*, — a life of jealousy of the Establishment, disputes, tea-meetings, openings of chapels, sermons; and then think of it as an ideal of a human life completing itself on all sides, and aspiring with all its organs after sweetness, light, and perfection!' (*Culture and Anarchy*, *Selected Prose*, Penguin, 1970, Chapter 1, p.216).

Such a life was 'so unlovely, so incomplete, so narrow, so far removed from a true and satisfying ideal of human perfection.' (p.217)

Arnold sighed not only for the last enchantments of the Middle Ages, as Oxford still sighed for them, but also for an ordered society, which he feared was disappearing from England:

> For a long time, as I have said, the strong feudal habits of subordination and deference continued to tell upon the working class. The modern spirit has now almost entirely dissolved those habits, and the anarchical tendency of our worship of freedom in and for itself, of our superstitious faith, as I say, in machinery, is becoming manifest. (Chapter 2, p.231)

And what is the answer to this uppity rabble who persist in doing as they like and in inventing their own religions?

'Culture', Arnold tells us, 'suggests the idea of the State.' Having been a devoted and diligent School Inspector much of his life, he is particularly horrified by the thought of an education system (or lack of system) which is not supervised by the State. He casts his eye longingly to Prussia, where an enlightened Sovereign endows schools out of his own revenues 'to be under the direct control and management of him or those representing him'. With envy he compares this State system, under the wise direction of great men such as Humboldt and Schleiermacher, with the English way:

> ... to have a sheer school of Licensed Victuallers' children, or a sheer school of Commercial Travellers' children, and to bring them all up, not only at home but at school, too, in a kind of odour of licensed victualism or of bagmanism, is not a wise training to give to these children. (Chapter 3, p.266)

The State is the only answer,

> Because a State in which law is authoritative and sovereign, a firm and settled course of public order, is requisite if man is to bring to maturity anything precious and lasting now, or to found anything precious and lasting for the future.
>
> Thus, in our eyes, the very framework and exterior order of the State, is sacred; and culture is the most resolute enemy of anarchy, because of the great hopes and designs for the State which culture teaches us to nourish. (Conclusion, p.294)

Arnold is well aware that even Prussia is not perfect and

reassures his readers: 'Now I do not say that the political system of foreign countries has not inconveniences which may outweigh the inconveniences of our own political system.' (p.266) But these foreign countries do have an idea of the State which not only wards off 'the intolerableness of anarchy' but permits a society to progress towards the perfection of its culture. Thus we can see in Arnold's essay the outline of how modern Britain was to develop, a sketchy outline perhaps but clear enough. His chosen concrete example is education — the field he himself knew so well – but the lesson can be applied to almost any area of human social activity. Only if the State takes the lead and institutes and presides over a national system can we progress in any serious sense. That is what Arnold wanted, and that is, by and large, a century or so later what we got.

But if Arnold laid down the first heavy bombardment, fusillades of no less damaging fire had already been heard from almost every leading novelist of the time. Let us first look at the attacks they launched at the Evangelicals, those energetic, muscular Anglicans who sought to wake up the Established Church from its long torpor and who in particular sought to communicate with, convert and educate the poor. In *The Call to Seriousness* (1976), Ian Bradley can think of only three Evangelical clergymen in the whole of Victorian fiction who are portrayed sympathetically: old Mr Clare in *Tess of the d'Urbervilles* and the poverty-stricken and saintly Amos Barton and Edgar Tryan in George Eliot's *Scenes of Clerical Life* (*Call to Seriousness*, p.63).

Against these relatively minor counter-examples of good

Evangelicals, what an array of cruel, grasping, slimy, hypocritical alcoholics we are presented with. There is the Rev Obadiah Slope, the scheming curate in *Barchester Towers* who 'perpetually exudes a cold and clammy perspiration' and whose worst crime appears to be his determination to turn an old men's hospital into a Sunday school (a great enthusiasm of almost all Evangelicals). There is the terrifying figure of the Vicar of Wrexhill in the novel of that name by Trollope's mother, Frances. There is Mr Brocklehurst, the cruel and insensitive headmaster of Lowood School in *Jane Eyre*. There is Charles Honeyman, the sanctimonious and hypocritical incumbent of Lady Whittlesea's fashionable proprietary chapel in Brighton, in Thackeray's *The Newcomes*. There is Mrs Jellyby in *Bleak House* who is obsessed with the welfare of the natives of Borrioboola-Gha on the left bank of the Niger and neglects her own children. And, above all, also in *Bleak House*, there is Mr Chadband.

You remember the wonderful passage in which Mr Chadband makes his appearance:

Mr Chadband is a large yellow man, with a fat smile, and a general appearance of having a good deal of train oil in his system. Mrs Chadband is a stern, severe-looking, silent woman. Mr Chadband moves softly and cumbrously, not unlike a bear who has been taught to walk upright. He is very much embarrassed about the arms, as if they were inconvenient to him, and he wanted to grovel; is very much in a perspiration about the head; and never speaks without first putting up his great hand, as delivering a token to his hearers that he is going to edify them

'My friends!' says Mr Chadband. 'Peace be on this house! On the master thereof, on the mistress thereof, on the young maidens, and on the young men! My friends, why do I wish for peace? What is peace? Is it war? No. Is it strife? No. Is it lovely, and gentle, and beautiful, and pleasant, and serene, and joyful? Oh yes! Therefore, my friends, I wish for peace, upon you and upon yours.' (*Bleak House*, Chapman and Hall ed., Vol. I, pp.314-15)

Again and again, Dickens tells us how oily and greasy Chadband is, how fat and flabby, how greedy and grasping. His physical repulsiveness is matched by his pomposity, his hypocrisy, his avarice and his gluttony. We are not surprised to learn eventually that he is also a blackmailer. In Dickens, a clergyman who seeks a following among the poor is always a confidence trickster, and his followers are always ignorant dupes.

But if the great Victorian novelists are contemptuous of Evangelical Anglicans, they are even more hostile to Dissenters. Whether Baptists, Calvinists or Methodists, Dissenting ministers are all presented with unfailing viciousness as ignorant charlatans. In his Preface to the 1847 edition of *Pickwick*, Dickens launches an all-out attack on religious cant and the pretence of piety and the 'audacious and offensive obtrusion' of the letter and not the spirit of Scripture 'in the commonest dissensions and meanest affairs of life, to the extraordinary confusion of ignorant minds'. Such preaching offered 'one of the most evil and mischievous falsehoods existent in society — whether it establish its head-quarters, for the time being in Exeter Hall, or Ebenezer Chapel, or both.' It was, Dickens added, 'never out of season to protest against that coarse familiarity with sacred things, which is busy on the lip, and idle on the heart.'

It is no surprise then that Mr Stiggins, the itinerant preacher in *Pickwick*, also known to Sam Weller and his father as 'the red-nosed man', should be an alcoholic leech who turns up completely sozzled at the monthly meeting of the Brick Lane Branch of the United Grand Junction Ebenezer Temperance Association. The meetings

> were held in a large room, pleasantly and airily situated at the top of a safe and commodious ladder. The president was the straight-walking Mr Anthony Humm, a converted fireman, now a schoolmaster, and occasionally an itinerant preacher; and the secretary was Mr Jonas Mudge, a chandler's shop-keeper, an enthusiastic and disinterested vessel, who sold tea to the members. Previous to the commencement of business, the ladies sat upon forms, and drank tea, till such time as they considered it expedient to leave off; and a large wooden money-box was conspicuously placed upon the green baize cloth of the business table, behind which the secretary stood, and acknowledged, with a gracious smile, every addition to the rich vein of copper which lay concealed within. (*Pickwick Papers*, Chapman and Hall ed., Vol. II, p.76)

In this passage, as in Dickens's treatment of Chadband, we see displayed all the elite's complaints against preachers of unorthodox religion: that they are ignorant, hypocritical, money-grubbing and, above all, coarse. 'Coarse' is a recurring insult hurled by Dickens and most other novelists of the period against the Dissenting clergy. They simply lack class, they are plebeian in their manners. By contrast, priests of the Established Church may be pictured as a little lethargic and out of touch, but they are always portrayed as gentle in every sense of that word. And their churches are beautiful, holy places.

By contrast, the chapels and meeting houses of the Dissenters are ugly red-brick monstrosities. Often their premises are no more than squalid attics and their manners rough and blasphemous (Mr Stiggins's appearance at the Ebenezer meeting ends in a hilarious brawl). But Dickens is only the most exuberant and unrestrained of the enemies of Dissent. Beneath his network of civilised irony, Trollope is just as contemptuous of the ignorant Puddleham in *The Vicar of Bullhampton*, which revolves around the plan to build a horrid red-brick Methodist chapel next to the ancient parish church — thus perhaps the first 'nimby novel' ever written. In Thackeray and Charlotte Brontë too, Dissenters are humbugs and loudmouths who bawl and snuffle and snivel in the pulpit. Thackeray indeed has a Mr Bawler, just as Dickens has his Melchisedech Howler. Only George Eliot gives her Dissenting characters a fair chance — even the wicked Bulstrode — but then fairness is her unrivalled virtue. Perhaps the least attractive of all the sustained onslaughts on Dissenters came from the Revd Sydney Smith, that otherwise lovable wit. Methodism, he said, led to insanity; it gave ploughmen and artisans too elevated opinions. He earnestly wished the Established Church 'a decided victory over the nonsense, the melancholy, and the madness of the tabernacle'. (Cunningham, p.224). Baptist missionaries were 'little detachments of maniacs', nothing more than devout tinkers. Methodism was not Christianity but 'debased mummery and nonsense'. Cunningham points out that Dickens named his fifth son Sydney Smith Haldiman Dickens.

Now abuse from the adored spokesmen for the well-to-do might not be enough in itself to choke off the rise of Dissent or indeed to precipitate its slow, steady decline which has lasted into our own day. But I would submit that the assault did have clear and lasting effects, not simply on the Dissenting faiths themselves but on the repute and self-confidence of the urban lower classes.

The assault saw to it, first of all, that the Dissenters made no recruits among the upper classes. They remained cussedly, defiantly common; they might be prosperous merchants, or they might be dirt poor, but they were socially inferior, and the upper classes were determined that they should remain so.

All the varieties of Dissent remained as they had always been, ineradicably unfashionable and unthinkable for the upper classes. Even as late as the 1960s, a friend of mine achieved the otherwise impossible feat of shocking her unshockable mother by becoming a Methodist. And for those who might be even momentarily attracted by these queer sects, a stream of propaganda, much of it anti-religious in a general way, denounced the churches of the people as narrow, parochial, unlettered, *unkulturny*. Harold Wilson, himself a

Methodist by upbringing, might say quite correctly that the Labour movement owed more to Methodism than to Marx. But while Catholicism was an acceptable alternative haven to Marxism for the disenchanted haute bourgeoisie, Methodism certainly wasn't.

To gain some idea of the ferocity of the onslaught, we need only consult E.P. Thompson's chapter on religion in *The Making of the English Working Class* (1963). It is entitled 'The transforming power of the Cross', but we are not to think that this transforming is a benign process. On the contrary, 'it is a phenomenon, almost diabolic in its penetration into the very sources of human personality, directed towards the repression of emotional and spiritual energies... The box-like, blackening chapels stood in the industrial districts like great traps for the human psyche' (p.404). John Wesley, Thompson claimed, 'appears to have dispensed with the best and selected unhesitatingly the worse element of Puritanism' (p.398)

'It is difficult,' he tells us, 'not to see in Methodism in these years a ritualised form of psychic masturbation' (p.405). 'These Sabbath orgasms of feeling made more possible the single-minded weekday direction of these energies to the consummation of productive labour' (p.406). 'It is difficult to conceive of a more essential disorganisation of human life, a pollution of the sources of spontaneity bound to reflect itself in every aspect of personality' (p.409).

Now within this violent onslaught there emerges something of a contradiction, one which Thompson himself partly admits: 'At one pole, the chiliasm of despair could reduce the Methodist working man to one of the most abject of human beings... On the other hand, as if to battle expectation, Methodist working men, and, indeed, local preachers, repeatedly emerged in the nineteenth century — in handfuls here and there — as active workers in different fields of working-class politics.' To which one must add that they emerged not just in those fields, but in industry and commerce and local government, some of these worthies becoming decidedly smug — which Thompson, like other critics of Nonconformity, repeatedly complains of too. So, far from being a demoralising force, Nonconformity seems to be rather energising, both in those directions Thompson approves of and those he doesn't. Far from sapping the practical idealism and self-confidence of working men, the practice of these queer faiths appears to ginger them up.

But Thompson's loathing of religion is too suffocating for him to linger here. He is, after all, interested in these matters only in so far as they contribute towards the formation of a revolutionary consciousness in the working class. And so it has remained. For most modern students of history and politics, Nonconformity remains merely an episode in the creation of the Labour movement.

This intense, almost hysterical class-revulsion of the intelligentsia and the elite had a secondary effect, that upwardly mobile Dissenters began to migrate from the faiths into which they had been born. They mostly joined the Church of England. Desmond Bowen argues that the defection of many of its most prominent members was one of the chief reasons why Dissent did not increase after the middle of the nineteenth century. (*The Idea of the Victorian Church*, 1968, p.379). Nonconformity provided a transitional creed for those who were rising in the social scale. Elie Halévy (*England in 1815*, p.424) goes further, seeing a progression that is almost automatic:

> The unskilled labourer becomes in turn a skilled workman, an artisan, the head of a small business, a business man possessed of a modest capital, and as he rises out of the barbarism in which the working class was plunged, he becomes a nonconformist. If he himself rises still higher on the social ladder, or if his children rise after his death, he or they go over to the Church of England. (Quoted in *The Idea of the Victorian Church*, p.379)

Money and social influence were jealously guarded by the Established Church. For those who despaired of beating it, joining it became an option which could easily be rationalised: one could do so much more to help the poor from within the Church of England.

We are familiar with this drifting away from Nonconformist origins in the careers of well-known politicians such as Margaret Thatcher, Harold Wilson and Selwyn Lloyd. In those three cases as in many others, gratitude for the moral and spiritual training of a Methodist childhood never faded, but the regular practice of the Methodist faith became socially inconvenient. In other cases, such as that of the remarkable novelist and headmaster, J.L. Carr, the breaking away was a violent wrench which left its scars. Carr kept the moral standards (including temperance) of his Wesleyan Methodist upbringing in Yorkshire when he became an Anglican headmaster, publisher and antiquary down in Northamptonshire, but there remained about him a fierce unsettling quality (well caught in Byron Rogers's biography, *The Last Englishman*, 2003). Methodism did not go quietly into oblivion. Those who sloped off into the gentler meadows of the Church of England were well aware that life had thereby lost some of its intensity.

Compare here the American experience. The Episcopalian Church may have been the predominant church among the early settlers and for that reason became the preferred church of upper-class Protestants in the nineteenth and 20th centuries. Yet the Constitution guaranteed equal treatment for all religious faiths, and membership of other churches was never regarded as so socially inferior as to inhibit the upwardly mobile. In recent years it is the Episcopalians who have been in sharp decline and the inheritors of the English Nonconformists who have made startling progress. George W. Bush, the last in a long line of Episcopalians, was born again as a Methodist — something more or less unthinkable for an Englishman from a similar social background.

At the same time as lower-class faiths were being so persistently denigrated, the State began to offer fresh competition to all the institutions founded and operated by the lower classes (whether dissenters, Anglicans or cheerfully heathen). Forster's 1870 Education Act was in many ways what we would consider as quite liberal or even neo-liberal. An option for giving parents 'tickets' or, as we would say today, 'vouchers', for their children's education was built into it. The new Board schools were intended only to fill in these supposed gaps in the existing network although in many cases they took over existing Church of England and Wesleyan schools. There was to be healthy competition between the old and the new schools, which, it was hoped, would stimulate higher standards. But, as E.G. West points out in *Education and the State*:

> This argument reveals a misunderstanding of the nature of competition. Competition which is socially useful requires that every single participant should be able to go bankrupt. Board schools were in a specially protected position and they enjoyed the advantage of always being able to dip into public revenues to cover their costs even when they went above those of their competitors. The expenses of the school board were paid out of what was called the 'school fund', and the 1870 Act provided that: 'Any sum required to meet any deficiency in the school fund, whether for satisfying past or future liabilities, shall be paid by the rating authority out of the local rate.' (Section 54) (*Education and the State*, p.154)

The Board schools could not go bust. The private schools could and did. The fees in the Board schools became lower and lower, as the subsidies to them rose — leading to complaints, even from Matthew Arnold, about public extravagance. Often the Board school would be in the next street to the Wesleyan school, but charging its pupils only 3d per week — and by the end of the nineteenth century nothing at all — while the church school might need to charge 6d or 8d. It was not difficult to prophesy the end result.

And indeed quite a few eminent observers at the time did descry the shape of the future, not merely that the independent schools for the poor would be crowded out but that this might have incalculable social effects. We have already quoted Brougham on the dangers of interference with the voluntary system, and in 1836 Gladstone himself warned:

> It appears to me clear that the day you sanction compulsory rating for the purpose of education you sign the death-warrant of voluntary exertions... If this be the true tendency of the system which my noble friend seeks to introduce, are we preparing to undergo the risk of extinguishing *that vast amount of voluntary effort which now exists throughout the country*? Aid it you may; strengthen, and invigorate, and enlarge it you may; you have done so to an extraordinary degree; you have every encouragement to persevere in the same course; but always recollect that you depend upon influences of which you get the benefit, but which are not at your command — influences which you may, perchance, in an unhappy day, extinguish, but which you can never create. (*Education and the State*, p.86)

There are darker fears lying behind those words than the mere apprehension of losing the cash provided by working-class parents. The great philanthropist Lord Shaftesbury put his fears in more emotional terms, after he had officiated at the annual prizegiving of the Ragged School Union in 1870, on the very eve of the Act becoming law:

> Never was I more touched, never more sorrowful. It is probably, the close of these Christian and heart-moving spectacles. The godless, non-Bible system is at hand; and the Ragged Schools, with all their Divine polity, with all their burning and fruitful love for the poor, with all their prayers and harvests for the temporal and eternal welfare of forsaken, heathenish, destitute, sorrowful, and yet innocent children, must perish under the all-conquering march of intellectual power. (*The Call to Seriousness*, p.133)

Something was going out of English life, something rare and unrepeatable, unprecedented since the replacement of the old Catholic Church by the Church of England. This time there was no Pilgrimage of Grace to protest against its passing. But unmistakably the life of the lower classes was changing. Beatrice Webb, raised among Unitarians, recognised how Chapel had once been a resting-place 'to the worn-out or failed lives' (Cunningham, p.95) and now the spirit had gone out of Dissent. She thought the new Dissenting Minister at Bacup:

> ...one of the 'new college men', with measured phrases and long words; a poor exchange for the old-fashioned minister 'called of God from among the people', no more educated than his fellows but rising to leadership by force of character... He has a certain influence over the people, through his gift of the gab; but even they half unconsciously feel that the

'real thing' is passing away, and grieve that there [are] 'na more plain men as *feel* the word of Christ'. (Cunningham, p.208)

What I want to draw particular attention to is the combined effect of these erosions of lower-class cultural independence. It was not simply that their chapels lost heart, nor that their schools began to close down, nor, as we have already seen, that the Friendly Societies at the peak of their numerical strength, popularity and usefulness should have been progressively taken over, manipulated and eventually strangled by the State. It is that all these things should have happened as a part of a single stream of events, a purposeful process directed by the State and a process for which the lower orders were expected to be grateful.

Let me add one more area of benevolent State encroachment and perhaps the most important of all: the housing of the poor. The slums — Dickens's rookeries — were a standing reproach to the active consciences of the nineteenth century. The Lodging Houses Acts of 1851 represented the first attempt of Parliament to confront the question. Dickens himself described it as 'the best measure ever passed in Parliament', and it was one of Shaftesbury's great achievements. Then came Disraeli's Artisan's Dwellings Act (of 1875), which for the first time empowered local authorities to sweep away insanitary dwellings and replace them with improved homes for workers. But this process really only took off after Lloyd George's legislation of 1919, followed by Neville Chamberlain's Housing Act of 1923. It is important to note here, as throughout this essay, that State intervention on behalf of the poor has never been confined to the parties of the Left — rather the reverse, if anything.

Public-sector housebuilding gathered pace from a total of between 20,000 and 100,000 a year in the 1920s and 1930s to over 200,000 a year in the early 1950s. This naturally had spectacular effects on the pattern of housing tenure in Britain.

Until 1938, less than 10 per cent of dwellings were owned by the local authority. This rose to a peak of 32 per cent in the post-war years, before rapidly dwindling again as Margaret Thatcher's policy of selling off council houses to their tenants began to take effect. We shall come back to that later. For the moment, what I want to note is the spectacular growth of council estates. Within half a century, they grew from a tiny proportion of the total stock — a fallback solution for those who could not house themselves — to represent a third of all dwellings. A third to which the lower orders were shunted off in a series of huge one-class ghettos in every town and city in the country.

These colossal enterprises were seen by planners and architects as a golden opportunity to realise their utopias, to promote their visions of community and order, just as Le Corbusier had taught them. Serious modern architects rejoiced in the fact that here lay the great opportunities to build as they liked and not as the wretchedly philistine client dictated, with his love of semi-detached houses in appalling retro styles.

What I want to emphasise at this point is not so much the

sadly mistaken nature of these utopian projects as the fact that nobody thought of consulting the people who were to live in them. Sensitive observers, even on the Left, were not slow to voice their unease. G.D.H. and Margaret Cole, the great socialist pioneers, in their book *The Condition of Britain* (1937), found 'incontestable proof of the continued existence of "two nations".' They agreed that 'the main body of the working class is absolutely a good deal better off today in terms of material goods' (pp.79-80), but they also foresaw (p.173) the problems of creating bleak, utilitarian estates on the fringes of the great conurbations, ill-served by community facilities, shops and local transport.

George Orwell, characteristically, went much further. In *The Road to Wigan Pier*, published in the same year, he accepted that:

> When you walk through the smoke-dim slums of Manchester you think that nothing is needed except to tear down these abominations and put decent houses in their place. But the trouble is that in destroying the slum you destroy other things as well. Houses are desperately needed and are not being built fast enough; but in so far as rehousing is being done, it is being done — perhaps it is unavoidable — in a monstrously inhuman manner... there is something ruthless and soulless about the whole business. (*The Road to Wigan Pier*, Penguin ed. 1962, pp.62-3)

Tenants were not allowed to keep their houses and gardens as they wished. They could not keep poultry or pigeons, or operate a small business from their homes. There were scarcely any pubs. All in all, 'It is a great achievement to get slum dwellers into decent houses, but it is unfortunate that, owing to the peculiar temper of our time, it is also considered necessary to rob them of the last vestiges of their liberty.' (ibid, p.64). All this in 1937, with the greatest boom in building council estates still to come after the war.

Orwell and the Coles were still writing at a time before council housing had come to occupy quite such a dominant role in the lives of the poor. And they therefore could not foresee some of its profoundest effects, many of which were embodied in the 'housing list'. Naturally the only fair way to allocate these precious new dwellings with all their modern conveniences was to set up a queuing system, to be calibrated according to need by a system of points — so many for being disabled, or elderly, or with dependent children. But such a list had two further effects: that it encouraged the queuers to show their wounds and to think of themselves as victims with entitlements rather than as agents with challenges; and it also meant that once having climbed to the top of the list and been allocated a house or flat, people didn't want to go through the whole business again (most councils were in any case slow to set up a transfer system) and felt inhibited from moving even to another part of the same town, thus becoming permanently dependent on the local authority. Sterner critics in the 70s and 80s came to argue that teenage girls deliberately became pregnant in order to qualify for a council flat, once the stigma of bearing a child out of wedlock had faded. I remain unpersuaded that this was the sole or even the prime reason in most cases; a deeper longing to give some meaning to one's life often seemed to be involved. But at the very least, in those many parts of towns and cities where council housing became for a generation the dominant form of tenure, there was inevitably a growing need to cultivate the goodwill of the town hall. Council tenants occupied their dwellings at the pleasure of the housing officers. In what sense was and is their position much different from the unfree lower orders under feudalism — the serfs and villeins — or from the tenantry of a great Whig landowner in their tied cottages?

I do not for one moment underestimate the huge improvement in living conditions enjoyed by most of the poorest over that period. I am the last person to undervalue indoor sanitation or the delights of central heating. But it must be remembered that these things did not come as free gifts from the well off to the worst off. On the contrary, the worst off were themselves paying for them, not only through rent and rates but also through taxation.

For the other great change that the onset of the Second World War was to mark was that, for the first time, the lower classes began to pay income tax. Until that moment, income tax, then standing at five shillings and sixpence in the £, had only affected the middle classes and above. And the Chancellor's annual revenue from it had changed remarkably little since 1918, averaging between £200-£300 million. All at once this figure took off, as both the rate of the tax and the number of people caught by it rocketed. By 1940, it had reached £1,000 million, by 1950 £1,400 million, by 1960 £2,400 million, by 1970 £5,700 million, and so on to the stratospheric figures of the present day. Much of this increase is, of course, due to the rampant inflation which became endemic for many years after the war. But much of it is not. The standard rate of income tax remained steady at about 25 per cent, between 1918 and 1939, then rose sharply to 50 per cent by 1945, falling back only very slowly after the war. In 1969 it was still 41 per cent, coming down to 30 per cent only in the early 1980s and finally to its present rate of 20 per cent. More to the point for lower wage-earners, the starting point for paying tax never kept pace with rising wages. Indeed, except during the years of the Rooker-Wise amendment, which inflation-proofed the personal allowance, the starting-point did not keep pace with rising prices either. Thus more and more low wage-earners found themselves paying income tax although their real wages might scarcely have increased — the notorious phenomenon of 'fiscal drag'. As Chancellor, Gordon Brown's large increases in expenditure on the NHS forced him back into the bad old habit of freezing the personal allowances, thus adding to fiscal drag.

In 2008-09, according to Inland Revenue statistics, nearly 31 million British citizens have been paying income tax, four and a half million more than were doing so when Gordon Brown became Chancellor six years earlier. This comes on top of the increased contributions to National Insurance, an income tax in all but name. Commentators of the Left, such as Polly Toynbee, like to argue that economic inequality is worsening because the British are 'undertaxed' (*Guardian*, August 27 2003). The truth is surely rather different, that the Downers are overtaxed in a way they never used to be.

This is familiar territory in political debate, hard fought over by the Conservatives as a means of undermining Labour's moral legitimacy. Labour believes that the Man in Whitehall knows best and must be allowed to spend a high proportion of the worker's income in ways that are supposedly good for him, rather than leaving it 'to fructify in the pockets of the people', in Churchill's phrase. Powers of choice and decision-making have been systematically removed from the poor over the past century and must be given back to them. It is predominantly but not exclusively Conservatives who argue in this way.

And a good argument it is too, but I cannot help adding that Conservative governments have themselves played an energetic part in removing powers of choice and decision-making and in hollowing out the lives of the lower classes. They too have shown by their actions that they have little faith in the abilities of the poor to make good choices and still less faith in those institutions which the poor devised for themselves. It was the Balfour Education Act of 1902 which placed both State and voluntary schools under political control. It was the Butler Education Act of 1944 which finally abolished fee-paying in schools and extended compulsory state education to the age of fifteen with a further extension to sixteen to be brought in later. It was Conservative-dominated governments in the 20s and 30s which raided the National Health Insurance fund. After the war it was a Conservative government that was in power during the early 50s when more council houses were built than ever before or since.

Clement Attlee was happy to concede, in a broadcast in 1948, that, 'in the building up of the great structure of our social services, all Parties in the State have borne their part.' In the same way, Conservatives ought to admit that their party too has played its part in the destruction of lower-class institutions and in the demoralisation of the poor.

I emphasise this because the argument is too important to be obscured by party point-scoring. Let us for the time being concede that all parties were soaked in the spirit of their times, as political parties always are, and that none of them had much conception of the harm they might be doing.

(ii) The growth of cultural condescension

To begin with, the erosion of lower-class institutions probably had only modest effects on the aspirations and self-confidence of the worst-off. Nor did it immediately eat away at upper-class expectations of what the lower classes might achieve, given the chance. As we have seen, working-class autodidacts embarked on the most arduous intellectual adventures without a backward glance. And those who were genuinely keen to urge them on would not have dreamed of dumbing down.

Take, for example, the great movement to make the treasures of the nation's museums accessible to the poor. It is often forgotten what intense efforts the early Victorians made to this end. Sir Robert Peel had insisted that one of the purposes of the new National Gallery should be to 'cement the bonds of union between the richer and poorer orders of the state'. Prince Albert agreed to support the 1857 Manchester exhibition only if the Lancashire mill owners would lay on transport to take their workers to it. The first report of the Victoria & Albert Museum describes it as a place where 'all classes might be induced to investigate those common principles of taste, which may be traced to the work of all ages'.

Mark Fisher, a Labour MP and a former Minister for the Arts, in a Slade lecture at Oxford (reprinted *TLS*, March 22, 2002) drew attention to these high ideals and energetic practical steps and compared them adversely with the present state of things. 'There is a danger that we are losing confidence in museums, even that some museums are losing confidence in the ability of their own collections to command attention.' This lack of confidence was already having visible effects:

> It is one thing for young artists to wish to free themselves from the constraints and weight of past traditions. It is another for those who fund and determine policy for museums to lose confidence in the relevance of, and interest in, the past. But that is beginning to happen. Museums and galleries in Britain, under pressure to fulfil their role as agents for social inclusion and to increase the number of schoolchildren visiting their galleries, are favouring exhibitions that will make good school projects over those aspects of their permanent collections that do not. How much easier it is to devise a school project around dinosaurs, in the wake of Jurassic Park, than one around eighteenth-century costume

or watercolours. (*TLS*, March 22, 2002, p.14)

The capacity of the lower classes to respond to the highest when they see it is increasingly doubted. The guardians of culture are under pressure to render their treasures accessible, not by admirable initiatives such as opening on Sundays or publishing cheap editions of classic books and classic recordings, but by abridging, simplifying, vulgarising and boosterising. A British Museum show of Yemeni artefacts must be billed as 'Treasures of the Queen of Sheba', though it is doubtful whether any such person existed.

My objection is not so much to the odd flash of vulgarity — Mr Darcy seen bathing nude in the TV film of *Pride and Prejudice* will do for example — as to the belief that the masses won't tolerate any classic fare at all unless it is sugared and salted in this way. Our grandparents were not afflicted by this panic about the inability of the lower orders to stick at anything difficult. Until well into the 60s, it was expected that educational opportunities could be expanded to reach the overwhelming majority of the population without any sacrifice of standards. When Kingsley Amis said, in 1960, 'more will mean worse', it was a genuinely shocking prophecy. And there was, after all, no intrinsic reason why it should invariably be true. The introduction of GCSE, despite all denials, did make exams easier in order to broaden the intake, but all over the Commonwealth children in much poorer, more 'backward' countries continued to take the old O Levels and many do so to this day.

Again when the BBC began in the 1920s, it was taken for

granted that the wireless would be a prime instrument in opening educational opportunities to all. Above the great marble hall of Broadcasting House, there are engraved above the lifts the words

DEO OMNIPOTENTI TEMPLUM HOC ARTIUM ET MUSARUM ANNO DOMINI MCMXXXI RECTORE JOHANNI REITH PRIMI DEDICANT GUBERNATORES PRECANTES UT MESSEM BONAM BONAM PROFERAT SEMENTIS UT IMMUNDA OMNIA ET INIMICA PACI EXPELLANTUR UT QUAECUNQUE PULCHRA SUNT ET SINCERA QUAECUNQUE BONAE FAMAE AD HAEC AUREM INCLINANS POPULUS VIRTUTIS ET SAPIENTIAE SEMITAM INSISTAT

which being translated means

In the year of our Lord 1931, with John Reith as director, the first governors dedicate this temple of the arts and muses to Almighty God, so that a good sowing may bring forth a good harvest, and that all impure things and those things harmful to peace may be expelled, and that the people, inclining their ear to whatever is beautiful and true and of good report, may tread the path of virtue and wisdom.

And that mission was taken with the utmost seriousness — and received with considerable pleasure. Percy Edwards, a Suffolk ploughmaker who later became the most famous imitator of bird calls on the radio, remembered that 'the day after the BBC broadcast *The Magic Flute* from Covent

Garden you'd have thought the Martians had landed there was such excitement' (Jonathan Rose, p. 204). Growing up in Shadwell, the roughest part of the East End, Louis Heren, later to be Deputy Editor of *The Times*, regularly listened to the Foundations of Music series. 'Later I was taken aback by sneers at Lord Reith's crusade to improve the quality of listening, and of life itself. No sneers were heard in our house' (ibid). The music-hall star Wee Georgie Wood was a dedicated fan of Beethoven, Mozart, Chopin and Schubert and hailed the BBC for bringing first-class music, played by great orchestras, to the masses. Jonathan Rose in *The Intellectual Life of the British Working Classes* gives many other such examples. Indeed I can scarcely recall an autobiography of any cultivated self-made man or woman of that generation who does not pay tribute to the role of the BBC in their development.

The BBC today still maintains orchestras and continues its unrivalled Promenade Concerts. But its TV channels have been largely given over to unspeakable, mindless docusoaps, celebrity chat shows and quizzes in bright colours with audiences primed to bray and emote. Programmes like *Big Brother* and *Celebrity Survivor* swamp all channels, demonstrating the relentless determination of every producer and controller to bring every minute of prime time down to the lowest conceivable level.

Let us take a typical evening's viewing on the BBC on a dreary night in late winter, February 28, 2003. At 7 pm on BBC1 we have *A Question of Sport* — a quiz show featuring past and present sporting celebrities. After *Top of the Pops* and *EastEnders* — two evergreen shows which generate celebrities for other shows, we have *Celebrity Driving School*, which speaks for itself. After a repeat of *Only Fools and Horses* and the news, we have a talk show, *Patrick Kielty Almost Live*, in which the star guests are Danni Minogue and Tom Jones. This is followed at 11.10 pm by *Liquid Assets: Elton John's finances* — a celebrity insider story transferred from BBC3, the new digital channel, which according to the terms of the licence granted by Tessa Jowell, the Culture Secretary, 'must deliver a mixed schedule of programmes embracing drama, entertainment, current affairs, education, music, the arts, sciences, international issues.'

And six-and-a-half years on, what is this amazing new channel broadcasting on the evening of Monday October 19, 2009, as I am updating this chapter? *Bizarre ER*: a lecturer who was stabbed in the eye; *Clever v Stupid – Cabin Crew*: a team of flight attendants take up the challenge; *Gavin & Stacey*: Bryn tries to organize a surprise for Gwen's birthday; *EastEnders*: Heather's waters break; *Coming of Age – Up the botty*: Ollie and Jas try a sexual experiment; *Family Guy* – he's too sexy for his fat. And so on and on. Was so much ever spent on such sustained vacuousness?

By contrast, celebrated long-running programmes devoted to culture and politics are perpetually under threat of being axed or relegated to graveyard viewing hours. Since 1995, for example, the BBC has dropped, among others, *The Late Show* and *Bookmark*, and in 2003 brought the 35-year run of *Omnibus* to an end. In 2009, ITV followed suit by axing the *South Bank Show* after 32 years. *Panorama* and *Newsnight* cling on, but other serious current affairs shows on radio and television have vanished, in most cases to be replaced either by occasional or much more lightweight interview programmes. *The Reith Lectures*, which once provided a series of oases for reflective thought on the Third Programme, have been shifted to Radio Four, the text shortened and the lecturer subjected to usually rather dim questioning from a studio audience. Wherever possible, sustained speech has been replaced by chatty, undemanding interviews. In music, the flip boosterism of the disc jockey has invaded even parts of the network that took their music seriously, such as Radio Three. But then taking things seriously is the new cardinal sin in the media. Perhaps the most ruthless exponents of the new flip are the presenters on Classic FM, who are likely to introduce a late Beethoven quartet with some such words as: 'Here comes old Ludwig again.'

Sir Jonathan Miller commented on the decision to drop *Omnibus*:

Unless it is a programme about how to decorate your house or chop up vegetables, it is impossible to get anyone in the BBC to commission your programme. The BBC is run nowadays by people who have done degrees in media studies and sit in glass boxes poring over ratings. Even when they do decide to make an arts programme, it is about Leonardo or Michelangelo, because those are the only artists they have heard of. There is a vast audience of intelligent people out there who can read without moving their lips, who they do not care about. (*Sunday Telegraph*, November 3, 2002)

Rather than rage on here at this collective dying of the spirit, I want to draw attention to the *purposefulness* of the process. Those sneers at Lord Reith's ambitions did not come from the poor. It was by the middle-class intelligentsia that the stiff, driven Calvinist giant was mocked. Compare Reith's unyielding seriousness with the light-hearted streetwise approach of Kenneth Clark when he was appointed the first Chairman of Independent Television. He thought the general level that ITV ought to aim for would be about the level of the *Daily Mirror*. The *Daily Mirror* then represented a rather more elevated level than it does today, but even so the ambition was not exactly Reithian.

That easygoing assumption that the lower classes really don't want anything more demanding has prevailed. Listen to the vibrations in the verdict of the philosopher A.C. Grayling on postwar culture:

> But after 1945 the culture of self-improvement declined, partly because of increased formal schooling, partly because of television and other distractions, and partly because increasingly rapid changes in cultural fashion have made self-taught classicism look conservative. In any case, it was always an avocation for a minority, and remained so even as the working class grew in prosperity and political confidence, taking with it a long ingrained mistrust of high culture and a natural loyalty to its own tastes, transfigured by the new medium of television (itself subserved by the tabloids) into a now familiar and characteristic demotic view of the world.

But although the masses do not choose to be interested in high culture, it is not undemocratic to promote it at the public expense. (*Guardian Review*, 13 July, 2002)

Note how subtly the blame is transferred from culture-producing bodies like the BBC and the schools to the working classes themselves. 'We' are simply giving 'them' what they have always wanted, and that is fine so long as They continue to be compelled to pay their taxes to support our elitist programmes.

Grayling goes on to say that the great Lord Reith was right in thinking that 'if you took horses to water, many of them would find how good it is to drink. Although the paternalism is no longer acceptable, he was otherwise right.'

But where is the 'paternalism' here? And why is it no longer acceptable? Reith was simply the man in charge, and wanted to see the BBC broadcast the stuff he thought was the best. How is that paternalist? Surely it is more paternalist to broadcast stuff which you know to be inferior on the grounds that the child-minds of the lower orders cannot handle anything more demanding.

And that is, in fact, the position of all those university graduates who commission and direct these programmes aimed at the mass audience. Experienced directors who were brought up in the school of Reith and Huw Wheldon have often described to me the wearisome process these days of showing rough cuts to a series of producers, each of whom insists that the action must be more violent, the pace faster, the music louder, the characters more stereotyped, so that any subtlety lingering from the original script may be ironed out. The coarsening process must be rigorously followed through until no hint of the difficult, the idealistic, the refined remains.

Anyone who is compelled to watch television continuously, when laid up in a hospital bed, for example, can only wonder how any viewer can survive without having their brains irreparably addled. Even so, viewers remain decidedly sceptical about most programmes they have viewed, frequently dismissing them as 'the usual rubbish' and preferable only to the rubbish on the other channels.

(iii) The indifference of capitalism

Characters in bottom-class milieux, those I have dubbed the Downers, appear abandoned. They have been left behind, and not only in the rat race for worldly success, for the rat race we have always with us. The Cabinet's special unit to help the bottom class describes them as 'socially excluded', which is not a bad phrase, but it omits to indicate who or what has done the social excluding. If they are left out in a way that the worst off in previous generations were not left out, what force or group is responsible for the leaving out?

We have dealt at some length with the contempt of the intelligentsia and the destruction of those institutions which the lower classes had built up themselves and which afforded some shelter against the rougher winds of fate. But there are other forces which need to be mentioned. There is, for a start, capitalism, free enterprise, the market economy, call it how you please. The market has been praised as a benevolent liberator of human energies and a great generator of prosperity. It has also been fiercely attacked as a callous destroyer both of communities and of individual human lives. The truth is that the market may have both those effects, but it has no *intentions* in either direction; it is simply a mechanism which can have no purposes but can only have consequences. For all the benefits that capitalism brings, its cold indifference remains hard to cope with, both in theory and practice. The defenders of market solutions won't hear a word against them; by contrast, the critics accept the prosperity unleashed by markets with a grudging nod but prefer to discern a systematic evil at work. *The Communist Manifesto* argues that

> The bourgeoisie, wherever it has got the upper hand, has put an end to all feudal, patriarchal, idyllic relations. It has pitilessly torn asunder the motley feudal ties that bound man to his 'natural superiors', and has left remaining no other nexus between man and man than naked self-interest, than callous 'cash payment'. It has drowned the most heavenly ecstasies of religious fervour, of chivalrous enthusiasm, of philistine sentimentalism, in the icy water of egotistical calculation. (*The Communist Manifesto*, p.82)

But this need not be true at all and very often isn't. All sorts of non-cash ties remain even in the most marketised of Western societies. 'Philistine sentimentalism' continues to flourish everywhere, especially in that nirvana of the capitalist bourgeoisie, the United States.

Yet it is true that full-blooded capitalism has certain natural tendencies which may make life for the poorest more insecure and unnerving, even if it makes them richer in cash terms.

There is capitalism's demand for flexibility in order to make the best of the available opportunities. The natural consequence of this is a tendency towards impermanent employment, job-changing and contract work. None of those is in itself an evil. Changing jobs, working for a series of employers, being your own master as a sub-contractor — each of these ways of living may have its own rewards and satisfactions. But the feeling of impermanence can be unsettling, as much the threat of it as the experience. On the whole, most people do not care for the thought that the job they are doing today may not exist in a couple of years time because of the increasing pace of technical obsolescence. The 'gale of creative destruction', as Schumpeter memorably described the way capitalism works, can be a biting wind.

In *The Corrosion of Character* (Norton, 1988), the American sociologist Richard Sennett argues eloquently that this demand for flexibility, with its aversion to stable, long-term arrangements, spills over into the private life of those who are subjected to it. Those human characteristics which contribute to the formation of a stable individual character and a stable society need to be marinated in time. Trust, loyalty, patience, tolerance are all much easier to acquire in contexts where you are not expected to change your job and therefore your house and your friends at bewilderingly short intervals. Sennett draws a telling contrast between Enrico the janitor whom he interviewed in depth 25 years earlier for a book about blue-collar workers in America, *The Hidden Injuries of Class*, and his son Rico, now a prosperous businessman in a smart suit with a computer in his briefcase. Enrico's lot had superficially been harder, a dreary grind in fact, but his life had at least been a coherent project, to save enough to buy a house out in the suburbs and to send his two sons to college. Rico by contrast was much better off, but was constantly having to shift from one job to another and found it much harder to bring up his children in the stable moral principles which had been drummed into him.

Less alluring still is the tendency of capitalism to de-skill workers, especially those at the bottom. We try to pretend that this is not so. The politicians and business leaders like to say that we need a much more skilled workforce. But that need applies mostly towards the top of the scale. Nearer the bottom, capitalism is continually finding efficiency gains by simplifying tasks for humans, while it complicates them for machines, so that all the business of calculating, measuring, estimating and combining is done by the computer, while the human is required only to press a small selection of buttons. Wherever possible, capitalism prefers to eliminate those quasi-artistic skills of hand and eye which marked out a craftsman and let the computer produce a standardised, infinitely repeatable solution.

Sennett describes a local Greek bakery which used to bake delicious bread by hand. The working conditions were hellish, and the racial exclusiveness of the Greeks was not exactly attractive. Now the Greeks are gone, and so are the skills required to bake a decent loaf. A floating population of assorted races passes through, needing only elementary skills to push the right buttons. And when the machine breaks down, unlike in the old days, they could not begin to fix it themselves but must send for a computer wizard.

Again, I do not want to exaggerate here. There are thousands of lower-class jobs which still demand the old skills — in building, painting and decorating, for example. It is also noticeable that people whose day jobs have been de-skilled take pleasure in devising tasks at home for themselves which do demand those very skills — decorating and gardening, for example. But, all in all, for the Downers the general effect of capitalism is to make work less demanding and more boring, thus to make it less of a satisfying centre to life. True, it tends progressively to eliminate the backbreaking elements of toil, simply because human muscle power is an unreliable and transient resource: workers get old, they get ill, they die. Where work cannot be wholly mechanised, it can at least be made physically undemanding. Power steering can be developed to such a degree that a woman can drive an articulated truck without undue strain. Indeed, a great deal of manual work can be feminised in this way. That has considerable advantages in opening up a whole new range of jobs for women, but it has a downside too, in that physical strength and endurance, once the principal selling quality for lower-class men, find fewer takers now. Male pride and sense of usefulness diminish correspondingly. We are uncomfortably aware that a job for life in a steel mill or even a coal mine is more of a man's life than a series of impermanent engagements to stack shelves in a supermarket.

On top of this general tendency to feminise work through technology comes also the rapid obsolescence of the old heavy industries. In Britain more than in any other industrial country, those industries — coal, shipbuilding, steel, the railways — had taken centuries to build up. Whole towns concentrated along the major estuaries of Wales, Scotland and Northern England had grown up around those industries, to serve their needs and conversely to depend upon them. Within a generation the coal industry had disappeared. The shipbuilding had diminished to a few specialist yards. The iron and steel industry, and the railways too, employed only a fraction of their former numbers.

The blow was shattering. Successive British governments did their best to fill the gap by encouraging new industries and overseas investment. There have been some striking successes, in Silicon Glen in central Scotland and in the huge new plants on Teesside, for example. By the time of the Millennium, unemployment in the worst black spots was much reduced and not greatly worse than in the rest of the country. In material terms, the government's response in Britain to such inevitable but terrifyingly quick technological change was not discreditable. By comparison, ten years after the Berlin Wall came down, unemployment in the old East Germany remained in the region of 20 per cent. The 'regional policy' of successive governments in Britain, much criticised at the time, has had its successes.

All the same, something has gone out of those great heavy-industrial conurbations — pride, morale, independence, a sense of confidence in the future, call it what you will. And the social consequences linger on. In a string of villages round Worksop in what was once the great Nottinghamshire coalfield, for example, heroin abuse has become rampant. Ninety-two per cent of people brought before magistrates by the local probation service are on the drug; five young people have died. Yet unemployment is as low as three per cent. It appears to be simply the case that pride and aspiration disappeared when the pits closed. A local charity worker, Sandy Smith of the charity Hope for the Homeless, says 'there's a failure of aspiration in families where dad, grandad and great-grandad were miners, but now there's no pit to go to any more. There's no tradition of moving away to try something else. And this is a generation which saw its parents very obviously defeated.' (*Guardian*, 21 September, 2002)

Once again I do not wish to exaggerate or overgeneralise. There are still plenty of jobs in every area which fully employ a man's muscles as well as his mind. And, to general surprise, several sets of statistics have found that the average length of service in a firm in the US or the UK has not changed nearly as much as we imagine.

But the imagination is where feelings of insecurity have their being. And there is no doubt at all that all the rhetoric about the workforce needing to be flexible and the warnings that no one should expect to stay in the same job all their life have left their mark. No doubt employers have always seen their workforce largely as instruments to be deployed or redeployed in the interests of efficiency. But it is only recently that we have all, as it were, become fully conscious of that instrumentality, aware of how little the economic system *cares* for its workers.

Many workers are relatively content with that unsentimental relationship, finding their satisfactions in their friendships with their colleagues and in their life outside work. But what if that outside life is itself stripped down and deprived of social meaning and satisfaction?

(iv) The infantilising of patriotism

No campaign has been more relentlessly pursued by the intelligentsia than its vendetta against national sentiment. Patriotism is a delusion, we are told. And it is a dangerous, insidious force, too. There is no worthwhile distinction to be drawn between the people swathed in Union Jacks at the Last Night of the Proms and the poisonous, murderous nationalists who scarred the 20th century with so many terrible wars. Any rational grown-up person must treat all the paraphernalia associated with this childish infatuation — flags, baubles, titles, Coronations, Kings and Queens, oaths and anthems, bowing and scraping — with the contempt they deserve.

More particularly, these absurd reverential antics are characteristic of the unenlightened lower orders, who simply don't know any better. In discussing the monarchy, Walter Bagehot in *The English Constitution* tells us quite plainly that 'the masses of Englishmen are not fit for an elected government' and this is why we need a visible symbol of authority because 'the fancy of the mass of men is incredibly weak and can see nothing without it.' And so we must

241

preserve the mysterious glow of royalty; in his most famous phrase, Bagehot tells us 'we must not let daylight in upon magic,' because otherwise 'the coarse, dull, contracted multitude' would see that they were being conned and that their glorious queen was simply a dumpy, not very bright, middle-aged German woman. Luckily, Bagehot concludes, 'the lower orders, the middle orders, are still, when tried by what is that standard of the educated "ten thousand", narrow-minded, unintelligent, incurious.'

Bagehot, I must remind you, was not some effete aristocrat but a hardworking banker and editor of the *Economist*, whose advice Gladstone valued highly and who has never ceased to be regarded as a leading authority on the British Constitution. And his attitude towards the monarchy and everything that went with it has also remained influential and highly representative among the intelligentsia.

The same aversions — and the same condescensions — crop up repeatedly. Charles Bradlaugh, the great Victorian atheist republican who refused to take the MP's oath of allegiance to the Queen, wrote in *The Impeachment of the House of Brunswick* (1873), 'I loathe these small German breast-bestarred wanderers whose only merit is their loving hatred of one another' — a sentiment we have heard again and again from republicans of our own day. The same applies to the verdict of the Marxist Social-Democratic Federation on the death of Queen Victoria: 'Her late Majesty was a very selfish and self-regarding old lady... she never took a single step towards improving the lot of the mass of "her" people.' Almost exactly the same words recurred in the letters columns and features pages of the *Guardian* on the death of the Queen Mother a hundred years later. Beatrice Webb could not see how Victoria's successor Edward VII, who was so 'unutterably commonplace', could be so popular with the masses.

That was just the problem. It might be, as Bradlaugh argued, that 'monarchy is government for children. Republicanism is for men.' Modern republicans like Stephen Haseler and Jonathan Freedland might argue that monarchy induces 'childish sensibility' and imprisons us in 'political infancy'. For the past 50 years — the whole of the present Queen's reign in fact — a stream of commentators has exhorted the masses to grow up. Kingsley Martin said that 'with the growth of science and democracy, people begin to realise that monarchy is a survival, surrounded by superstitions which must be outgrown.' Malcolm Muggeridge complained that 'true religion is in danger of being driven out by the royal soap opera'. The masses were hypnotised by fairytales about beautiful princesses in glass coaches. In the late 1980s, Tom Nairn in his sparkling polemic *The Enchanted Glass* was still lamenting that 'people enjoy the monarchical twaddle and show very little sign of being robotised or "brainwashed".'

Now you could argue that, on the contrary, people of all classes continue to enjoy such things for the very good reason that they are visible symbols of national continuity and unity. In other countries, including republics such as France and the United States, such symbols are cherished and revered without inhibition or embarrassment. A capacity for symbolic thought is not simply a hangover from our primitive animist past when we worshipped rocks and trees; it is the basis of all art and language, indeed of the human capacity to engage with and celebrate the world. This is not necessarily to insist that constitutional monarchy is the most brilliant or indispensable system of government, though it has plenty of merits. It is to say only that it is one such system which quite a few nations have found usable and which accordingly has over the years garnered the loyalty and affection of those who live under it.

Uniquely in Britain, monarchy and patriotism are used as sticks to give the lower classes another beating up. The reverence of the masses shows how infantile they are, how easy to bamboozle. We have seen how Virginia Woolf and George Gissing — and many others — load their pens with particular venom when they describe scenes of national rejoicing — the Armistice, the Jubilee. You would think that these were scenes from hell, rather than harmless expressions of relief and gratitude.

And how miserable the intelligentsia was when the lower classes (and including large numbers of the well-to-do as well) showed that even now in the post-post-modern age they had not managed to kick the habit. The extraordinary outpouring of grief at the death of Princess Diana could plausibly be presented as an expression of anti-royalist sentiment, but it was an expression of royalist sentiment too. The crowds wanted to show that they thought the luckless Princess had been vilely treated by her in-laws, but they also wanted the Queen and the rest of the royal family to repent of their supposed sins and so become adorable once more; 'Show us you care, ma'am,' as the tabloids implored. And by the time of the Golden Jubilee and the Queen Mother's funeral, normal adoration had indeed been restored.

Thus the monarchy and patriotism more generally provide yet another occasion for the intelligentsia to sneer at the masses, but there is more to it than that. The republican discourse is strongly motivated and unremitting, and its long-term aim — of demolishing the monarchy — is supported by a variety of tactics. The first is to argue that all these traditions are *invented*. The so-called national identity is an artificial construct put together over centuries to reinforce privilege and the political status quo. In such works as Benedict Anderson's *Imagined Communities* and *The Invention of Tradition*, edited by Eric Hobsbawm and Terence Ranger, the process of nation-building is taken to pieces and the soaring pillars and majestic draperies revealed as shoddy pieces of painted canvas and plywood. Subtler historical accounts such as Linda Colley's *Britons* describe how the supposed dupes actually take a conscious part in building the sort of nation they can identify with, but even in such books our attention is directed to the inventing and reinforcing process rather than to any long lasting continuities in national feeling and loyalty.

As a matter of fact, medieval historians convincingly trace English national feeling back to the Venerable Bede at the beginning of the eighth century, but you won't find much tracing of that sort in constructionist (really deconstructionist) histories.

If these patriotic symbols are invented and illusory, it follows that they ought to be discarded. The monarchy must be stripped down, shorn of its flummery and its medieval accoutrements. It must be so deconsecrated and deprived of its rituals and traditions as to be scarcely distinguishable from the unadorned republic which is to succeed it.

Thus once again the lower classes are on the receiving end of a double whammy. They are reviled for the infantile, primitive nature of their loyalties. At the same time they are to be deprived of any occasion for expressing those loyalties; the monarchy is to be dis-anointed and transformed into a modest political convenience.

There are obvious political dangers to any such deliberate undermining of the focus of national loyalty. But there is another dubious consequence too. If you bleach out the numinous element of monarchy (or any other focus of collective loyalty) from a nation which is already secular and materialist to a degree unthinkable in previous generations, you leave that nation in rather bleak surroundings. In a world already so disenchanted, how desirable is it to remove any lingering social experience of the transcendent, leaving the metaphysical imagination in the purely private realm? Let me add here that I am not 'doing a Bagehot' in recommending the continuation of popular illusions which I do not myself share; I do share these feelings and would hotly contest that they are illusions. Indeed, it is a category mistake to describe such feelings as an illusion, just as it is a mistake so to describe A's love for B: she loves him, loves his conversation, his blue eyes; there is nothing illusory about the feeling, it is simply a matter of taste and affection.

Republicans may regard these questions as piffling or sentimental. I can only refer them back to the mass grief expressed at Princess Diana's funeral. This extraordinary phenomenon provoked an almost equally extraordinary out-pouring of academic and semi-academic cultural studies, few if any of which cared to confront the fact that that terrible wailing, those mountains of flowers showed in what desolation millions of our fellow citizens live and how Princess Diana, for all her faults or perhaps because of them, had acted as a comforter to so many who felt abandoned by modern Britain.

The intelligentsia, after all, do not need patriotism. It was one of the illusions of Marxism that the proletariat was international and could not be expected to feel any great loyalty to the nations in which they lived. That illusion was famously exposed at the outbreak of World War One, when the lower classes in their millions offered the most extreme expression of loyalty by volunteering to fight for their country. Conversely, the last years of the 20th century marked the growth of a new international elite ready to live and work anywhere and do business in the new international language, which turned out to be English. It was widely said that, just as the new multinationals owed no allegiance to any one country, so their managers became detached from the national loyalties they were brought up in.

Actually, I have my doubts in both cases; when they are up against it, most multinationals show a decided preference for the factories, offices and employees of their country of origin;

and the new international citizens are often no more international in outlook than the old servants of Empire who still regarded Britain as home and the motherland, however far they might roam and even if they continued to live out East after retirement.

But at any rate the new elites have a choice. They can decamp to Tuscany or New York. Even if they settle in the English countryside, they can live a detached life there, living as it were in a charming playground, while the most vital part of their existence takes place elsewhere, and is reached via Boeing or the Internet. By contrast, those who do not belong to these roaming elites may feel more intimately connected to the place where they live and, by a process which is entirely rational and grown-up, come to attach more value to that connection. Thus on this front too it is the Downers who are most likely to feel uncomfortable and beleaguered when they are told that such attachments are childish and outmoded. To find values which have been taken for granted all your life peremptorily devalued is at best bewildering, at worst a desolation.

(v) Fragile harbour

So what are the people at the bottom left with? Their churches have been derided and strangled, their schools and hospitals and savings schemes have been taken over by the state, they have been herded into mass housing (largely paid for by the tax deducted from their own pay packets), and in return for modest improvements in their real take-home pay they remain subject to the bleak disciplines of capitalist enterprise. Their old loyalties to Queen and country — and indeed to county, town and trade union — have been belittled. In return, they are fed by the media with a stream of degraded pap which for the most part leaves them dissatisfied and feeling that they have been gulled.

In what area of life then can they be said to be free, independent, autonomous? Where is their own space? The answer to that question is easy: it is within their own home, and their own family. If ever freedom for the working class existed in the great pulsating, protesting collective — as the romantics of the Left, from Marx to E P Thompson, have always dreamed — it certainly does not any more. People at the bottom have long since lost confidence in mass action as the guarantor of authentic freedom and justice. If happiness is to be found, it is to be found in the pleasures of private life, above all in love.

Thus the people at the bottom lead a life whose vitality resides entirely in personal relations. Curiously, what does this condition remind us of? Surely it is the gospel of the Bloomsbury Group, that personal relations are what matter most in life; friends come before country, we are to believe in the individual not the mass. Of course, the Bloomsberries had in mind a group of highly educated, sensitive persons of the upper class; they did not envisage extending this freemasonry of the emotionally refined to the lower orders.

And in noticing this weird similarity, one is struck by the cruel differences. For the Bloomsberries it was a personal decision to adopt such an intimate and civilised way of life —

a decision cushioned by modest private incomes and an ineradicable class confidence.

For the lower orders, the concentration on family life is a psychological and material necessity. The family becomes, in the title of Christopher Lasch's memorable book on the subject, 'a haven in a heartless world'. And marriage becomes (as it was not for the Bloomsberries) the governing principle of the haven. I can do no better here than quote again (as I did in the introduction to *The Subversive Family*) what D.H. Lawrence wrote in *Apropos of Lady Chatterley's Lover* (London, Phoenix edn 1961, p.27):

> It is marriage, perhaps, which had given man the best of his freedom, given him his little kingdom of his own within the big kingdom of the State... It is a true freedom because it is a true fulfilment, for man, woman and children. Do we then want to break marriage? If we do break it, it means we all fall to a far greater extent under the direct sway of the State.

By 'true fulfilment' I take Lawrence to mean that marriage and parenthood at their best are complete satisfactions in themselves; they refer to nothing beyond and provide a joy and sense of achievement which are their own reward.

There are moments today as ever when you catch that joy on the wing: seeing a little girl standing in a shopping trolley singing a nonsense song or a chortling urchin toepoking a football past the toppling figure of his father in the park. The jingling tills in the run-up to Christmas bear witness to the reality that doing your best for your children is a British ruling passion, which seems to intensify if anything the further you travel down the social scale. 'Family life' is occasionally offered in a puckish spirit as his recreation by some notable in *Who's Who*. Among people at the bottom it is not so much a hobby as a vocation or a lifeline, the importance of which easily surpasses any other project in life.

Yet the sheer intensity with which this project is pursued brings its own perils. The more hope and love are invested, the more desperate the disappointment caused by failure. And it has to be said that the social, legal and fiscal environment in Britain today sharpens the risks and adds to the pressure. Never have people at the bottom put more into family life, and sadly never has it been more difficult to maintain that family life intact.

Making divorce easier had several attractions to liberal-minded people in the 1950s and 1960s. It would release unhappy couples from marriages which had 'died' years earlier. It removed the humbug and pretence from divorce proceedings — and it was hoped, some of the acrimony too. It would enable long-standing unions between people who were devoted to each other to be legitimised, and the children of those unions could be absolved of the stigma of bastardy.

As the welfare state developed, the poor were enabled to enjoy that freedom to divorce which the rich had already enjoyed for many years. Abandoned mothers and children would now be automatically supported by the State — in straitened circumstances, it is true, but they would no longer starve.

All these arguments were and are appealing. The opponents of reform sounded hard-hearted and old-fashioned. I would not myself have felt like voting against any of the measures of divorce law reform which were presented to Parliament in those years.

It is, however, difficult to deny that something happened in subsequent years which the sober reformers had not anticipated (though they were certainly warned of the possibility). The freedom of divorce did not happen in isolation. It was part of the current of individual fulfilment which had been flowing, erratically but unstoppably, ever since the French Revolution. Saint-Just's remark that happiness is a new idea in Europe is perhaps the most astute harbinger of what was to come. The freedom to bury a dead marriage and embark on a new one was certainly regarded as an essential part of that pursuit of happiness which had been so prominent in the American Declaration of Independence.

Thus marriage began to acquire a more impermanent, provisional character. The couple still promised to stay together 'till death us do part', but that commitment could be trumped by the commitment to the pursuit of happiness. And happiness, like pain, can only be measured by the person himself.

At the outset, there were still objective tests of when a marriage had broken down. Proof of adultery, or of impotence, or of specific acts of cruelty and brutality might be offered. But as the years went by, those tests came to seem too mechanical. Such criteria alone could not determine how unhappy one partner to the marriage, or both, had become.

So 'no-fault' divorce, or something approaching it, became the general rule. Moralists of an old-fashioned sort objected to this removal of blame and hence of responsibility. In practice, the 'no-fault' principle reached even wider, for it tended to erase any kind of objective criterion, leaving only the states of mind of the individuals concerned, something which by definition could not be reliably ascertained by outside observers, such as solicitors, judges and marriage guidance counsellors.

So from being a guarantee of security the married state became an insecure condition, an arrangement that had to be 'worked at', one which might demand considerable effort to 'save' and which could, with surprising ease, be deemed to have 'irretrievably broken down'.

At the same time, the climate in which these arrangements were undertaken had undergone such radical alteration as to be scarcely recognisable. Everything was sexualised — fashion, women's magazines, television soaps and dramas, books, films — with an overt, knowing, yet at the same time yearning eroticism previously confined to dilettantes of exotic tastes. It was not exactly that everyone was now expected to have an interesting sex life — although some people did feel that and worried about it. What happened more was that an introspective, Rousseau-like quality began to permeate relationships. People began to *think* more about their marriages, which naturally added to the weight of expectation placed upon them. The expectation included sexual fulfilment; wives, and husbands too, were instructed to minister to their partners' fantasies. But there arose a more general expectation of contentment. Marriage and the family had to bear an unprecedented weight of longing, particularly among the worst-off. Hopes and aspirations that once might have been spread elsewhere were now concentrated. 'Focus' in Latin after all only means 'the hearth'. And now the focus really was the focus.

And thus the temptation to look elsewhere when your existing arrangements seemed a little less than perfect was greatly added to. The not unusual feelings of lust for someone you didn't happen to be married to now carried a certain moral, indeed scientific justification. It was almost your duty to find out whether B rather than A could achieve the crucial life goal and make you happy.

Estrangement, separation and divorce are horrific experiences for people in all classes. While going through the now grimly familiar process, people are usually distraught, sometimes more or less deranged. But the whole agony is surely even worse for those at the bottom who have few other projects and distractions. A middle-class person has still the hope of becoming a consultant or a director after he has 'been through' the divorce; he may still be singing in the Bach choir or replanting the shrubbery. Down at the bottom there are fewer consolations.

And the revenge taken may be terrible. Week after week we read of the estranged husband who pesters his wife mercilessly and then finally snaps and murders her and the children too, wiping out in one appalling night the whole evidence of failure. The horrific brutality of second husbands to their step-children leaves the old warnings of the fairytales seeming pallid.

Oh, such things have always happened, we shall be told. Terrible things have always gone on inside marriage, and few marriages have been without their moments of fury, disillusionment and even violence. But have there ever been such numbing stories of utter despair as now seem commonplace?

The breakdown of lower-class marriage has left reservoirs of bitterness and rage which take years to drain away, if they ever do. And that rage is not so far from the surface. In almost every public place in Britain now — schools, hospital accident and emergency departments, supermarkets, motorway toll booths — you see signs saying that 'anyone abusing the staff will be prosecuted'. And this in a country which was once famous for public politeness.

In 2002, the Chief Inspector of Schools, David Bell, reported that a rise in the number of disturbed children was threatening school standards. Teachers found it difficult to keep order in classrooms. Even a small number of disruptive pupils could make a class unmanageable (*Times*, November 11, 2002). Children were showing disturbed and violent patterns of behaviour at increasingly young ages. At one school, more than 90 per cent of staff claimed to have been verbally abused by their pupils. According to a report by the National Association of Schoolmasters and Union of Women Teachers, at 71 schools over the previous eighteen months, teachers had threatened industrial action because of difficult pupils. The government was clearly at its wits' end, being at first determined to reduce the number of children excluded from school for fear that they would roam the streets and drift into crime, then realising that unless head teachers had effective disciplinary powers, the schools would become even more violent and chaotic places.

But the origins of this implacable and growing problem clearly lie in family breakdown and in particular the growing tendency of lower-class marriages to come apart while the children are still in their early school years.

And, as Lawrence warned, the consequence of marriage breakdown is to throw people back on to the State. The tax support for marriage has, unlike anywhere else in Europe or in the United States, been whittled away by successive Chancellors — 'an anomaly', Kenneth Clarke called it — and the benefit support for the victims of marriage breakdown (or of the absence of marriage) has grown vastly in its place. In the case of single mothers and abandoned mothers too, the State is quick to provide housing as well, thus reducing independence to the barest minimum. Once such systems are in place, it is extremely difficult to alter them so as to encourage self-reliance again, as all governments have found.

What I want to emphasise here is how the eagerness of the State to gather the casualties of broken marriages under its wing undermines the permanence of existing marriage, and it is that permanence, that quasi-eternal quality, which gives to a marriage and to the children born of it the character of a work of art, the only true work of art most of us ever accomplish.

It is not perhaps surprising that young couples increasingly shy away from making a commitment which seems at once so perilous and so undervalued by government — easy to dissolve, no longer much supported by tax or other privileges, and, when broken down, replaced by increasingly generous State support. At first optimists derived some consolation from the fact that, although Britain had just about the highest proportion in Europe of children born out of wedlock, in most cases both parents put their names to the certificate and continued to cohabit. Alas, it turns out that about half such cohabiting parents split up within a few years and in many of those cases the father quite soon drifts out of touch. Once again, all these things are most painfully experienced at the bottom of the heap, where the father being low-paid or unemployed has less to contribute to the family in the first place and when pursued by the Child Support Agency is more likely to disappear than to pay up. Above all the disappearance of any serious social role for young lower-class men has had catastrophic results, which are easily measured in the statistics for drug abuse and civil disorder.

If there has been in the past 20 years any single action undertaken by Government or any single trend emerging in society which has effectively bolstered lower-class marriage, I should be very glad to hear of it. The wind has been blowing in one direction only, against marriage as a necessary or unbreakable commitment, and it is the worst off who feel the bitterest of the after-effects.

VIII
The Present State

(i) What about poverty?

Some may prefer a simpler diagnosis and a simpler remedy —
and a more obvious villain. So far we have mentioned the
subject only glancingly, but we can go no further without confronting it more directly. The subject is poverty. The difference
between the rich and the poor, as Ernest Hemingway pointed
out to Scott Fitzgerald, is that the poor have less money. This
shortage of cash permeates their lives, shrivels their expectations and cripples their spirit. Sociologists may distinguish
between absolute poverty and relative poverty. But the poor in
modern Britain suffer from both. In poor families, especially
single-parent families, it is an increasingly hard struggle to
feed and clothe the children and keep up with the rent. Real
wages for the worst-off have scarcely increased since the
1970s. In 1970, when Polly Toynbee first tried to see how
the poor live, an experience recounted in *A Working Life*,
she earned £12.50 a week as an orderly in a hospital ward,
the equivalent of £210 a week today. Yet when she returned to

do the same job in a new hospital thirty years later, she earned only £174 a week — a substantial decrease in real terms (*Hard Work*, Bloomsbury, 2002, p.56). Middle-class followers in Orwell's footsteps who have attempted to live on the minimum wage today all agree on what a miserable grind it is; like Toynbee, Fran Abrams, in *Below the Breadline; Living on the Minimum Wage* (Profile, 2002), argues that the minimum wage is set far too low to lift the worst-off out of genuine poverty. That no doubt is why until the Credit Crunch there was no dire effect on levels of employment predicted by free-market economists. Set the minimum wage a couple of pounds higher than the present modest level of £5.80 an hour and those earning it would be a little nearer the comfort zone, but there would be fewer such jobs offered. At the same time, the level of middle-class pay has purred along keeping well ahead of inflation, while the pay of top executives has disappeared into the stratosphere. Thus while suffering the daily practical misery of not quite making ends meet, the poor also have the humiliation of seeing how little the society they live in values their efforts. Their ever-increasing relative poverty entrenches feelings of worthlessness and inferiority.

For those on the Left, writers such as Nick Davies and the late Paul Foot, and for the remnant within the Parliamentary Labour Party which feels passionately about poverty, both the question and the answer to it are straightforward. The social revolution has not gone far enough. In fact, it was stopped dead in its tracks and partly reversed by eighteen calamitous years of Conservative rule. A return to the redistribution of wealth will finally abolish child poverty and bring us closer to a condition of economic equality. And increased public expenditure will revive the Welfare State and produce the schools and hospitals that we dreamed of.

It is accordingly a matter for lamentation that, as we have seen, even during most of the Labour government's period in office, economic inequality actually increased and the fat cats continued to award themselves obscene pay increases without the government lifting a finger. Gordon Brown's tax credits for working families do help to underpin low wages, but they are really only an extension of the scheme first brought in by Keith Joseph and the Tories, and they have a pernicious effect in that they actually encourage employers to offer low wages. This disastrous practice can trace its origin back to the 'Speenhamland system' of the 1790s, in which well-meaning Berkshire magistrates ordered public subsidies to be paid to starving farmworkers. Then as now, the effect is to pauperise and demoralise the workers, instead of paying them a fair day's wage for a fair day's work. In financial terms, therefore, the poor in Britain today have not advanced all that much. And the answer remains as it always has been, that it is the government's task, one way or another, to transfer wealth from those that have a superfluity to those that presently have far too little.

Now there are several hard-nosed objections that may be put to this diagnosis, some of them put by fair-minded observers like Toynbee herself. Poverty today is rather different from what it was even in 1970. Then only 37 per cent had central heating, now 92 per cent do. Then only 42 per cent had telephones, now it is 98 per cent. Car ownership has not reached the very poor, but it is spreading from around half of all households to about three quarters. Although some of the poor may still live in damp basements, the general standard of accommodation has risen in line with Parker-Morris standards.

In the same way, although we still complain bitterly about the shortcomings of our schools and hospitals, billions have been steadily pumped into them, even during the notorious Thatcher years. NHS hospitals, for example, offer to everyone medical techniques that were not available thirty or even ten years ago. I don't mean simply life-saving breakthroughs in the treatment of cancer and heart complaints but operations that make life more bearable — hip replacements, cataract operations, pacemakers and so on. There are waiting lists for many such operations, but they have shrunk and even six months of continued pain is at least better than an infinity.

But it is not my purpose here to argue that the poor in Britain today aren't really so badly off in material terms. Nor am I trying to argue that there is no room for levelling up their wages. On the contrary, there is a decent case not only for upping the minimum wage but for introducing special higher rates for expensive areas like London and South-East — a modification, I think, rejected by the Treasury only because it was too complicated. Better still, I believe, is to raise the starting point for income tax, so that we come closer to the prewar situation in which only the middle and upper classes paid any income tax at all.

But this essay is about something different. Far from arguing that the poor are no better off (or even a little worse off) than they were 30 years ago, we are asserting that the Downers of today are *much* worse off than the Downers of 1970 or even the 1930s. What we have called their cultural impoverishment blots out any modest material improvements. Yes, social inequality, material hardship and unemployment following the collapse of heavy industries were all infinitely worse in the 1930s, but there was no social breakdown, very little disorder, and the psychic hurt took the form of injured pride rather than surly demoralisation.

It is tempting for disenchanted modern observers today to look back nostalgically to the 1960s and 1970s when the Welfare State was still intact and inequality was at its lowest. Yet Jeremy Seabrook tells us that the demoralisation of the people at the bottom was palpable in those years too before Thatcher came to power and already the early signs were visible — the decay of standards in State schools, the degradation of the worst council estates, the rise of the drug culture.

It may be possible to point to one or two deviations that do correspond to changes of government. For example, I have seen a set of statistics that purport to show a rise in suicides under Conservative governments. Certainly you would expect to see a worsening of the misery index and a rise in petty crime in periods of high unemployment — although again no such trends were observable in the 1930s. But as a general rule the most obvious indicators of the unhappiness of the worst-off seem to suggest that the trends are not greatly influenced by a change of government.

So if greater economic equality and higher expenditure on

public services are part of the answer, they don't sound like the whole answer, or even the most important part of it. And, though the safety net for poor working families that has been woven over the past 20 years by governments of both parties may have the defects mentioned above, it happens to be the system that most reformers have recommended as the best method available of helping the working poor.

But there is another, perhaps more cogent argument for saying that the redistribution of wealth does not look like the prime means of relieving the demoralisation of the poor. Quite simply, by everything they say and do, it is clear that the representatives of the Left — politicians, think tanks, administrators alike — no longer believe that to be the case.

On the contrary, for some time now the problem has been recognised by the Left as not solely or even primarily an economic one but a socio-cultural one. Progressive reformers no longer appear to think that all would be well if the worst-off enjoyed a rather larger slice of the cake, if the differences between their earnings and the earnings of the middle class were sharply diminished.

The new conventional wisdom of the Left is very different. It is that, by one means or another, the Downers must be coaxed and chivvied, bullied and bribed to behave better. Loutish families who terrorise council estates are to have Antisocial Behaviour Orders slapped on them. Rowdy schoolchildren are to be excluded from school and sent to special units. Young hoodlums are to be tagged or subjected to curfews. Respectable citizens are to be encouraged to sneak on their neighbours who drink and drive or behave in other offensive and dangerous ways.

All this has a strongly medieval flavour. In the Middle Ages, communal disapproval was an important weapon of social control, in many ways more effective than the then rather sparse official forces of law and order. And public humiliation — such as placing a miscreant in the stocks — was an inexpensive method of punishment. To revert to such methods now is a remarkable retrogressive step.

After all, the whole Beveridge philosophy pointed in the opposite direction. The poor were to be assisted to stand on their own feet, to become sturdy autonomous citizens. That is still the orthodoxy today, but the practice seems to be somewhat different, as indeed it always was. Even during the great post-war flowering of the Welfare State, there was always a strong interfering element. The itch to manage the lives of the lower classes was never entirely absent.

(ii) Managing the lower classes

The remarkable thing in fact is that as the Welfare State moves into its second century, this itch appears to be sharply intensifying. After the war the number of middle-class persons appointed to oversee the behaviour of the lower classes was relatively modest. There was the health visitor, who checked on the wellbeing of young mothers and their babies and kept an eye out for signs of abuse and neglect; for those in difficulty, there was the social worker; for those in serious trouble, the probation officer. That was about all.

These officials might now and then be intrusive and

annoying to their 'clients' — a weasel word to disguise the true nature of the relationship — but they often had useful advice to offer, and isolated young mothers in particular often found the visits of the health visitor very welcome. But the remits of these public officials were limited and specific to certain circumstances of life. They were not all over the place.

The situation now is very different. There is now a huge army of officials to manage the Downers. The best place to review this army is, notoriously, the Wednesday 'Society' supplement of the *Guardian* — an unconsciously ironic title, since the voluminous pages of advertisements in the supplement are designed to service people at the other end of the social scale from Society in the old-fashioned sense. The supplement regularly carries 100 pages or more of ads for public posts in the field of health, housing, social care and the environment, the majority of them working for local authorities. On a typical Wednesday (September 18, 2002), Oldham required a Community Drug Support Worker; Walthamstow was looking for a Smoking Cessation Adviser; Lambeth needed a Manager for its Social Inclusion Service; Wolverhampton was short of a Domestic Violence Prevention Officer; Waltham Forest was advertising for a Young Lesbian and Bisexual Women's Health Worker; Brent Community Alcohol Services was looking for a Team Manager.

These are, of course, only the most picturesque outriders of the more traditional infantry: the Youth Workers, Social Workers, Probation Teams, and Truancy Officers. But they all share certain characteristic features: that the successful candidates are likely to be more highly educated than those they seek to help and that their services will be directed almost entirely towards the bottom class. The well-to-do are no doubt equally vulnerable to alcoholism and other drug addictions, but they have their own clinics and doctors to help them kick the habit. Husbands beat their wives in Belgravia no less often than in the Balls Pond Road. But you will not often find the Domestic Violence Prevention Officer knocking on doors in Eaton Square.

Perhaps the most startling of these efforts to correct the habits and manage the lifestyles of the Downers was the news that the Labour Party was proposing to deny treatment on the NHS to overweight people and heavy smokers unless they mended their ways (*Times*, June 3, 2003). These proposals outlined in policy documents to be put before the Labour Party conference were, I suppose, a logical development of the existing plans to fine patients who missed appointments. Heavy smokers and the very fat are disproportionately lower-class, of course, being less inclined to frequent the gym and less able to pay for it. But if this proposal were to be taken seriously, which it wasn't (can one really imagine the government refusing treatment to voters?), it would mean that in some cases refusal to diet or give up smoking might amount to a death sentence. Nothing could show more clearly the extent of the Uppers' exasperation with the fecklessness of the Downers. The lower classes may no longer keep coal in the bath, but their insistence on continuing to shovel junk food in vast quantities down the hatch is seen as no less reprehensible. Once again the difference between the plight of the Downers and the insulation of the Uppers is embarrassingly clear. There might be private doctors who would refuse to go on treating patients who stubbornly rejected their advice, but a couple of doors down Harley Street there would be other doctors who would gladly take on any such unco-operative patients.

I certainly do not mock the desire to help the worst-off. Many of my best friends undertake serious training (especially after their own children are older) and find a satisfying vocation in these new careers. My concern here is simply to point out the net effect of this huge wave of assistance pouring into the council estates and back streets. Indeed, the more soft-voiced and sympathetic these social missionaries are, the more they identify the bottom class as helpless social patients, whose manners and morals require as much improvement as their physical surroundings. My objection is not to nannying per se. After all, the upper classes have nannies too. But to make such a comparison even in a playful spirit lays bare the painful disparity. Upper class nannies may be fired at a moment's notice. Nannies for the lower orders are sackable only after an exhaustive disciplinary process, and then, of course, not by the people who use their services.

Again and again, one is struck by how *different* the services offered to the lower orders are, often different in kind rather than degree. It is true that less money is spent on these services than on those that the well-to-do pay for out of their own pockets. The amount of money spent on the education of each State school pupil has been in recent years roughly half the amount spent on a pupil at an independent day school, although since Labour's generous increases in expenditure, the proportion has improved quite a lot. And most fairminded observers would have said, until recently, that this figure was too low to attract decent teachers to State schools and keep class sizes to a tolerable level. On the other hand, many classes at leading public schools are pretty large, and not a few of the teachers I endured in my own expensive education were hopeless duds. Money is not the whole story. What compounds the shortage of funds in State schools has been the peculiar nature of their ambitions — certainly in more recent decades. Since the 1960s, many if not most of them have provided not simply a poorer education but a different type of education from that which is offered by the public schools, by the former direct grant schools and by the best of the comprehensive schools in middle-class areas. Educational reformers took the opportunity of the introduction of comprehensive education to imbue the new schools with a different ethos, one opposed to competition, rote learning and marking, hostile to compulsory sport, to religious indoctrination and to respect for traditional values. In place of these outmoded fustian features was to grow a co-operative, free, communal spirit in which pupils discovered things for themselves and learnt to question and criticise.

That 'progressive' approach captured the hearts of not only education theorists but also the Department of Education, HM Inspectors of Schools and the teacher training colleges. In many of the latter redoubts it still has its adherents. Take for example an article by Professor Trevor Kerry of Lincoln University on his vision of education in 20 years time:

I envisage schools in which pupils choose for themselves when to attend and when to work at home or in a resource centre via a virtual classroom. I look forward to classes in which pupils are encouraged to experiment, explore material and ideas, question, and create ideas of their own. The teacher's role will be changed from that of a conveyor of syllabus-prescribed information to a resource-facilitator, guide, software guru and life-skills adviser.

...Homework will be obsolete, replaced by learning contracts in which pupils agree with their teachers what needs to be done but choose their own time, place and speed. (*Daily Telegraph*, November 3, 2001)

Such an approach is now in retreat. The Labour government, like its Conservative predecessor, is all for competition and testing; the protests of parents that their children simply were not learning the basic skills finally percolated to the political world. But it is worth noting how long the whole process took (it is far from complete today). It was a quarter of a century ago that James Callaghan in his 1976 speech at Ruskin College became the first Prime Minister to admit that State schools were failing and failing badly. Seven years earlier in March 1969, the first Black Paper on Education, which made similar criticisms, had been rubbished by the educational establishment, including the then Secretary of State, Ted Short.

But this is not the place to rehearse that sorry story. My point here is a simple and incontrovertible one: that the type of education provided for the bottom class was deliberately *different* from that provided for children of parents who paid school fees. The bottom class was and is well aware of this, as was shown by the fact that those who managed to clamber out of it took care that their children should attend either fee-paying schools or good State schools, by which they meant those which insisted on discipline, competition and uniforms. One may well argue that such 'traditional' schools can be ghastly in all sorts of ways and often may not live up to their academic pretensions. But that is not the issue. What matters for our present purposes is that most parents who could afford to chose not merely better financed schooling for their children but schooling of a different type.

One final example of class differentiation in schooling. Local authorities have jumped at the opportunity to sell off State-school playing fields for development — rather than reschedule agricultural land, of which there is now a huge surplus. Most independent schools, by contrast, glory in their playing fields and have to be very financially hard-pressed before they think of selling off any part of them.

Of course, the comprehensive school movement was and is basically a movement of the Left. But the Conservatives have been at least acquiescent in the process; Margaret Thatcher is said to have closed more grammar schools than any other Secretary of State for Education. At the peak of the comprehensive movement, Conservative-controlled county councils seemed just as relaxed as Labour-controlled borough councils about the fact that the bottom class was now being educated in a quite different ethos from the children of the well-to-do.

And within that comprehensive ideal lurked an assumption which was and is not quite so idealistic: namely, that the Downers stood in greater need of being 'socialised', because of their defective parenting skills and lack of any neighbourhood support network. In racially mixed State schools, for example, particularly strenuous efforts needed to be made to teach tolerance and respect for one another's cultures. No such efforts would be made in, say, the average English public school, although it too might contain a fair sprinkling of pupils from overseas or immigrant backgrounds.

In all such efforts, behind all the good intentions, it is not difficult to detect an overall assumption, all the more potent for never being overtly stated, that the bottom class need to be *managed*. This implicit assumption is such an inbuilt feature of debate about education and welfare in this country that it is hard to convince people that they suffer from it.

The best I can do is to point to France and Germany where everybody seems to be taught in much the same way — I don't say to the same standard. There are still a large number of State-supported Catholic schools in France — which have survived President Mitterrand's campaign to deny them funds — but the basic methods of teaching, highly academic and competitive, don't seem to be very different in them from those of the secular schools. In Germany there is a strongly academic approach in the technical schools just as in the schools for the more academic pupils, with written exams as well as practical work in most departments. Again, I am not particularly recommending Continental methods here. My only aim is to point out that educational methods there don't seem to be divided by class.

As indeed they never used to be in Britain. We have seen in earlier chapters how in the nineteenth century the schools for the poor might be staffed and paid for by the poor themselves. But their aims were not different in kind from the schools paid for and staffed by the middle classes. And even when the Board Schools began to dominate and force out the private schools for the poor, they were still attempting to teach the sort of curriculum that most of their parents would have approved of. That, I think, continued to be true even of the Secondary Moderns which educated the mass of working-class children until the coming of the comprehensive schools. Whatever may be said of their achievements, their methods were mostly traditional and basic, and it was middle-class educationalists who mocked them rather than the parents of the children who actually attended them.

It needs to be emphasised, therefore, how very recent is this deliberate apartheid in education. Yes, I know the abolition of the 11-plus was supposed to abolish division in education, but in many places it merely introduced a different and more insidious kind of division.

In the same way, we often forget that the most spectacular growth of council housing occurred in the postwar years, especially under the Conservatives. It was in those years rather than the 1930s that it became a general assumption that the lower classes would be living in council estates because they were incapable of housing themselves.

Thus it is only yesterday in historical terms that the lives of the bottom class became quite so hollowed out and that the middle classes felt able to sneer at them in a way that would not have been decent before the war. Before the war, after all, the vast majority of the working classes were fending for themselves in almost all aspects of life and were enduring extremely difficult circumstances with patience, good humour and orderliness. Even today nobody dares to mock the men and women of the 30s.

We are, I think, uneasily and increasingly aware that something has gone wrong. It is painful to admit it, but, despite all the material improvements and social securities which are enjoyed by the worst-off today, there now exists a kind of cultural impoverishment which, though not unknown in the 30s, was then confined to the most cripplingly poor sections of towns and cities worst hit by the depression and which is widespread today far beyond areas that are technically defined as deprived. We may blame different causes — Margaret Thatcher, the demoralising effect of the welfare state, the shattering impact of industrial decline. But anyone who cares to look cannot help seeing it.

What I do not think many people have yet woken up to is that the working class has been subjected to a sustained programme of social contempt and institutional erosion which has persisted through many different governments and several political fashions. That idea is a little slower dawning.

(iii) Glimmerings

All the same, it has begun to dawn, though very slowly and hesitantly. And politicians of both parties have been slower still to act on their inklings. The idea that a good society depends for its survival on a sturdy, self-reliant citizenry is an ancient one. That has always been the self-image of the 'free-born Englishman'. The huge readership of the works of Tom Paine took it for granted. But that self-image was eclipsed by the rise throughout the nineteenth century of another image: that of 'the proletariat', whose members were individually helpless but collectively irresistible, a mass whose wants and aspirations could be realised only through the actions of the State.

As we have seen, the State itself developed a professional self-interest in cultivating this belief and shutting out any corrective or alternative view. It was therefore only when failures of State action became too glaring to be glossed over any longer that such alternative views were likely to gain a hearing.

Perhaps the first glaring drawbacks to be noticed in public debate were those of the council estates. The early misgivings expressed by Orwell and the Coles did not catch on for decades. The reason for this was simple. The new council flats provided much better accommodation than the unimproved slum dwellings they replaced. They were properly heated, equipped with modern conveniences and often quite spacious. These advantages were maintained by strict regulations against subletting and overcrowding — restrictions which helped to maintain the housing shortage and so made the council flats even more desirable. They were built to Parker Morris specifications, higher than the building specifications previously applied to private spec builders. Mr Justice Parker

Morris, the father-in-law of Roy Jenkins, was insistent that the housing of the poor should be carried out to a standard the nation could be proud of. Such feelings were an admirable characteristic of postwar progressive thinkers. Yet of course the effect was to bind council tenants ever more tightly into the embrace of the State.

The tenant was dependent on the favour of the council, was deterred from moving to a new job in a different town for fear of not qualifying for another council house there, was increasingly confined in a single-class environment with poor shops, schools and other amenities. The more energetic tenants gradually moved out to buy their own homes or at least gravitated to the better estates, leaving the weakest, most vulnerable and depraved tenants to congregate in the sink estates, which were soon recognised as such and avoided by everybody else. Estates full of fathers who had not worked for years and single mothers struggling to cope cropped up in every town and city. The worst weren't necessarily confined to the older industrial areas which had been devastated by the closure of local heavy industry but could be found in prosperous southern cities such as Oxford. The notorious Blackbird Leys estate, for example, is physically not such a bad place, backing onto open farmland, but it has become subject to the vicious circle of degeneration to be found on similar estates in any borough.

Not only did that process take some years to reach its full effect. There were still new council estates going up all over the country, the opening of which gave pride to the local council and sometimes immortality to leading local figures

275

after whom the blocks might be named. And there were still thousands of new tenants moving in after years of struggle in damp privately rented basements. The view that council housing, with all its faults, was a noble thing and should continue to be encouraged was thus constantly reinforced until right up to the moment when Mrs Thatcher's new legislation, the 1980 Housing Act, forcing councils to sell homes to their tenants, came into force. At least 20 Labour councils refused and had to be threatened with legal action, and even Conservative-held councils were decidedly uneasy about being forcibly deprived of a social resource they continued to think essential. It had always been legally possible for local authorities to sell their properties, but most had been highly reluctant to deplete their stock. The demand for house ownership turned out to be huge. Within three years, about half a million homes had been sold to their tenants by local authorities, New Town Corporations and housing associations — more than had previously passed into private ownership in the entire postwar period. By the time the Conservatives lost office in 1997, over one and a half million tenants had exercised the right to buy, and sales have continued under Labour, although some discouraging restrictions on the discounts were introduced.

Today the disadvantages of council estates are recognised across the political spectrum. Disagreement continues as to how large a stock of 'social housing' needs to be maintained for the most vulnerable tenants and for special emergencies. But only the most obdurate refuse to accept the social damage caused, largely inadvertently, by grouping the bottom class together in under-maintained and under-policed estates without any incentive to maintain or improve their surroundings.

I want here to stress the slow 'recognition time' which may be inevitable in a process still continuing even while its downside is already emerging. In the same way, local education authorities were continuing to build large comprehensive schools for years after the drawbacks of such schools had already emerged. Some of those drawbacks were not inherent at all. There is no need for a school which has a comprehensive intake to abandon competitive testing, competitive sports, school uniforms, streaming — or any of the other characteristic features of a large independent school of the same size. Those features derived from an ideology which was not simply egalitarian in tone but argued that equality was the crucial priority in education.

Still, for children who found themselves at such schools the precise amount of ideological input was a rather academic question. Their experience was what counted, and at the worst comprehensives the ideal of equality seemed sadly equivalent to indifference. So little was expected of the children in the lower streams or, where there was no streaming, of all the children. The failure of so many perfectly bright children to acquire the basic skills of literacy and numeracy was well known to parents and employers years before politicians condescended to take notice. Even in the early years of the Thatcher Government, Secretaries of State for Education felt it their duty to make encouraging noises and each summer to congratulate the nation's schoolchildren on their superb exam results. As I have already described, it was not until the Labour Party conference of 2002 that we heard a Labour Secretary of State, Estelle Morris, fullheartedly confess the extent of her disenchantment with the comprehensive system and heard too both Morris and Tony Blair tell us that we were now moving into 'the post-comprehensive era'.

Yet local working-class opinion is to play no more part in the end of the comprehensive system than it played in its introduction. There is no sign that this latest reform, or any other presently being contemplated, is to be used as an opportunity to diminish the impotence of the Downers.

Nor was there much sign that pouring extra money from Whitehall into the worst inner-city schools is producing any results remotely equal to the public cost. Ofsted reported in 2003 that the Excellence in Cities programme, personally launched by the Prime Minister in 1999, had so far shown no sign of closing the gap with pupils in more privileged areas. The *Times* was told that the effect of spending £800 million in both primary and secondary schools in 58 selected urban authorities had been 'pretty negligible'. More damningly still, 'it has had an effect but not on attainment. It's mainly been on changing attitudes of disadvantaged kids, basically making them feel better about underachieving at school' — that is, far from kindling ambition and self-esteem, the Department of Education has simply confirmed the Downers in their down-ness. At the same time, the £650 million spent so far on initiatives to reduce the school truancy rate had had no impact. In fact, the number of pupils who played truant in secondary schools had actually increased by 25 per cent from

423,000 in 1996-7 to 566,000 in 2001-02. In 2008 truancy rates were reported to be the highest for ten years.

Downer life has come to involve traipsing from one large publicly owned facility — the council estate — to another — the comprehensive school — then on to other large institutions such as the supermarket, the office and the factory, which may be privately owned but which offer the Downer equally little room for consultation or participation in decision-making. Instead of the undoubted affluence of the 1950s and 60s offering people in the bottom class a greater say over their lives, in some respects their lives have become more 'massified', less responsible than those of their parents and grandparents.

Efforts to find in the educational sphere an equivalent empowering device to the sale of council houses have so far failed. Sir Keith Joseph, as Education Secretary, toyed at agonising length with the idea of education vouchers or 'tickets' as envisaged in Forster's Act 100 years earlier, but eventually ducked the challenge, finding the practicalities too fraught. The Conservatives reintroduced a modest measure of diversity into the State school system with City Technology Colleges. Labour currently has more plans for diversity on the same lines, such as specialist schools and City Academies. These may well provide an improved route for lower-class children to reach university. But for all their pretensions to independence, these are likely to be essentially 'top-down' institutions inspired by and largely financed by the State. The idea that the lower classes might have a say in the education of their children comparable to that routinely expected in the upper classes remains strictly verboten. How would such schools maintain standards? What would happen if such a school went bankrupt? I am wearily familiar with the usual questions thrown at would-be reformers by civil servants in the Department of Education — all of which boil down to: how on earth can you imagine that the lower orders could ever run a school better than we can? And yet there have been sink schools and schools which have effectively gone bust for lack of pupils under the most impeccably State-controlled system — and there always will be.

The State won't let go. And this refusal to relinquish control has a perversely self-reinforcing effect. For as long as the State refuses to let go, it can persuade the public, more or less, that the lower classes are not fit to manage their own affairs. There are, after all, no counter-examples on view.

The lower classes can scarcely be blamed for tending to accept this view of themselves, since the people who are sent to manage so manifestly come from a superior world with access to all sorts of mysterious knowledge. There is, however, a limit to mystification in education, and that limit is clearly reached when children have failed to learn to read and write at the age their parents learnt. The whole apparatus of repeated testing and the consequent improvement in literacy in primary school did not spring from the world of the educationists but sprang rather in opposition to them, from the sustained indignation and frustration of parents.

In many other respects, too, lower-class complaints remain as impotent as ever. Ever since I can remember, people in poorer districts, who are the principal victims of crime, have been calling for more bobbies back on the beat. Over and over again, they are told by their Chief Constables that putting policemen to walk the streets and the estates is not an efficient method of policing. To which the lower orders would like to respond 'We'll be the judges of that,' but no one is listening. To subject police forces to genuine local control is thought to be to open the force up to bias and corruption — as though there had never been a bent copper under the status quo.

Since these people are not fit to be trusted with the most elementary powers and decisions, such as those involving their children's education, they are therefore incapable of understanding anything demanding, difficult or noble. We must therefore feed them pap.

In television, film and newspapers, only the crudest effects, the simplest plots, the crassest themes may be employed. A good story must reach the lowest common denominator. Anyone who deviates from these rigorously maintained rules is a paternalist, a Reithian, a pompous, stuck-up, outdated prig and snob. We must pursue the highest possible ratings, and the vulgarest techniques are the way to achieve these ratings, because if we do not, in the case of the BBC there will be a clamour to abolish the licence fee, and in the case of ITV the advertisers will abandon us. It is pleasant to report that both things have happened none the less, while all the terrestrial channels desperately pursue the audience as it flees to cable and video.

But the consequence is that the ruling classes find their worst suspicions confirmed as they surf channels desperately looking for something even half worth watching: people who watch such stuff must be subhuman clods. It would be madness to let them anywhere near the glittering levers of power. As for taking the major decisions in the lives of their own families and communities, that is a sentimental fantasy. The vicious circle of condescension whirls on, and those who are carried along by it — the managing classes — remain unaware that they are helping to bring about the thing they claim to dread — an ignorant, irresponsible underclass, potatoes incapable of levering themselves off the couch.

This is itself a twisted form of paternalism, one which permanently infantilises its victims, refuses to engage with them as equals, or as time goes by to engage with them at all. The gated community of middle-class residents is the most scandalous instance of the managers cutting themselves off from the managed, but even those of us who live in normal streets are not much more interlocked with the lives of those at the bottom.

Let us go back to *Sybil* and read once more the famous words which I have already quoted twice, but read them slowly, not sliding over them but pausing to ponder whether matters are really any better today: 'Two nations; between whom there is no intercourse' — not much certainly, perhaps less even than there was then — 'and no sympathy' — less overt hostility today we may hope but not an obvious flood of fellow feeling — 'who are as ignorant of each other's habits, thoughts and feelings' — indifferent might be a better word than ignorant today — 'as if they were dwellers in different zones, or inhabitants of different planets' — well, we do dwell in different zones, more so than ever, because of the rise of large one-class estates designed specifically for Uppers as well as for Downers — 'who are formed by a different breeding, are fed by a different food, are ordered by different manners, and are not governed by the same laws.' We must plead guilty to most of those indictments still: the public schools and the comprehensive schools breed differently, the Connaught and McDonald's feed us differently, our speech and manners have not converged as much as we pretend, and if we are in theory governed by the same laws, it cannot be said that the authorities treat us in quite the same way. How many men in pin-stripe suits do you see being stopped at the roadside by the police, how many social workers do you see ringing the doorbell in South Kensington?

Yes, today we are at least conscious of these differences, uneasily conscious, uncertain how to cope with them: whether to ignore them, or to atone for them by extravagant imitation of the Other, or to hope that things are slowly improving and that One Nation is just around the corner. The only trouble is that many of us have been hoping along these lines for up to half a century and the best we can see of that dawn even today is its first glimmerings.

By now it ought to be obvious that only a more robust proactive daring is likely to efface this bleeding shame. Only a wholehearted, even reckless opening up of genuine, sub-stantial power to the bottom classes is likely to improve either their self-esteem or the view which the managing classes take of them — which is what makes the managing classes so reluctant to effect any such transfer.

However, let us not be deterred by that unlikelihood. Polemical essays normally end in one of two ways: either in a fruitless lament without hint of remedy; or in a sober, responsible list of modest improvements, carefully costed and thought through. There is, however, a third way, normally followed only by anarchists and other crazies, which is to throw out a wild scatter of ideas, many of which readers will find either absurd or repellent. The idea is not to appeal to policymakers but to stir the cerebral juices and make people think and argue about what might conceivably be done in the real world. This is the method, or rather anti-method, that I propose to follow.

(iv) Unlock and allot — a rough guide to the future

How then do we open society — or reopen it — to those at the bottom of the heap? What are the principles that we should keep in our minds and what are the most likely practical techniques and the handiest devices to bring them into action? Straight away, I think we need to empty our minds of party-political aversions and allegiances. For both the relevant principles and the usable techniques are likely to be drawn from and to appeal to almost all the active political traditions in this country: Labour, Conservative and Liberal certainly, but also the Co-operative movement, the Greens, the Distributists, the Anarchists. At some moments our suggestions may appeal to Fabians, at others to members of the Freedom Association, at still others to nobody much at all. These last suggestions may well be the best.

284

The first basic principle has long been incorporated in the idea of 'a property-owning democracy' — a phrase dating back at least to Sir Anthony Eden in the 1950s, although the idea of people possessing 'a stake in the country' was a commonplace in the eighteenth and nineteenth century. Individuals and their families at all levels of society and in all income brackets should be assisted to acquire property, both through bricks and mortar and through savings. Even the poorest should have the prospect of a modest 'independence' — the use of that word in this sense goes back to 1815 and again reminds us how longstanding this ambition is. It is the ownership of property that imbues people not only with self-esteem but with a sense of responsibility. Property which is owned by some large impersonal collective is in effect owned by nobody.

That is the basis of Aristotle's criticism of Plato's *Republic*, that in such a political brotherhood, affections are diluted. 'Of the two qualities which chiefly inspire regard and affection — that a thing is your own and that you love it — neither can exist in such a state as this.' A modern example is the green space surrounding many council estates. Critics of the planners and architects who designate such amenities argue that they are 'confused' spaces, lacking both specific purpose and assigned ownership. If they were broken up into individual back gardens, they would be more carefully tended. This principle of ownership does not always operate in the direction of the individual. It may sometimes be better to hand over a green space to a dedicated group of local volunteer gardeners. The Culpeper Garden round the corner from us in Islington run by a volunteer trust is one of the most beautiful gardens in London.

In the same way, State schools may be handed over to a parents' trust. And those self-governing hospitals within the National Health Service which are already owned by Trusts may be given full-blooded independence. The key is to revive Forster's principle of the 'ticket' — or, as we say today, the voucher — which in the case of schools entitles every child to, let us say, £5,000-worth of education at a secondary school and £3,000 at a primary. It would be easy enough to open up most of the public schools with their rich resources of teachers and buildings by allowing parents to spend their vouchers there too, provided that the school guaranteed to take at least half its pupils from State primary schools. Public schools which refused to accept this condition would either close for lack of custom or become very, very exclusive indeed. Middle-class parents are already finding it intolerably hard to pay full fees as well as their taxes and are likely to find it harder still in future. Those who dislike giving the well-to-do any help at all may be appeased if we make the voucher taxable for the rich. Similarly we may open up private hospitals by letting patients for routine operations spend their vouchers there up to a certain standard value.

The purpose of these initiatives is twofold. First, by giving back to the Downers the controlling say in the education of their children, we restore to them the self-confidence and sense of responsibility which has been filched from them over the years. At the same time we make it virtually certain that the gap in the nature of the services provided will be swiftly closed. Schools where most of the pupils come from poorer homes will have the same aspirations, rules and methods as independent schools and schools in more prosperous areas. At present the government is trying to achieve something like this, in the teeth of sustained opposition from the educational Establishment, but when the parents themselves are calling the tune the change in atmosphere is likely to be more whole-hearted and more irrevocable. Similarly in hospitals and other welfare and local government services the more we can make the Downers genuinely 'clients' and 'customers' rather than 'patients', the sooner they will be treated with respect and civility.

Now this sort of approach is familiar to us. Both political parties have been playing around with it for years, although the results on the ground are fairly modest to date. But rather than elaborate such schemes here, what I want to bring out is the principle underlying such nostrums, because we may find ourselves able to apply that principle more widely.

In a phrase, the underlying principle is what I would call 'unlock and allot'. It is quite distinct from most of what Tony Benn and other reformers of the Left used to advocate, namely, 'a massive transfer of wealth and power to ordinary working people'. That demand certainly included some appealing proposals in the co-operative tradition (one or two experiments being carried out by Benn himself, when in office, alas rather hamfistedly). But the dominant urge behind it was to remove wealth and power from the undeserving rich and transfer it, whether through taxation or nationalisation, to the poor or to the nation as a whole with the intention that the poor should thereby obtain their fair share.

In the 'unlock and allot' principle, nothing is removed from anyone. The idea is simply to unlock the value that is already theoretically the property of the Downers and to allot it to them specifically by name, whether as individuals, families or voluntary groups. I say 'allot', that is, assign as a lot or portion, mark out for you what is theoretically already yours. This is not to be confused with 'allocate' or 'allow' which carries some suggestion of grace and favour. An allowance is, after all, something that is granted by its proper owner and may be withdrawn at that owner's whim. Allotment is different. It is a share-out of entitlements. We understand this well enough when existing shareholders are allotted new shares in a rights issue. These allotments are due to the people on whose investments the company was founded. The principle has not been so clear to us in, say, the case of municipal garden allotments. Local councillors have been inclined to preen themselves on their benevolence towards deprived tenants who will benefit from the fresh air and exercise. But the principle is really much the same. A piece of ground — often a rough patch running down to a road or railway line and not much use for anything else — became collectivised when the local authority bought it or, quite often, woke up to the fact that they owned it. Now it is being handed out on rent or lease to some of the individuals who compose that collective — in short, unlocked and allotted.

Which brings us to a much more sweeping and much more controversial part of my proposals, namely, that to bring the Downers back into the nation we need to unlock and allot land on a far wider scale than anyone in this country has so far contemplated.

Land ownership in Britain is much more concentrated than in any other major country I can think of. It is not simply that so many of the great estates have survived to a remarkable degree unparallelled anywhere else. If the Buccleuch and the Norfolk and the Devonshire estates are shadows of their former selves, they are very substantial shadows. Yet these are only the most prominent representatives of a pattern of landownership which is, so to speak, large all the way down. The squires have many more acres than smaller proprietors elsewhere. And the average size of farms is bigger too. The smallholdings which are such a feature of life in many parts of the Continent and (as a result of land reform under British rule) in Ireland too, both North and South, are in Great Britain the exception rather than the rule.

At the same time, ever since the 1947 Town and Country Planning Acts the landscape has been frozen. Development of any kind is permitted only after the exhaustive procedures of planning permission; even the most modest change of land use has to go through these procedures. The pressure for building land, especially in South-East England but in other desirable areas, too, eventually forces the process to disgorge a few parcels of land, mostly to the large developers who build up their own 'land banks' for the purpose. The outcome is predictably that land prices rise to stratospheric levels and the number of houses built falls steadily over time, thus forcing up the price of new houses too. In the South-East it is reckoned that nearly 40 per cent of the price of a new house may be accounted for by the cost of the site. It is no coincidence that the average number of houses built each year has dwindled from well over 300,000 in the 1960s and 1970s (and indeed in the mid-1930s) to less than 200,000 in the Nineties and the Noughties — while the population has risen by several million. And house prices have risen from the long-running average of three and a half times a person's annual income to nearly five times — higher still in some areas.

Now the social consequences of all this are obvious and well noted: the housing shortage generally, and in particular the difficulty for young couples of finding a house or flat they can afford. Governments make repeated efforts to force county councils in the South-East to disgorge more land for building, and in particular to redevelop every available acre of brownfield land. John Prescott left his mark with his massive plans for new cities along the Thames Estuary and the M11 corridor and around Milton Keynes and Ashford.

But all this is to be done within the confines of the existing planning legislation, thus ensuring that the price of land and of new houses remains as prohibitive as ever. The whole business is strongly reminiscent of the way De Beers keeps up the price of diamonds, by controlling the supply and releasing gems onto the market in carefully calculated batches so that the price is never in danger of collapse.

Suppose, though, that we wanted to extend diamond ownership to the poor. We would release large stocks onto the market to crack the price and allow fresh entrants into the business to keep prices low by ensuring competition.

Suppose therefore that we want to help the Downers break

out of their ghettos and enjoy some sort of stake in the country. This may sound an implausible, idealistic ambition. Yet we have to recognise that in some countries it is not implausible at all. In Ireland or France or the United States or Italy, quite poor people own a patch of land, and when they have a few bob to spare they get hold of a pile of bricks and begin to build — a bungalow for their daughter when she gets married, a workshop, a retirement home or just a holiday chalet to look at the sea from.

You can't do that in Britain, I shall be told, this is a small and crowded island, and there is no land to spare. If we are to preserve what's left of the English countryside, the tightest planning controls must be maintained.

Yet what happens in practice is that almost every available acre of countryside is devoted to agriculture. We may perhaps have abandoned the worst excesses of the Dig for Victory mentality. Whitehall no longer subsidises farmers to drain the wetlands or plough up the stoniest hillside. But the presumption in favour of total agriculture remains, long after any conceivable economic justification for it has disappeared.

As a result, we are suffocating. Playing fields are repeatedly sold off for housing estates and supermarkets because the surrounding farmland is taboo. Unless you move to northern England, cheap housing of the sort that was once freely available all over England is disappearing. Bristol commuters now have to trek to the heads of the Welsh valleys to find a modest terrace house.

And at a less tangible level the sense of possibility is strangled. Governments of both parties fuss about, offering increasingly complex packages for small businesses, but all most people often want is a shed or a small yard to rent for a fiver a week. The idea of building your own house used to be a straightforward possibility for a competent handyman with a few friends. Now you need to invoke the assistance of one of the Prince of Wales's Trusts, which enable (admirably, I have to say) exceptional people to do things which ordinary people once thought nothing of.

The present system entrenches a selfish and blinkered idealism in its determination to preserve the English countryside as it was in 1910 — an ambition both doomed and perverse.

I propose instead:

That every council tenant should be given the choice of a freehold or a lease on his dwelling, to sell or enjoy as he pleases.

That tenants' associations should run their estates, drawing on the expertise of local housing associations. Lottery grants would help them to lease or buy land for playing fields from the nearest farmer.

Every village and town should be allowed to set up 'plotlands' on old farmland or brownland, to be leased out at low rents to local residents to do whatever they fancy — build a house, set up a workshop, keep caravans, plant vines.

Every landowner should be allowed to sell off ten per cent of his land for development up to a maximum acreage of ten acres (the planning authority would have the right to decide which acres he could sell).

These devices may seem a little fanciful now, but similar things are commonplace in other countries. And there have been attempts to start such ventures in Britain too. In Dunkeld, Perthshire, a Community Land Trust planned to buy a twelve-acre site and hand over plots to local people to build their own homes. It seems odd that such an initiative needed to be supported by distinguished architects and ecologists, seeing that Dunkeld is surrounded by acres and acres of valueless heather. Yet planning restrictions had pushed local house prices over the £100,000 mark, nearly half of that being swallowed by the cost of the bare plot. Hopes were placed in the Scottish Land Fund which had begun to buy up large estates and whole islands such as Gigha for public benefit. But at Dunkeld no grant was made, nothing was built and, on checking recently, I could find no trace of the Trust.

In fact, the whole campaign to buy land for the people has gone rather quiet north of the Border, not least because of the shortage of public funds after the Credit Crunch. But in England the Conservatives are talking eagerly of unleashing local Community Land Trusts and of giving local authorities 'a general power of competence' to undertake any type of activity which is not specifically forbidden to them. In a year or two, the more enterprising authorities could use such schemes to make it possible for local people who are at present priced out of the market to start housing themselves. But of course if the planning laws were eased, there would be much less need for such elaborate schemes of community ownership. Even after we had excluded from any such relaxation the existing green belts, national parks, areas of outstanding natural beauty, sensitive locations and any other areas we wanted to preserve, much more land would become available for building and land prices would tumble.

More bizarre and far less popular is the initiative of developers in several counties — Hertfordshire, Kent, Sussex, Hampshire, Buckinghamshire, Suffolk — who have bought farmland from farmers who no longer see much profit in farming them and have divided the fields up into plots ranging from half an acre to five acres and sold them on to individuals who are willing to pay as much as £35,000 an acre for them. Most of the land is in the Green Belt and the plots carry no planning permission. Yet city-dwellers have been snapping them up. Why? Obviously the purchasers are placing a long-term bet on some change in the planning laws which might enable them one day to build a house with a decent garden there. Till such day many of them seem happy to come down for the occasional picnic and bask in the thought of owning a piece of the country. These initiatives have been severely criticised by the Green Belt lobby, and some local MPs are clamouring for them to be banned. The Campaign for the Protection of Rural England regards them with undisguised horror. Parish and district councils are up in arms against them. Planning authorities have discovered to their delight that they can slap an 'Article 4' direction on these sites under the Town and Country Planning Act of 1995. Once these directions are in force, the site is frozen and plot-owners cannot put up so much as a picket fence ('Fields of Dreams' by David Cox, *Times*, January 3, 2004):

Such speculators are now regarded as villains by respectable opinion. Yet I have sympathy for them and hope that one day they will come to be regarded as admirable pioneers. Not simply does small-plot landscape offer opportunities for self-expression to people who are not well off. It can offer enrichment to the land too. That doyen of housing revolutionaries, Colin Ward, points out that 'low-density housing is the best way of conserving land'. He recommends do-it-yourself new towns, driven by the energies of the settlers rather than the dictates of the planners, and quotes the alluring solution of John Seymour, father of the self-sufficiency movement:

'There is a man I know who farms ten thousand acres with three men (and the use of some contractors). Of course he can only grow one crop — barley, and of course his production *per acre* is very low and his consumption of imported fertiliser very high. He burns all his straw, puts no humus on the land (he boasts there isn't a four-footed animal on it — but I have seen a hare) and he knows perfectly well his land will suffer in the end. He doesn't care — it will see him out. He is already a millionaire several times over.' (*Talking Houses*, Colin Ward, 1990, p.33).

Compare that with Seymour's alternative:

'Cut that land (exhausted as it is) up into a thousand plots of ten acres each, giving each plot to a family trained to use it, and within ten years the production coming from it would be enormous. It would make a really massive contribution to the balance of payments problem. The motorist with his *News of the World* wouldn't have the satisfaction of looking over a vast treeless, hedgeless prairie of indifferent barley — but he could get out of his car for a change and wander through a seemingly huge area of diverse countryside, orchards, young tree plantations, a myriad small plots of land, growing a multiplicity of crops, farm animals galore.' (Ward, pp.33-4).

The beauty of such developments is that they can prosper on poor and currently neglected land safely removed from any Green Belt or Area of Outstanding Natural Beauty. And for those who like to look back to the past, such miniature landscapes would recapitulate the diversity of the medieval countryside with its strip fields of assorted crops, its coppiced woods, fishponds, rabbit warrens and dovecotes. Something of the sort survives in the 'hortillonages' on the banks of the Somme within a pleasant evening walk of Amiens Cathedral. This collection of market gardens, orchards and weekend cottages intersected by tiny canals covers 300 hectares and dates back to Gallo-Roman times. It is one of the sights of Amiens.

In Britain we can look back to the original 'plotlands', one of the most original social developments in our history which was killed stone dead by the Town and Country Planning Acts of 1947. From the agricultural depression of the 1870s onwards, auctioneers found so few takers for poor agricultural land that they would often split the fields up into smaller plots and sell them off for somewhere between £5 and £50 to people who wanted to start a chicken farm or put up a home for holidays or for retirement.

You can still see these plotlands around the country — a mixture of allotments, chalets, bungalows, old railway carriages and so on, some of them gradually evolving into ordinary little settlements but others defiantly untidy to this day. They grew up in all sorts of places where the land was poor but the view was pleasant — Canvey Island, Camber Sands, the Wirral, along the Thames and the banks of Loch Lomond, up the east coast from Essex to the Humber and the Tyne.

Such places are full of happy memories for those who grew up in them or spent their holidays there. But to the sensitive and the privileged they were regarded as blots on the landscape and, moreover, represented an uppity intrusion of the lower orders into their rural idyll. How the Bloomsbury Group abhorred the threat of Peacehaven — just a short walk over the Sussex downs from their own mellow cottages and farmhouses.

Ever since the Enclosures of the eighteenth century drove cottagers off common land, country dwellers no less than townees have found access to the land increasingly barred to them — sometimes literally when rights of way (a meagre enough network in any case) are not maintained or are actively obstructed by the landowner. The right to roam across country that is not under growing crops seems to me only a bare minimum. The spread of land ownership is a great good cause, much neglected in England. It is time to revive it.

If you stop to think, is it not, after all, a remarkable thing that, with the almost accidental and fleeting exception of the plotlands (and that was scarcely a movement in the political sense), there has been virtually no serious campaign to encourage wider land ownership? Left and Right, earls and ideologues alike, automatically assume that large-scale land ownership, whether by landowners, local authorities, developers or public bodies such as the National Trust and the New Town corporations must automatically be a good thing. This is as bizarre as though it had been taken for granted that all our homes should belong either to the State or to the Duke of Westminster. The aesthetic of the frozen landscape that results is a strange and stifling constraint on human potential — all the stranger because it is so seldom identified or questioned.

Perhaps a more obvious source of property rights — and one long discussed by socialists and liberals — is the workplace. Why should not the workers by hand and brain — to quote the old language of the British Labour Party's constitution — enjoy a share of the enterprise for which they toil? The co-operative ideal has had a history not unlike a typical British day — mostly clouded over, with the sun breaking through here and there, and occasional prolonged sunny spells which we remember ever after with misty eyes. Government-sponsored attempts to set up co-operative ventures have mostly collapsed in ignominy; Tony Benn's misguided efforts at Upper Clyde Shipbuilders and Meriden motorcyles gave the idea a bad name. Clearly there is little hope of survival for such enterprises when the market for their products has just collapsed. Much more successful have been cases where a benevolent founder has bequeathed to his workforce a large, or even controlling share of a prosperous business; the John Lewis Partnership chain of stores is the best known example. This can also work well with a relatively small-scale business which has local ties and sound prospects. The well-known oyster bar on the shores of Loch Fyne was founded by the local laird, Johnny Noble, and on his death the Baxi Partnership of St Andrews, which finances workers' buy-outs, holds half the shares in trust for the employees until they can pay back out of profits. Variations on such schemes are now popping up all over Britain and have, I think, a bright future and should be further encouraged by tax breaks.

Moreover, such co-operative enterprises, however funded and financed, need not be confined to little islands of partnership in an inhospitable capitalist sea. One can imagine areas in which clusters of such businesses become the norm rather than the exception and generate their own financial support institutions. Dominic Erdal of the Baxi partnership points out (*Evening Standard*, May 2, 2003) that in the Mondragon region of Spain the majority of businesses are now employee-owned, comprising 40,000 people in more than 100 companies. Specialist banks in the region will only finance co-operative businesses. It should also be pointed out that it has taken nigh on half a century to reach this critical mass. If we are to be serious about introducing a co-operative strain into the pattern of business, we shall need patience and determination.

But can we move in this direction on a wider front, rather

than leaving it to the benevolence of individual proprietors (or their heirs) and the initiative of charitable bodies? The Labour government and its allies have been fiddling about with the notion of stakeholding without ever seeming clear about its exact meaning. Schemes to encourage workers to take up shares in their firm have been advanced somewhat timidly, I think, for two reasons: first, New Labour, being still uneasy in its new-found sympathy for capitalism, is nervous of being caricatured as plotting to undermine free enterprise. And then hard-headed observers point out that, in terms of strict financial prudence, investing your savings in your own firm is a classic case of putting all your eggs in one basket. If the firm collapses, you lose your savings as well as your job.

All the same, I think the benefits of owning a slice of your firm should outweigh both factors. If we assume that workers do accumulate implicit rights in a firm for which they have worked for some time, then surely it is reasonable to unlock those rights at a time when a firm is proposing to expand its capital base. At such a time, the worker-partners should legitimately be given an opportunity to become shareholders in the enlarged company. Quite a few firms already do this, but it would surely be possible to make it a routine procedure (again promoted by tax breaks) that at least 20 per cent of any new share offer should be reserved on favourable terms for the workers. Again, when proprietors retire or die, their holdings could be tax-exempt if bequeathed to the workforce. Ingenious minds will, I am sure, be able to think up many other schemes. The cumulative effect should be, in a piecemeal fashion, to reach a situation in a decade or two in which a company which did not have at least a substantial minority worker shareholding would be regarded as a bit freakish.

In more general terms, the joint-stock company with limited liability has become absurdly dominant. This model has many brilliant qualities of flexibility and efficiency, but it need not be the best or only option. For many types of enterprise, the family firm, the partnership and not least the co-operative or semi-co-operative offer a better way of balancing the interests of all concerned and making a decent profit too.

The principle of 'unlock and allot' can be applied not merely to individual property rights, but to other sorts of rights and to groups as well as individuals. One may, for example, unlock certain powers currently exercised at higher levels and allot them directly to local bodies.

Policing powers, for example, are presently exercised in an oblique, complex way by three bodies: the police themselves (operational matters), the local police authorities (strategic and financial matters), and the Home Secretary (structure, finance and professional training). Suppose a directly elected local police committee controlled all except obviously national matters. Suppose even that the chief constable was elected at local elections.

This is presently regarded as unthinkable and liable to corruption and incompetence. Yet it has been standard practice in the United States for a very long time. Nor is it as if direct control by the Home Secretary had prevented the Metropolitan Police from being periodically riddled with corruption. If the local population, which is, after all, paying

301

for the police service, wants to see bobbies on the beat, why should they be denied the right to have them?

Why should not other responsibilities — and modest taxing powers to go with them — be devolved to parish councils? Again the levels of these taxes could be subject to approval at local elections — a likely inducement to voters to turn out. The usual objections — incompetence, corruption — can be applied with just as much force to large local authorities. Indeed, some of the largest have been the most corrupt and useless.

The present government has at least been toying with proposals to devolve power to lower levels, but the bureaucracy's itch to retain control always spoils the best intentions. And in some cases, notably that of John Prescott's efforts to kickstart regional government, the net effect is to draw power up from lower-level traditional bodies such as county councils into remote large-scale bureaucracies which are bound to talk the same language as and take their cue from Whitehall.

Nor need the 'unlock and allot' principle be confined to mainstream democratic bodies. It is noticeable, for example, that in many of the worst areas of major cities it is the churches that are the last bodies to withdraw from the front line. It is one of the most tragic effects of the demoralisation of working-class areas that the churches which used to offer asylum from the surrounding wretchedness are now themselves targets for the resentment and criminality. Violence against members of the clergy is now commonplace and has increased by a third over the past four years. Break-ins and thefts and vandalism are rising just as fast (*Times*, March 11, 2003). Some parishes are now thought of as no-go areas and find it difficult to attract ministers. Any revival of the social fabric must surely go hand in hand with a return of the church. It is not too much to imagine that some districts might prefer to see certain welfare services detached from the remote and inflexible local authority and allotted to the local churches. Perhaps churches and other 'faith communities' might be allotted out of public funds the equivalent of Victorian tithes to expand their schools and other existing community activities in poor inner-city areas. The aim here is not simply to deliver services more effectively — though we hope that would be the effect — but also to bolster intermediate associations of every kind. In the same way, the use of lottery money to endow council estates with playing fields — a quasi-country estate of their own in fact — is not simply to lick the residents into shape physically but to make it possible for the most deprived to create their own sporting and social clubs on the sort of scale that was so impressive in even the poorer parts of Victorian Britain.

Our aim is to de-massify the masses by rebuilding the little platoons. But in encouraging the revival of intermediate associations, it would be absurd to neglect the most intimate form of association. Any set of proposals to re-found civil association among the Downers must also take account of the State's record over the past 20 years of sullen hostility towards marriage. There is a paradox here and a disgraceful one. Over that same period, reliable research has demonstrated over and over again that a stable marriage is the best environment to bring up children in and that, on average, children in two-parent families are likely to lead longer and happier lives.

Ever since Norman Dennis and George Erdos, both life-long ethical socialists, published *Families without Fatherhood* (IEA, 1992), it has been impossible to pretend that the decline of marriage can be a matter of indifference to those who care about the welfare of children. Yet over the same period the State has progressively eroded to vanishing point the married couple's tax allowance and removed almost all other prefer-ential treatment for the married state. Occasionally Ministers will permit themselves a nervous word or two in favour of marriage in the foreword to some official pamphlet. But the kind of serious assistance offered to married couples in most other advanced Western nations appear to be too embarrass-ing to contemplate. Indeed, the 'M word' is increasingly banned from public political discourse.

This is clearly insane. The married couple's tax allowance must be reinstated along with the other legal and fiscal recog-nitions of marriage. I am also attracted by Peter Mandelson's suggestion of a generous marriage bounty — a grant to be paid when a couple wed. After all, the State is happy to pay a funeral grant to cover your expenses when you die, so why not a grant when you undertake the even more expensive business of getting married? Apart from its material appeal, it has the charm of making the couple feel a treasured part of the nation.

It is sometimes argued that young people today are so attached to their independence and accord it such priority in their life project that mere material incentives would have no effect on them. I find this argument odd, since we expect people to respond to material incentives in every other aspect of life. In any case, other countries where the marriage incentives have not been removed or where they have actually been reinforced recently, such as France, find that the willingness to marry has scarcely diminished and may even be increasing.

There is here a more delicate mission which it is hard even to outline without sounding both pompous and sentimental. But part of our undertaking is by one means or another to reawaken a common national conversation. And in this undertaking it is difficult to avoid such words as 'allegiance' and 'patriotism'. It is even more difficult to avoid making comparisons, between the services offered by BBC Radio for example and those offered by BBC Television, or between the celebrations arranged for the Millennium and those organised for the Queen's Jubilee.

BBC Radio offers a wide range of services, highbrow, middlebrow and lowbrow, but all seem somehow rooted in the national culture. Television, on the other hand, tends to inhabit a tinny depthless world which acknowledges no historical resonances and no national characteristics. It is, in short, akin to the Millennium Dome in its empty content, its flavourless message. My original solution was to replace the Chairman and Director-General of the BBC and replace them with people who had a clearer sense of the Corporation's national cultural mission, which does not of course mean being uncritical or sycophantic about the government of the day. The Chairman and Director-General were indeed replaced but for other reasons. It is hard to detect any improvement in the output of BBC TV as a result. But the renewal of the Charter remains a golden opportunity to set the BBC off on a fresh course with which Lord Reith might be reasonably content.

Beyond the narcissistic world of broadcasting, however, it is harder to make more specific recommendations for overcoming the halting, awkward quality of our national conversation. It is not after all an easy thing to play freely upon the shared national memory without falling into mawkishness. I can only say that other countries — France, the United States — manage to devise public manifestations of pride in their traditions, both on exceptional occasions and in the daily run of things, without experiencing anything resembling embarrassment. Indeed, it is our obsession with avoiding any occasion for embarrassment which has rendered us virtually incapable of expressing any national feeling without apologising first. In a supposed age of uninhibited self-expression, this is the one emotion that dare not speak its name. And this repression, I think, bears hardest on those who have fewer other consolations in their lives. The snobbish refusal of the bourgeoisie to share in the patriotism of the lower classes is one more estranging element — and not the least important — in the growing gulf between them.

And if it is difficult to talk about things that are really quite simple, like patriotism, then it is even harder to discuss more problematic questions like the decay of family life and the gulf between the classes. Serious, thoughtful debate on these and other vexed questions is scarce on our airwaves, or anywhere else.

But then it is an uphill task to persuade the Uppers to see that in some ways they are no less snobbish than their grandparents and a good deal smugger than they were. It is equally hard to make them see that the frozen English landscape protected by the 1947 Act is an embodiment not of their aesthetic sensibilities but of their selfishness. For the truth is that the Uppers like it this way. They don't want to wave flags alongside the Downers and they don't want to share their view with them either.

IX
Becoming Visible

Let us recall once again the conventional, now traditional version of the story we are told. Modern Britain, the society we live in today, emerged out of a benighted nineteenth century assisted by three great processes. The first, we were told, was the rising standard of living generated by technological advance and (if you like — plenty still do not like) by the energies of capitalist entrepreneurs; the second was secularisation, the gradual obliteration of Christianity from its central role in social and political life and its replacement by a scientific, materialist outlook; and the third, according to the conventional version, was the fulfilment of democracy, by the extension of the franchise to all adult men and women, from which naturally flowed the State's assumption of the leading role in education and welfare. These processes are presented as natural and cumulative, surging irrepressibly forward — assisted, of course, by modern-minded, public-spirited leaders of opinion and resisted only by reactionaries and obscurantists. The resistance was mostly token and negligible. It was, after all, futile to resist the steamroller of history.

It didn't seem quite like that at the time. On the contrary, viewed from the point of the lower classes, there seemed to be a different sort of war on, a war waged with considerable ferocity and no little deviousness against their faiths, their institutions, their principles and occasionally their existence. They were patronised, insulted, elbowed aside and ultimately neglected by their social superiors. That is not the story still told by middle-class philanthropists, who prefer to cast their fathers and grandfathers and indeed themselves in the starring role in an epic of social progress. In their eyes, all the great changes of the past century and a half have been undertaken with the wellbeing of the lower classes at heart.

But the lower classes could be forgiven for taking a different view, which some of them did at the time — being occasionally angered and outraged, but more often bemused and saddened by what was represented to them as pure progress. At times, it must have seemed to them that while the first 70 years of the nineteenth century had been devoted to building up the civilisation of the lower classes, the next 70 years and beyond were devoted to dismantling that civilisation.

The first and most striking instance of this was, as we have seen, the persistent belittling by the intelligentsia of the characteristic religious institutions of the lower classes, that is to say, the Nonconformist churches. Modern historians often miss this or glide over it, because they are more occupied by what seems to them a greater battle, the one between the atheists and the believers, most notably between the Darwinians and the creationists. For modern observers, it is the clash between Thomas Henry Huxley and Bishop Wilberforce that is crucial and fascinating. But at the time, for Anglican writers it was Dissent that really made the blood boil — and most of the writers we have heard of were brought up as Anglicans, even if they too heard the melancholy, long, withdrawing roar of the tide of faith (not the most apt metaphor in Matthew Arnold's *Dover Beach*, since tides have a way of coming back in again).

This was the first hollowing-out of lower-class life and was soon to be followed by the gradual State takeover of the secular institutions, such as the lower-class private schools and the friendly societies, and the gradual erosion of the traditional forces of social inclusiveness, such as patriotism and the monarchy, forces that gave the lower classes an equal place in society which might in some degree mitigate their abysmal economic inequality.

Even at this late stage in the argument, some readers may still be saying impatiently: but they have the vote, don't they, and the health service? And what is all this about the lower-class lack of self-confidence? Surely what we see much more of these days is 'working-class swagger' (to use Mr Anthony Howard's striking phrase). It swills out of the pubs on to the pavement and spills on to the television pop and celebrity shows, loud-mouthed, uninhibited, colourful.

Yes, but doesn't all this seem a little like bluster, a boisterous façade concealing a deep-lying uncertainty and lack of self-worth? The young have always roamed the streets in gangs, unnerving their elders. But nobody pretended in the old days that this was all there was to their lives or ever would be. The peer group was not thought of as the determining social factor, let alone the foundation of society. From the Middle Ages on, it was expected that the yobs (for there were always yobs) would on closer inspection turn out to be connected to guilds, clans, religious and social orders, from which they would derive part of their identity and purpose in life (even while jeering at the greybeards who ran such institutions).

But now those connections seem thinner and frailer, for the lower classes anyway. When I talked about this essay to the American sociologist Richard Sennett, now a British citizen, he said thoughtfully that the thing that struck him about the lower-middle classes in Britain is that they didn't seem very *visible*. And that, I think, sums up the outcome of the historical process I have been trying to describe. In much the same way that women have been steadily 'becoming visible' in our national life (there is even a book of that title describing the process), so the Downers have receded from view and as actors have been written out of the script.

In his recent book, *Respect: The formation of character in an age of inequality* (Allen Lane, 2003), Sennett continues his investigations into how ordinary working men may win honour and respect in a society which offers them only modest material prospects. He suggests that respect can be earned in one or more of three ways: there is self-development (making the best of your potential), there is self-sufficiency (looking after yourself so that you are not a burden on others) and, most important of the three, there is mutual exchange, giving something back to others. A good violinist may have devel-

311

oped her potential to the utmost, a successful businessman may be self-sufficient, but neither of them will earn our warmest respect and admiration unless they give something back to others.

At present all well-meaning attempts to help the Downers are concentrated on the first two tasks: helping them to stand on their own feet and somehow or other to explore their potential. Yet more important still if we are to be reunited into one nation is that civil society — the world of association and mutual aid — should be opened up to them. This mutual aspect of working-class life — the society of chapel and institute and trade union — was once such a vibrant consolation for material hardship. Now it has gone dead, and the Uppers have few ideas and not a lot of interest in how to revive it. Even the idealism of the young Uppers is directed only fitfully to this or most other domestic social problems.

One final vignette: a performance by the London Shakespeare Workshop of *King Henry VI Part Three* in the chapel at Pentonville Prison in February 2003. Professional actors take the main parts, but all the other actors in this violent swirling enactment of the Wars of the Roses are prisoners or ex-prisoners, the red-rose Lancastrians in the raspberry track suits that are the prison uniform, the white-rose Yorkists in silver-grey. The zest of the cast during the performance and their boyish friendliness before and after are deeply moving. We tumble out through the sequence of locked holding rooms into the biting February air with feelings of having been touched and cleansed, of having experienced that catharsis which the ordinary theatre so seldom achieves. For us comfortable Uppers — many of whom have never been inside a prison before — the experience was clearly something of a secular communion. Yet the occasion — a unique one, no full-length play had been performed there in front of an audience before — was surely of more lasting significance for the prisoners. It was not simply that the whole business of volunteering and rehearsing must have relieved the boredom of prison life and might perhaps help their chances of early release; it was also that the performing may well have been an opportunity for mutual exchange that was unprecedented, not merely since their conviction but in their entire adult lives. Had they ever before had the opportunity to do something for people outside their immediate families? Had we in our comfortable, largely automated lives ever had the surprising pleasure of receiving such an uncovenanted favour from people we otherwise had so little contact with? The enthusiasm of our clapping and their clapping at our clapping had the intensity of a long thirst being quenched.

Yet such an experience remains as rare for us as for them. The end of the British Empire did not lead to a renewed concentration of middle-class energies on the plight of the poor at home. On the contrary, that concern which was so earnestly felt by the Victorian middle classes and still burned brightly through the first half of the 20th century seems now to be flickering at best. What reserves of compassion we can muster are now reserved for the starving millions of Africa and Asia. Those are the realms of poverty which draw the young in search of spiritual awakening. Destinations for the gap year of middle-class students have become more and more distant, as though philanthropy or even mere curiosity became more meritorious, the more air miles you clocked up. The lack of curiosity about events in Bootle was matched by a corresponding quickening of the pulse at the mention of Bulawayo or Burma. Mrs Jellyby's great-grandchildren travel everywhere except north of Watford. The bottom classes are visited, it is true, but mostly by professionals who have come to manage them in one way or another, to stop them smoking and drinking and knocking their wives about. Nobody in their right mind expects to learn anything from the British poor in the way people expect to learn from the poor of India.

And how ready are we to make the practical changes that might make the lower classes visible? I don't mean merely to let them run their own schools and hospitals and parishes — though only a tiny minority of Conservatives and Liberals and even fewer Labourites are ready to contemplate such things.

I mean also letting the lower classes become visible in the most obvious sense, by allowing them to lease plotlands and build their own market gardens and make the messy splashes on the landscape that almost every civilised person revolts in horror at the thought of. Only a few old-fashioned anarchists are game for that kind of liberation.

The sort of untidy landscape in the Veneto where workshops and shacks and garages mingle with Palladio villas would not, I fear, be thought tolerable in the Home Counties. Freezing the English landscape continues to be regarded as the highest political virtue.

When it comes down to it, most of us are perfectly pleased

that the lower classes should be reasonably prosperous and healthy, so long as we don't have to see them or hear them. In a less flamboyant style, we are little better than those eighteenth-century noblemen who employed Humphry Repton and Capability Brown to beautify their demesnes by removing whole villages which were obstructing their view across the park. The oft-heard complaint that this is the age of the common man and that we are governed these days (more's the pity) by proletarian values is only a pretence. In practice, the lowest class is 'cabined, cribbed, confined' to its physical and social ghetto, offered only the alternatives of staying quiet or escaping through higher education. No mass embourgeoisement has occurred, because it was never really offered.

This is not an attack on or a defence of any political party. Both sides have had factions which genuinely wanted to see 'a transfer of wealth and power to ordinary working people' (Labourspeak) and/or to 'set the people free' (Toryspeak) — even if one might not always approve of the methods they recommended. Usually such persons in either party are dubbed 'eccentric' or 'maverick', as Keith Joseph and Tony Benn were. At all events, such views have had only a modest impact on events (mostly though not exclusively during the premiership of Margaret Thatcher). Otherwise, for the past 50 years, we have lived on a moderately benign managerialism which believes that, so long as the lower orders are pacified at regular intervals by tax cuts or increases in benefits, not much notice need be taken of them.

The thought that the lower orders might be 'conversable', that a certain comity might exist between all of us, is unsettling and, on the whole, to be dismissed as sentimental. Yet what is it that people find so attractive about life in France or the United States — two countries so different from one another? It is, I think, that, for all the huge differences in wealth in both countries, a certain assumption of commonality prevails. There are snobberies certainly, some of them no less absurd than those in Britain, but it is taken for granted that all are fellow-citizens, members of one nation.

Eager republicans will chip in at this point and assert that we shall never become citizens until we cease being subjects. It is, they claim, the monarchy that divides us from one another. I find that implausible. The assumption of *commonality* is just as strong in the monarchies of northern Europe — the Dutch, the Danes, the Swedes — as it is in the republics of southern Europe.

The historical circumstances of modern Britain — our religious quarrels, our early industrialisation and urbanisation — have left us, along with many blessings, an unexpiated curse, which is the curse of class division. In almost all societies, it is possible to grade people into classes of one sort or another, but Britain stands nearly alone in maintaining to this day so sharp a division between the Uppers and the Downers. The numbers of the Uppers have grown hugely over the past century, the numbers of the Downers are much depleted by upward mobility, but the divide is still there.

We can remove that divide if we really want to. But it will not disappear until we make it disappear.

INDEX